THEY TOOK THEIR STAND

The Founders of the Confederacy

They Took Their Stand

The Founders of the Confederacy

MANLY WADE WELLMAN

> . . . Names in my ears,
> Of all the lost adventurers my peers,—
> How such a one was strong, and such was bold,
> And such was fortunate, yet each of old
> Lost, lost! . . .
> —Robert Browning, *Childe Roland to the*
> *Dark Tower Came*

G. P. Putnam's Sons   New York

© 1959 by Manly Wade Wellman

Library of Congress Catalog Card Number: 59-7844

MANUFACTURED IN THE UNITED STATES OF AMERICA
BY THE COLONIAL PRESS INC., CLINTON, MASS.

Contents

Foreword

HISTORY, as it strives to interpret events, often oversimplifies to dullness the characters of the men and women who created those events.

The citizens of the Confederate States of America were, like all human creatures, complex and sometimes contradictory. Each of them had three dimensions, five senses and numerous characteristics. The bleak warrior Stonewall Jackson knew moments of deepest tenderness; the word-valiant secessionist Edmund Ruffin wanted to fight with more than words; the proud, articulate Jefferson Davis could be humble and confused. Mary Boykin Chesnut and other hoop-skirted, bright-eyed women who echoed the dreams and ventures of their men were not always fragile in their graces, not always empty in their laughter, not always weak in their tears.

These history-makers, each a fabric of infinite variations, differed widely from each other. There was no typical Confederate man or woman. Confederates were wise and foolish, gay and gloomy, rich and poor, suave and awkward, brave and timid. The land they sought to make independent was a land of meadows, mountains, swamps, forests, seashores, rivers and prairies. Here it knew hard frost, there it was subtropical and lush.

Various, too, were secession's motives. The first states to leave the Union did so in an effort to preserve a way of life that seemed honest and pleasant, and looked hopefully toward peace in their new nation. Those that followed did so in protest at what they felt was tyrannical aggression, and went headlong into a desperate conflict.

Despite staggering odds of numbers and armament, the Confederacy almost won its war and its independence. Losing both, it perished, and left behind it the most dramatic and tragic memory of all American memories. But this is smug appraisal long after the fact; the Confederacy was organized in an atmosphere of triumph foreordained, of tingling excitement and high gallantry, and the bitter future had not yet become the present.

Many have assisted generously and importantly in this present effort to look into the natures and emotions of those who saw the Confederacy's beginning and who waged the war that was the Confederacy's chief history.

First grateful acknowledgment must be made to the Louis Round Wilson Library of the University of North Carolina, and to Director Jerrold Orne, Associate Librarian O. V. Cook, and their able staff. Dr. James Welch Patton, director of the library's Southern Historical Collection, and his assistants were wise and sympathetic in making available numerous manuscripts and in frequent good advice as to profitable avenues of study.

Photographs of Mary Chesnut, Stonewall Jackson and Edmund Ruffin are from the files of the Southern Historical Collection.

At the Howard-Tilton Memorial Library at Tulane University, Mrs. William J. Griffith, archivist, and others were unweariedly helpful to a researching stranger, as were Miss Virginia Rugheimer, librarian of the Charleston Library Society, and her staff, and Mrs. Granville T. Prior, secretary of the South Carolina Historical Society at Charleston, and her associates. As with past projects, valuable assistance was readily afforded by the Library of Congress, the Confederate Museum and the Virginia State Library at Richmond, and the Municipal Library of New York City.

Houghton Mifflin Company of Boston generously granted permission to quote several passages from Mary Boykin Chesnut's *A Diary From Dixie,* as edited in 1949 by Ben Ames Williams.

In the notes, this work is cited as *Mrs. Chesnut 1949*, with indication of direct quotation.

The portraits on the dust jacket, of Thomas Jonathan Jackson, Edmund Ruffin, and Mary Boykin Chesnut, are reproduced by permission of the Southern Historical Collection of the Louis Round Wilson Library at the University of North Carolina.

And special thanks are due these individuals for special help:

To Mrs. Mildred Bone Barkley of New Orleans, for loaning the letters of her soldier-grandfather Dr. Robert D. Bone; to Mr. Sam Boone of Chapel Hill, North Carolina, for skillful photoduplication of pictures, maps and documents; to Dr. Hugh Holman, chairman of the Department of English Literature at the University of North Carolina, for a penetrating assessment of literary tastes in the ante-bellum South; to Mr. Nathaniel C. Hughes, Jr., of Chapel Hill, for calling of attention to Edmund Kirby Smith's correspondence as it concerns the formation of the Confederacy; to Miss Lilly Belle Dameron of Warrenton, North Carolina, for use of a typescript of the unpublished memoirs of Maria Florilla Flint Hamblen; to Mr. John R. Peacock of High Point, North Carolina, and Mr. George F. Scheer of Chapel Hill, for permission to use their splendid private historical libraries; to Mrs. Panthea M. Twitty of Warrenton, North Carolina, for making available the results of her research on the origin of the Stars and Bars; and to Mr. Wade Wellman of Chapel Hill, for research into the appearance of a comet in Virginia skies in the early summer of 1861.

All told, hundreds helped in many ways; and all are partners and partakers in the labor and the result.

MANLY WADE WELLMAN

Chapel Hill, North Carolina
January 1, 1959

THEY TOOK THEIR STAND

The Founders of the Confederacy

I

Marching On

IT was December 2, 18̸5̸9, and the men rose before seven o'clock that morning in the deceptively quiet little town of Charlestown in western Virginia.

The weather promised to be pleasantly mild—"very favorable," remarked a visitor, as though he looked forward to a hunt or a picnic. A soft haze, like that of Indian summer, draped the mountain peaks that strung the horizon. This was the day that Sheriff James Campbell would bring John Brown of Osawotamie out of the double-guarded jail and hang him high.

Hangings were public affairs in those times, and usually well attended. Sometimes the spectators brought lunch baskets and whiskey jugs and fiddles, the better to enjoy such events. But from this extraordinary hanging of an extraordinary man the public had been told to stay away.

Almost the only ordinary thing about John Brown was his name. He had proved himself the most violent of all violent abolitionists. Aiding the Underground Railroad had early proved too tame for him; he had preferred to butcher pro-slavery settlers in Kansas and to free, by force, Negroes in Missouri. Under such aliases as Shubel Morgan and James Smith he had skirmished and rioted with such conspicuous success that President James Buchanan had offered a reward of $250 for his capture. His career as a self-elected flail of the Lord had been crowned and closed on October 17, when he and a band of only slightly less battle-hungry followers had raided the United States arsenal at Harpers Ferry.

In their effort to seize arms and free slaves, they had shot down citizens and gathered captives, had barricaded themselves in the enginehouse of the arsenal. But Virginia militia had besieged them until a company of United States marines, with Lieutenant Colonel Robert E. Lee of the Second Cavalry to direct them, stormed the enginehouse and killed or captured fifteen of the raiders. Brown had been convicted of treason, insurrection and murder, and this was to be his last day of life.

The whole South execrated him. Senator Jefferson Davis of Mississippi felt, and said, that Brown deserved to hang for inciting slaves to murder women and children. Senator Robert Toombs of Georgia called Brown a bearer of armed warfare into Virginia, and insisted that other abolitionists differed from him only in degree of resolution. Senator James Mason of Virginia added that Northerners deplored Brown's raid only because it had failed, and advised that Southerners prepare to meet violence with violence. Members of several pro-slavery state legislatures spoke out frankly and relishfully for preparation for war.

Southern women in magnificent old plantation houses locked doors that never had been locked before. Southern men looked askance at slaves who might not be devoted after all, and met to organize new volunteer companies of rifles and dragoons. Mary, wife of Senator James Chesnut, helping pack at Mulberry Plantation in South Carolina for a trip to Washington and the opening session of the Thirty-sixth Congress, added to her vocabulary a new and uneasy verb: to Brown—that meant to raid, to incite slaves to rebellion. Mulberry Plantation swarmed with slaves— were they loyal?

Opinions of diametrically opposite nature resounded in the North. Above the Mason-Dixon Line, it seemed, John Brown was viewed not as a fanatical killer but as a holy martyr. Henry Ward Beecher and a host of less celebrated divines applauded the Harpers Ferry raid as a wholesome example of militant abolitionism. A motion that the Massachusetts legislature adjourn in honor of the doomed man failed by but three votes. In his Cambridge study, Henry Wadsworth Longfellow wrote that December 2 was "the date of a new Revolution—quite as much needed as the old one." Concord in Massachusetts planned a "martyr service" for two o'clock in the afternoon, with addresses by Henry David Thoreau, Bronson Alcott, and Ralph Waldo Emerson. Other meetings to mourn and extol Brown were announced in Boston, Cleveland, and Philadelphia. In large towns and small throughout the free states, bells tolled as for the passing of a national hero.

A rare expression of moderate opinion was offered by an ex-congressman from Illinois, speaking that day in Troy, Kansas. "We cannot object," he said soberly, in commenting on Brown's sentence to the gallows, "even though he agreed with us in thinking slavery wrong. That cannot excuse violence, bloodshed and treason." The speaker was Abraham Lincoln, trying to decide whether he would seek next year's Republican nomination to the presidency.

Virginia's governor, Henry A. Wise, had heard from a variety of quarters that throngs of Brown's disciples would converge on Charlestown to set their hero free, and Wise urged all private citizens to stay home, while two thousand Virginia militiamen gathered at Wise's order to make certain that John Brown would hang by the neck as scheduled.

They had been at Charlestown, those militiamen, for three or four days. They outnumbered the fifteen hundred whites, free Negroes and slaves who inhabited the little town, and they filled all available quarters to capacity. Some of the amateur soldiers disliked sleeping seven and eight in a room. None seem to have voiced any regret that John Brown must die.

Brown himself had eaten a farewell supper with his wife the night before, in the sitting room of the humanely sympathetic jailer John Avis. Before dawn of December 2 he was awake, writing affectionate last words to his family, drawing up his will, inscribing his well-worn Bible to a friendly Charlestown confectioner named John H. Blessing. Earlier in his imprisonment he had harshly refused the proffered prayers of Virginia preachers —their upholding of the institution of slavery put them outside the pale of his religion. But he said a prayer himself, then talked cordially with Sheriff Campbell, Jailer Avis, and the guards. Several of these men shed tears. Outside the jail waited the host of militia.

Best-disciplined and best-officered of all the armed units concentrated in and around Charlestown was a detail of eighty-five cadets from the Virginia Military Institute, under command of their professors. These men had slept in their clothes the night of December 1, each with his ready-loaded musket beside him. They ate breakfast at seven-thirty, fell in an hour later, and by nine o'clock were marching to the rise of ground southwest of Charlestown, where the gallows had been built.

It was a gaunt and unlovely structure, that gallows, with steep openwork steps that mounted to a platform of boards with a trap door in its center. Above this, a bleak horizontal spar dangled a noose of stout rope.

Colonel Francis Smith, the rawboned superintendent of the Military Institute, was in command at the spot. He and his staff of fellow professors sat on borrowed horses. Arriving, the cadets formed in line behind the gallows. They looked colorfully handsome, even dashing, in caped gray overcoats buttoned back to show red flannel shirts and white crossbelts. Twenty-one of the most proficient had been assigned as artillerists, and trundled forward two twelve-pound howitzers, one to each end of the formation. Lieutenant Daniel Truehart, instructor in engineering, had charge of the gun at the left. Beside that on the right stood the Institute's professor of physics and instructor in artillery, Major Thomas Jonathan Jackson.

Major Jackson would be thirty-six years old in January. He stood straight and tall and square-shouldered. His features were strong and regular, his eyes pale blue, his complexion ruddy. A thick brown beard grew upon his firm chin. A certain stiffness of manner, at once prim and awkward, kept him from seeming wholly assured. "Fool Tom Jackson," some of his less respectful cadets called him. But he had graduated high in his class at West Point. By spectacular gallantry in the Mexican War he had won praise and promotion. Various thoughtful women considered him handsome, and various clear-eyed men found him impressive. Like his fellow professors present around the gallows, he wore a brass-buttoned blue frock of military cut, dark trousers, and a visored garrison hat.

The sixty-four cadets who formed with Commander William Gilham as an infantry company behind the guns found that their color guard had been increased by one volunteer. He looked old enough to be the grandfather of the oldest cadet there, with his withered face and his gnarled little body. White hair cascaded from under his borrowed cadet cap to the shoulders of his borrowed overcoat. Fumblingly he tried to match the snap of the smartly drilled youngsters, and his unsure manual of arms dated back to the War of 1812. The boys told each other who he was —Edmund Ruffin.

Ruffin was the Virginia planter who had taught the whole South how marl replenished soil drained by the greedy roots of cotton and tobacco, who had edited with success and distinction the *Farmers' Register,* who for a decade had preached the causes of States' rights and secession. Two years earlier, *De Bow's Review* had offered in serial form Ruffin's long and furious condemnation of the Northern states as exploiters of the Southern. Ruffin had bewailed the taxing of the agrarian South for banks, tariffs, and bounties for fisheries and ocean steamers. He had charged Northerners with "hostile and incendiary action" against the slave states. He had urged disunion, to begin in the Deep South where slaves were most abundant and important, then to be followed in the border states of Virginia, Maryland, and Kentucky. "In this manner," he argued, "without risk of bloodshed, the separation of our present Union with our worst enemies may be effected, and the subsequent construction of a Southern and slaveholding confederacy. . . ."

Why had this ancient zealot wheedled his way into the ranks of the Institute cadets? Why should such a man play soldier under the shadow of the gibbet yonder?

Bracing to attention, smolderingly triumphant, Edmund Ruffin knew his own reasons and his own harsh satisfaction.

He felt that he was coming into his own. In 1858, when the

peerless Alabama orator William Lowndes Yancey had formed the League of United Southerners to protect slavery even to the point of disunion, Yancey had proclaimed the league to be the inspiration of "that profound thinker, that practical farmer and statesman, that true and fearless patriot, Edmund Ruffin." Alas, the voices of Ruffin and Yancey and their extremist comrades had all but faded from hearing—leaders North and South had striven rather for harmony. But now, John Brown's violence and John Brown's execution would mark a return to life of the secession gospel, and Ruffin would be heard and honored again as among the foremost of its missionaries.

Brown had scared the slaveholders. The North approved of him. Compromise would be vain. Ruffin had come to Charlestown to see Brown's death with his own bitter eyes. If the rumors were true, if abolitionists should try to snatch Brown away and were mowed down by volleys of militia cannon and muskets, so much the better for Ruffin's dream.

Two volunteer companies marched in and formed their lines at angles, right and left, to the cadets. These were kid-glove units from the state capital, Company F in fire-gilt buttons and gold-banded sleeves with sword-wearing sergeants to close the files, and the Richmond Grays in splendid dress uniform as though for parade. Governor Wise's son Jennings, the fashionably intellectual editor of the Richmond *Enquirer,* was a private of the Grays. With him stood another young private recognizable to many, an actor at a Richmond theater who had played truant from the stage to shoulder his musket. He was of graceful medium height and figure, with a profusion of dark curls, burning eyes, a classic profile. Booth was his name, John Wilkes Booth.

More companies, variously uniformed, converged on the gallows knoll. They bracketed it on all sides, an ordered living rampart ribbed with gleaming swords and muskets. Outside of the great hollow square of infantry gathered mounted detachments. An officer on a magnificent white horse cantered here and there to post his troopers. His swarthy face and torrent of dark beard reminded observers of an Arab chieftain. Captain Turner Ashby from up in the Shenandoah Valley, that was who he was;

and his hard-riding lieutenant on the black horse, that was his brother Richard.

Time had passed, and it was nearly eleven o'clock, with units still arriving to fit into place around the scaffold, when word came from town that John Brown was on his way to his death.

Emerging from his cell, he had called down the blessing of God upon the imprisoned survivors of his raider band. He had shaken hands with Sheriff Campbell and Avis, asking each to accept from his personal stock of weapons a Sharps rifle once purchased to kill slaveholders. To one of the guards he handed a folded paper. Then he came into the open, and on to where the rope awaited him.

Three final companies of infantry militia marched as escort to an open wagon, drawn by horses as white as Captain Ashby's splendid charger. Brown sat on the lid of his walnut coffin. With him in the wagon rode Campbell and Avis. The driver checked his team at the foot of the gallows. Brown hopped down to earth, with the sheriff and the jailer at either side of him.

Brown, like Ruffin and Booth, was recognizable to hundreds of the militiamen present. A great frill of gray beard lent patriarchal dignity to his flinty, aquiline face. His erect figure was clad in a black frock coat and loose black trousers, and on his head was a soft, broad hat, such as a preacher might wear. His feet were shod in what appeared to be red-trimmed carpet slippers. As he mounted to the platform above the heads of the troops, those nearest to him saw that a cord had been looped around his knobby elbows, drawn tight, and knotted behind his back.

Up the stairs he climbed and up, to stand upon the stagelike level. He managed to lift a hand, despite his tether, and pull the hat from his grizzled head. He dropped the hat on the planks beside him and faced southward. Sheriff Campbell drew a white cap down over the set face, the blazing eyes.

"I can't see, gentlemen," came Brown's muffled voice. "You must lead me."

Avis and Campbell did so, far enough forward so that Brown stood upon the shaky trap door. They stooped to tie his legs.

They set the noose around his bared throat and drew it snug, the knot under the ear. Campbell asked if he should give a signal before releasing the trap.

"It does not matter to me," replied Brown, "if only you do not keep me too long waiting."

But he had to wait. Those three companies of his escort, amateurishly drilled and officered, found it difficult to gain their assigned positions in the hollow square. Fully ten minutes went past while clumsily they countermarched, halted, and dressed each in line. Blindfolded, pinioned, helpless, John Brown stood like a lance on the threshold of death. Thousands of eyes watched him for a sign of fear or nervousness. Did his knees tremble? . . . No. That was only a fluttering of the cloth of his trousers, caught by a puff of breeze that sighed over the gallows and the waiting host.

At last: "We are ready, Mr. Campbell," announced Colonel Smith from where he sat his horse.

Campbell did not seem to hear.

"We are all ready, Mr. Campbell," repeated Smith, more loudly, and the sheriff turned and walked down the steps.

Edmund Ruffin's old eyes fixed themselves intently upon Brown. Surely, said Ruffin in his heart, this man's life was forfeit several times over. Brown exemplified Northern abolitionism. His adventures and disaster had opened the eyes of all the South to peril of violence. Secession must follow now, to insure the rights of every slaveholding state. . . .

Aye, but Brown had animal courage, he was flawlessly brave in the face of certain death. Ruffin, himself a zealot, could appreciate that kind of bravery, could understand it, could and must admire it.

Major Thomas Jonathan Jackson, beside his howitzer, stood motionless, straight and soldierly. He had seen death before this, had seen it come violently and tragically. In his heart he felt the admiration Ruffin admitted, and the Christian pity Ruffin refused to allow.

What, wondered Jackson silently, were John Brown's chances of salvation? Jackson knew how harshly Brown had rebuffed

the Virginia parsons who would have prayed for him, condemn-
ing their belief in slavery as false and pagan. Jackson himself
owned several Negroes, considered himself justified legally and
morally in doing so; Brown would have forbidden Jackson's
prayers, too. But what said Holy Writ of the unrepentant, the un-
prepared? *Depart, ye wicked, into the everlasting fire.* . . .
Silently, Jackson offered his plea to the Almighty that this
doomed captive's soul be accepted into paradise.

Campbell swung a hatchet. Its keen edge severed a taut cord.
The released trap flew downward, and Brown dropped suddenly
through the floor, then bounced upward again as the tautened
rope at his neck yanked him violently back.

Tensely motionless, the lines of men saw Brown's arms strive
upward against the tethering at the elbows, the fists clench and
quiver, the bound knees crook and squirm. Brown quivered
spasmodically, and again and again, with lessening violence. At
last his hands relaxed and sank to his sides, his legs went limp.
The wind swung him this way, then that.

Silence, oppressive and awed, to be broken by the voice of
Major J. L. T. Preston, Latin professor with the cadets of the
Institute:

"So perish all such enemies of Virginia! All such enemies of
the Union! All such foes of the human race!"

After that, Brown hung by his broken neck, halfway through
the opening in the platform, for long minutes. Surgeons mounted
to him and examined him carefully. At last they pronounced him
dead. His body was cut down and deposited in the coffin, to go
under guard to Harpers Ferry and thence by rail to North Elba,
New York, where it would molder in the grave.

Noon had passed as the various units marched away. Very few
in the ranks could have felt any great appetite for dinner; but
Private John Wilkes Booth of the Richmond Grays was heard
to remark that he needed a good drink of whiskey.

Booth, at twenty-one years of age, and Edmund Ruffin, at
sixty-six, had less than five years and five months to live. To
Thomas Jonathan Jackson remained less than three years and
six months; to Captain Ashby, a little more than two years and

seven months; to Private Jennings Wise, a little more than two years. The blood of these and of hundreds of others present with them around the gallows knoll, and of more than six hundred thousand more Americans besides, would be required to complete the baleful sacrifice which John Brown's deed and death made certain of celebration throughout the land.

Back at the jail in town, the guards read that last note their prisoner had written:

I John Brown am now quite *certain* that the crimes of this *guilty land*: will never be *purged away*: but with blood. . . .

Martyr he may have been, or traitor, robber and murderer, but no doubt but that he was a prophet. His unquiet soul went marching on, toward fields loud with guns and littered with slain young men.

II

Where They Were Born In

JOHN BROWN died in the awareness that he had not failed utterly. His adventures and his death had demonstrated that a great majority of Northerners viewed slavery with earnest abhorrence. But his raid on Harpers Ferry, where the proportion of slaves was fewer than one in fifteen of the town's population, had been no stab at the real heart of the institution he hated.

The true slave power dwelt deep in the South, was anchored on the Atlantic coast by South Carolina and Georgia, with, below these, the sparsely peopled Florida peninsula. Westward lay what, no more than a generation before John Brown's hanging, had been the frontier—the fat black soil of Alabama and Mississippi, now cleared of forest and cloaked white with cotton. Beyond Mississippi was Louisiana with its heritage of French names and French manners, fashioned by American method into another cotton principality.

Semitropical that land was, with here and there an enchanting loveliness, but vigor was in its soil and climate. Dramatic contrasts obtained—one might emerge from a shadowy cypress swamp or from a country road darkened to twilight by the interlaced boughs of trees, into spacious fields of cotton ready for picking, of corn ripe for harvest, a sudden impact of blazing white or gleaming gold that was like a physical blow to the senses.

Here, past the old towns of the East, were only state capitals and shipping communities on sea or river; other than these, a few scattered hamlets, little clutches of dwellings around a church, a courthouse, a crossroads store or tavern, a mill. Great families lived in white mansions braced with pillars, among broad holdings. The smaller folk had farmhouses and cabins.

These six states of the Deep South were inhabited by some 2,200,000 whites, some 36,000 free Negroes, a few civilized Indians, and more than 2,150,000 slaves—nearly as many human chattels as free people. In South Carolina, Negro slaves outnumbered the whites by better than four to three, in Mississippi by better than eight to five.

But only a small portion of the Deep Southern white men were masters of an overwhelming majority of the slaves. By 1860, a mere 160,000 citizens throughout the six states claimed Negro property, and of these only 26,754 owned twenty slaves or more and could be considered as belonging to the planter class. If each slaveholder headed a family averaging five in number, less than 135,000 of the Deep South's 2,200,000 free citizens could pretend to plantation aristocracy, and only 800,000 belonged to slaveowning households.

This ownership of half a population by a privileged few of the other half had perhaps its most sentimentally friendly literary discussion in John Pendleton Kennedy's *Swallow Barn*, and its bitterest indictment in Harriet Beecher Stowe's *Uncle Tom's Cabin*. The phenomenon was eight generations old in the land, and planters of the hot, palmetto-tufted Deep South insisted that it was justified by Holy Writ and by legal and customary precedent modern and classic.

Boldly spoke the senators from slavery's stronghold. Thin, ascetic-featured Jefferson Davis of Mississippi was reckoned by many the most brilliant, personable and influential of them all, though his earlier record had been conservative. Robert Toombs, the burly, profane Georgian, had his own following and his own pungent arguments. Plump Judah P. Benjamin of Louisiana was plausible and persuasive among the sophisticates of the nation's capital. Stephen Mallory earnestly upheld Florida's right to prosper through slavery, Benjamin Fitzpatrick and Clement Clay were Alabama's champions. Mary Chesnut noticed that James, her senator husband, forgot his earlier Union bias and spoke and labored for the preservation of Negro servitude in South Carolina. These men were loudly seconded in the lower House of Congress, and by governors and legislators in their home states.

The States' rights gospel was no new fury; John Brown had but caused it to grow loud and strong again. Congressman William Lowndes Yancey, five feet six of opinionated eloquence, had frightened his fellow Alabamians more than a decade earlier by urging secession as a cure for overmuch control from Washington. Robert Barnwell Rhett, as a South Carolina senator in 1850, had called openly for his state to leave the Union; then, when defeated by the calmer logic of A. P. Butler, he had retired huffily from politics to edit his savage Charleston *Mercury*. And Edmund Ruffin, neither officeholder nor publisher but only a dedicated bearer of the disunion banner, had spread broadcast in Southern reviews and newspapers his essays on the rights to hold slaves and to secede.

Ruffin, Yancey and Rhett, in particular, had come to be viewed as quaint anachronisms of political philosophy. After Harpers Ferry, however, almost every Deep Southern leader began to talk about secession.

As John Brown's body was cut from its rope, South Carolina's state senate considered a resolution to reopen the African slave trade, forbidden by Federal law since 1808. Rising from his seat on December 10, mighty-muscled Wade Hampton, owner of three thousand slaves, spoke soberly and movingly against the measure. Hampton declared that he heard with sorrow the cries for disunion, and urged upon his fellow senators the employment of humanity, moderation and common sense. The resolution was tabled, as was another that looked toward secession. But in Alabama and Mississippi were enacted laws preparing for revival of the slave trade, under the euphemistic title of contract labor.

Up in Washington, Davis, Benjamin, and Yancey outorated the Northerners, as once Northerners had been outorated by Virginians. Deep Southern argument, alternately lofty and sharp, vibrated the walls and ceilings of both Houses of Congress. Back home, the slaveless majorities of the states were echoing and endorsing the pronouncements of their representatives in Washington.

For ambitious men could rise on sable shoulders to wealth and importance. Jefferson Davis himself was the cabin-born son of Kentuckians not unthinkably more monied or otherwise more fortunate than the parents of that troublesome Illinois lawyer Abraham Lincoln who now rallied the new Republican party toward what looked like victory; but the Davises had gained plantation riches and plantation prestige. Wade Hampton was the grandson of an Indian fighter and Revolutionary War hero who had pyramided cotton profits into a literal kingdom of slave-cultivated holdings in three states. Nathan Bedford Forrest, subliterate son of a Mississippi blacksmith, was a millionaire by 1860 through trading in Negroes. Light-pursed Virginians and Marylanders had become fine gentlemen when their work gangs had cleared vast acreages in the Gulf States forests and upon those acreages had sowed and reaped magically profitable crops.

Shrewd hopeful eyes looked, therefore, to the new West across the Mississippi, where surely would open another frontier of fortune for those strong and bold enough to win it.

Beyond the great river, Texas listed only 182,566 slaves out of a total population of more than 600,000, and slaveowners numbered but 21,878 in a culture more of the ranch than of the plantation; but the soil still unplowed promised new slave-produced wealth when Alabama, Mississippi, and Louisiana, too, had grown poor under the greedy drainage of too many cotton years. Texas would be of the Deep South, spiritually and economically. Of the Deep South, too, would be the territories on the far side of her.

For cotton, as these ambitious men assured each other, was not only king but absolute monarch. Let abolitionists complain their fill about slavery; New England's textile mills, and the mills of Europe as well, must have cotton. And cotton could be produced only by slaves. Cotton and slavery must go on forever, hand in hand. Let the Union perish before slavery perished.

Slavery cruel? Mississippians and Alabamians were ready to

argue that free white men, too, felt whips on their backs in the nineteenth century. American soldiers and sailors were flogged at the direction of courts-martial. Minor criminals, North and South, went to the public whipping post. School children were taught to the tune of a hickory stick. Apprentices got the lash for laziness or impudence. Parents backed their authority with the rod.

And slaves, argued Deep Southerners, were part of the family and were punished or rewarded family-style. Sensible masters fed and clothed and sheltered their chattels well, kept them vigorous and cheerful for the most practical reasons. The law, too, required masters to care for sick or old slaves. Who did as much for worn-out workers in New York or Massachusetts factory towns? Egad, a Negro was better off as a slave than as a freedman.

Thus strong in the sense of their own deserving righteousness, South Carolinians sent Christopher Gustavus Memminger to Virginia in January, to declare official South Carolina sympathy and to urge a conference of Southern states to prepare against any further aggressions of the John Brown sort. Indeed, the South Carolina legislature had appropriated $100,000 toward military defense. Memminger, who had been the penniless orphan child of German emigrants and who had made one of those Deep Southern climbs to power and wealth as a banker for rich planters, spoke forcefully.

He had come hoping for response in Virginia. Throughout the state, people expressed horror at Brown's attempt, delight at its failure. A song had risen, a burlesque of hymnody:

> In Harpers Ferry section
> There was an insurrection,
> John Brown thought the niggers would sustain him,
> But old Master Governor Wise
> Put his specs upon his eyes,
> And he landed in the happy land of Canaan.

The refrain winked toward that Charlestown gallows knoll as

it promised reprisal, at once flippant and grim, on any further raiding abolitionists:

> Oh—me!
> Oh—my!
> The Southern boys are a-trainin',
> And we'll take a piece of rope
> And march 'em up a slope,
> And land 'em in the happy land of Canaan.

But that was a song for excited, excitable youth as it joined the militia companies. With Virginia's mature leaders, though they had been shaken by events—perhaps because they had been shaken by events—a mood of caution was strong.

Slavery was legal in those latitudes, but masters were not utterly insistent upon its sanctity. Few more than 52,000 Virginia masters held 491,000 slaves, and these slaves were less than a third of Virginia's total population. In Maryland, where Memminger's message evoked only mildly courteous interest, slaves were as one to six of the population, and of 902,000 North Carolinians little more than a third were slaves. The proportion was smaller still in Tennessee and Kentucky. Westward, in Arkansas, slaves were slightly more than a fourth of the whole population, and in Missouri approximately a tenth. In tiny Delaware, the state law permitting slavery advantaged but 587 masters, with 1,798 slaves.

In the Upper South, too, sound business considerations prevailed. Slaves were fewer because less profitable. Their owners and the neighbors of their owners found themselves able quietly to imagine, in some cases even quietly to foresee, the approach of emancipation.

That may have explained why Virginia's mannerly legislature did not give official approval to Memminger's suggestion for a conference, though it did appropriate money for improvement of its state armament. Nobody spoke desperately for or against slavery in Virginia, or in Maryland, North Carolina or Tennessee. Barnwell Rhett of the Charleston *Mercury* editorialized in angry disappointment but yet with clear recognition of how those upper slave states thought:

They may live and thrive without slavery, and with them slavery or its abolishment is a question of expediency—a choice of different instrumentalities of prosperity. To us the institution is indispensable. We must maintain ourselves in the contest, or be utterly destroyed; and it is, so far as we are concerned, vain and cowardly to look to the Frontier States to lead the South in the recovery of her independence and security. The Slave South proper—the cotton States—must look to themselves alone for defense.

Strong in this conviction, Deep Southerners fiercely sparked rebellion among pro-slavery delegates to the National Democratic Convention that was called to meet in Charleston in April. When the Northern Democrats declined to support a demand for Congressional assurance of continued slavery, Yancey led his followers of the Alabama delegation out of the hall. The Louisianians followed, then the delegates of South Carolina, Florida, Texas, Arkansas, Delaware, and Georgia. These called a convention of their own, to meet at Richmond on June 11, while those still left in their seats at Charleston adjourned to meet in Baltimore on June 18.

At Melbourne, his Virginia plantation home, hard-bitten Edmund Ruffin applauded the party split but publicly execrated his own state for failure to withdraw also. His political experience had been limited to four undistinguished years in the Virginia State Senate, but in the past he had assailed, not without mordant wit and not wholly without attention, some of the greatest public figures. When William Henry Harrison died in 1841, after a single month as President, Ruffin had loudly declared his gratification at the news, saying that this early death in office was Harrison's most valuable service to his nation. Andrew Jackson he had accused of trampling on the Constitution, and Abraham Lincoln, now emerging as the Republican leader, he saw as a puppet of his party's bosses. As for Virginia—well, maybe the Mother of States and Statesmen needed another John Brown raid to teach her the facts of political and economic existence.

But if Virginia did not express appreciative agreement with the white-haired apostle of secession, South Carolina did. In March, Rhett's *Mercury* had republished from *De Bow's Review* salient passages of Ruffin's 1857 plea for departure from the Union under Cotton State leadership. When South Carolina chose delegates to the new Richmond convention, Ruffin appeared at Columbia in gray homespun, his chosen uniform of regional patriotism. Flatteringly the South Carolinians drank in his sermons on Southern independence, and he harangued other delegates on the train going home. As the convention met, Ruffin headed for White Sulphur Springs in Virginia, where he planned to heckle rich planters out of their holiday lethargy.

The Northern Democrats nominated Lincoln's doughty adversary Stephen A. Douglas, and the Southern Democrats called for personable Vice-President John C. Breckenridge, the pro-slavery Kentuckian who was rather more noticeable in Washington than Vice-Presidents usually are. The Constitutional Union Party, heir to Know-Nothingism, chose as its candidate John Bell of Tennessee. Lincoln was the nominee of the Republicans, and the division of his adversaries' strength assured his election.

SLAVERY was the most fascinating subject of all Deep Southern political talk that summer, and, after slavery, secession.

Earlier in American history, most secession murmurs had come from New England. Indeed, during the second war with Great Britain the commerce-starved New England states had all but grumbled themselves out of the racked Union. Only during the 1850's had Southerners spoken seriously and in great numbers of reclaiming their independence.

Independence, personal and regional, had become precious to them. They were prone to say so that summer, with all the meaning they could put into it. In a land of few and small towns, rural life made individuals of men, whether of great estate or small.

A rich planter's son, looking to inheritance of many dollars and slaves, was educated for address as for learning. He was expected to ride thoroughbred horses in dashing mock tournaments, gracefully to dance the night away under crystal candelabra, to handle arms with skill in the hunting field or, if need be, on the field of honor. His manners were overpoweringly ceremonious. He might wager at cards or at a main of fighting cocks or at the race track, winning and losing fortunes with an air of gallant distinction. If he was not naturally witty, he strove at least to be picturesque. That he was brave must be understood without his insistence upon it. His class produced the wordy champions who defied Yankeedom with massed claims of sacred rights.

Men of less wealth also maintained good opinions of themselves. A yeoman's son rode well, too, on less expensive mounts. He could shoot as straight to the mark, he could dance as happily at a barn-raising as at Charleston's St. Cecilia or the Rout of Comus at New Orleans, and he could risk as daringly his handful of hard-earned half dollars. A man was a man, by a variety of his own definitions, or he was nothing.

If among men the ideal was mannered prowess, among women the ideal was mannered beauty.

It is entirely possible that, dispassionately considered, the South did not produce women actually more lovely than the women of the North; but consideration of beauty cannot be dispassionate. Beauty, says the ancient aphorism, rests in the eye of the beholder, and the eyes of Southern beholders were notably wide open to see beauty, as were the mouths of Southern beholders to speak beauty's praise. Such admiration elicited its response. Plantation wives and daughters pored over news of Paris fashions, experimented with puffed and ringleted coiffures, bleached white skins whiter, walked and gestured as though to the heart-heard music of violins and flutes. The era's ballroom toilettes made the most of femininity. Upon the crinoline's domelike pedestal rose the waist's tight-corseted stem, and above this the low-cut bodice emphasized the bosom's white upper curve, the round smoothness of bare shoulders and arms. Bangles, necklaces, fans and scarves completed the equipment of these radiant creatures. Their voices were soft, their conversation elegantly coquettish, sometimes bright without enough wisdom to disquiet side-whiskered courtiers.

The loveliest and most graceful of such women married the richest and most famous men. Frequently the difference in age was great between sparkling wife and noted husband. Jefferson Davis was seventeen years older than his winsome Varina. Francis W. Pickens, hurrying home in 1860 from his ambassadorship at the court of the Russian czar to run for governor of South Carolina, was married to the blond and galvanizing Lucy Holcomb of Tennessee, young enough to be his daughter. Senator Benjamin Fitzpatrick of Alabama had taken as his second wife Aurelia Blassingame, plump-cheeked and blooming, twenty years his junior. Nor were riper attractions absent. Eugenia Phillips, lady of an Alabama congressman, vied successfully with her grown daughters for the compliments of Washington sparks. Similarly praised was the thirtyish wife of another Alabama senator, hazel-eyed Virginia Clay, star of amateur theatricals. And with a special magnetism restrained by steady luster shone Mary Boykin Chesnut, the wife of Senator James Chesnut of South Carolina.

She was thirty-seven in March of 1860, well-seasoned for a society charmer by judgment of the time, and she would be the first to admit that never had she been a tearing beauty; but men of sense had always found her fascinating. Small and of a compact but symmetrical figure, with slender wrists, small hands and fine white shoulders, she did justice to those society crinolines. Great clouds of dark hair framed her oval face. Her nose was straight, her chin firm, her mouth large but shapely and good-humored, and her eyes magnificent.

Mary Chesnut knew and liked the best of Southern society, and she was adroit at the fragile graces of bantering small talk, the shuttlecock exchange of half-meant flatteries. She would listen to jokes and gossip that in some circles were thought racy, in others downright indecent. Though considerably better read than most ladies, North or South, she had the wit to avoid being thought a bluestocking. She liked, though she never seemed to encourage, the attentions of personable men, and she loved her husband tenderly, even when she found him irritating.

Undoubtedly to the disappointment of both, James and Mary

Chesnut had no children. Therefore the lady gave warm affection to young relatives and to the sons and daughters of her friends. A special favorite was James Chesnut's gay young nephew Johnny. Sprightly youths offered her sincere compliments, and young belles sought her out as hostess or chaperon.

A very few of her intimates knew that she kept a diary, in which she wrote the vivid truth about the people and places and events she observed; about herself, too, setting down her own praise and her own weakness, revealing herself as wise, brave and sensitive. Along with all the rest of the nation she watched the progress of the presidential campaign.

Newspapers in South Carolina, Louisiana, and Alabama foresaw Lincoln's election, with secession as a sure result. Some in the upper slave states still argued for moderation. W. W. Holden of the North Carolina *Standard*, a sober Unionist, published in his paper a warning that secession and war would appear hand in hand, and crystal-clear was his precognition of what such war would mean:

Disunion would be fraternal strife, civil and servile war, murder, arson, pillage, robbery, and fire and blood through long and cruel years. It would unsettle all business, diminish the value of all property, put the lives of both sexes and all ages in peril, and launch the States on a sea of scenes which no eye has scanned and no navigator sounded. It would bring debt, and misrule, and oppressive taxes, to be followed, perhaps, by the military rule of titled tyrants. It would wrench apart the tenderly twined affections of millions of hearts, making it a crime in the North to have been born in the South, and a crime in the South to have been born in the North. . . .

But already it was a crime in one section to have been born and bred in the other. Men might even fight about it, and in the South, anyway, fighting meant killing.

Polished cotillion leaders and rugged possum hunters alike considered that if two men were angered to the point of physical combat the matter had gone beyond simple fist-and-skull pummeling. Settlement of serious differences of opinion meant pistols and twenty paces measured off by solemn seconds, or knives out in a barroom, or rifles leveled from a mountain ambush. As to war, hot-natured Southern youngsters thought of war as something romantic and glorious. Not many living Americans had been to war—only occasional volunteers for the Indian and Mexican campaigns, grandsires who had driven the British back from New Orleans, here and there an ancient survivor of Cowpens or King's Mountain or Yorktown. The militia companies welcomed new recruits and began to drill more frequently than four times a year. At banquets of such organizations a new and heart-quickening toast was honored: "The sword. The arbiter of national dispute. The sooner it is unsheathed in maintaining Southern rights the better."

In Virginia, the lesson of John Brown's raid was not forgotten so utterly as Ruffin complained. With the money appropriated by vote of the legislature, new weapons were secured and tested. A notable event was the trial in July of a new rifled cannon, under direction of Professor Thomas Jonathan Jackson at the Military Institute.

Artillery had existed since the Middle Ages, but Frederick the Great had developed it as a maneuverable arm only a century before, and only under Napoleon had it come into its own. By 1860 it was a proud science and its officers were among the elite of the regular army. Indirect fire, with solid shot and explosive shell, had become accurate, though for the most part cannon stood in battle before or beside supporting infantry rather than behind. The rifled piece, invention of Captain R. M. Parrott at the West Point Foundry, had not gained enthusiastic attention in Washington, but Jackson, veteran of fire fights in Mexico, saw at once its superiority to old smoothbores. His enthusiastic report on experimental firings led to the purchase of twelve Parrott guns by Virginia's Commission for the Public Defense.

His survey over, Jackson took his brown-eyed wife Mary Anna on a vacation to Northampton in Massachusetts, where he felt that mineral baths improved his health, and conversation with a New England Baptist preacher improved his spirit.

At White Sulphur Springs in the western Virginia mountains, Edmund Ruffin probably was the least fashionable and most stubbornly serious visitor. He belabored his fellow guests with arguments for disunion and, more secretly, made a renunciation. Like many another wealthy widower, he had thought of marrying a beautiful young wife, and a girl present at the White Sulphur seemed to pluck a melody in the strings of his heart. But secession, meditated Ruffin, was a jealous mistress. He introduced the charmer to his son, and the two young people made a match of it.

Ruffin comforted himself with the spectacle of Company F, the gilded young militiamen from Richmond who had stood with him under the shadow of Brown's hanged body. They were at White Sulphur, going through the motions of military training. Martial, too, was the echo of pistol shots from a gallery. The racket drowned out what might have been the music of a May-December romance. Ruffin savored the sweet promise of war with the abolitionists. His military experience, a bloodless tour with a volunteer company during the War of 1812, was as limited as his political experience, but he felt he knew what war would mean. With a happily expectant scowl he waited for election day in November.

November came, and Monday the fifth was the eve of election. In Columbia, capital of South Carolina, excitement built to a tingling peak. A full thousand accompanied musicians through the streets, to serenade one notable secessionist after another.

James and Mary Chesnut heard brassy melody outside the window of their hotel, and the senator leaned from the window above a street packed with people. He addressed them ringingly, and as fire-eatingly as Barnwell Rhett himself. Lincoln, said Senator Chesnut, most assuredly would be elected on the morrow, but:

"I would unfurl the Palmetto flag, fling it to the breeze," he told the crowd, "and with the spirit of a brave man, determine to live and die as became our glorious ancestors, and ring the clarion notes of defiance in the ear of an insolent foe."

Did that mean a declaration of war? Chesnut hastened to say that he thought not. ". . . The man most averse to blood might drink every drop of blood shed."

Congressman William W. Boyce urged a similar course. "If you intend to resist," he harangued the serenaders, "the way to resist in earnest is to act; the way to enact revolution is to stare it in the face. I think the only policy for us is to aim as soon as we receive authentic intelligence of Lincoln's election."

These things echoed all the way to Marlbourne, where Ruffin savored the publication of his curious effort at fantastic fiction, *Anticipations of the Future*. The time was past when he predicted peaceful secession. His book described a breaking up of the Union, war ending in Southern victory, and a woeful decay of the beaten North. On November 6 he went to the polls, cast his vote for Breckenridge, and boarded a train for Columbia.

Thomas Jonathan Jackson also voted for Breckenridge. Other Virginians to the number of 74,321 likewise marked their ballots for Breckenridge. Douglas, the Northern Democrat, got 16,290 Virginia votes, and Abraham Lincoln was the choice of 1,929 stubborn Virginia abolitionists, mostly in the west of the state. Virginia's electoral vote went to Bell, who showed 74,681 popular votes, a plurality of but 360.

Eleven other slaveholding states returned majorities or pluralities for Breckenridge. Kentucky and Tennessee went to Bell, Missouri to Douglas. Lincoln carried every free state. In Delaware, Kentucky, Maryland, Missouri, and Virginia, Lincoln reaped a total of 26,430 votes. No slave state other than these recorded a single vote for him.

As the South Carolina legislature met to consider election returns and take momentous action, Mary Chesnut departed for Florida to visit her mother. On November 7, while the cars rolled into Fernandina, she heard a woman's voice cry out: "That settles the hash!"

Mary glanced up inquiringly. Her servant, standing near, said: "Lincoln's elected."

"How do you know?" demanded Mary.

"The man over there has a telegram."

The whole car buzzed with talk. A man rose in the aisle like an orator at a political barbecue. "The die is cast," he said, gloomily trite. "No more vain regrets; sad forebodings are useless. The stake is life or death."

"Now that the black radical Republicans have the power," offered someone else, "I suppose they will Brown us all."

Everybody knew what it would mean to be Browned, and nodded dolefully. The train paused at the Fernandina depot. From her car window, Mary saw young men run a flag up a pole. It spread to the breeze, a palmetto device. "South Carolina has seceded!" she heard the flag raisers howl.

It was not true yet, but it was going to be. While Mary rode through Florida, Columbia musicians played admiringly in front of the Congaree House, where Ruffin had checked in. The white-maned old prophet of disunion hated to make speeches, but you spoke when called on, or you lost prestige. He emerged upon the balcony.

"The defense of the South, I verily believe, is to be secured only through the lead of South Carolina," he managed to bawl out. "As old as I am, I have come to join you in that lead."

Back in his room, he met students from South Carolina College and promised to visit them but not to orate. Surely he liked the look of one of them, spectacled young Charles Woodward Hutson, who wore Southern-made gray homespun like Ruffin himself. Others, then, were renouncing Northern weave.

On November 11, James Chesnut telegraphed his wife that he had resigned from the United States Senate. A single wretched word in her diary: "Alas!" Mary had loved Washington society. She came back to South Carolina, to Mulberry Plantation outside Camden. Things were dull there, she thought.

Things were not dull in Charleston, where Ruffin journeyed from Columbia. On November 16 another band serenaded him, another host of admirers dragged him out upon a hotel balcony. He shrugged off stage fright and spoke from a furious full heart.

"If Virginia remains in the Union, under domination of this infamous, low, vulgar tyranny of Black Republicanism," he assured the audience in the street, "and there is one other State in the Union that has bravely thrown off the yoke, I will seek my domicile in that State and abandon Virginia forever." He knew what state would throw off the yoke: "If Virginia will not act as

South Carolina, I have no longer a home, and I am a banished man."

The listening gentlemen cheered, the listening ladies waved handkerchiefs. Ruffin stormed down to Georgia, bent on talking more secession there. As he left Charleston, another man appeared there. He was Major Robert Anderson of the United States Army Engineers, come to command and improve the forts in Charleston Harbor.

FIFTY-FIVE YEARS old, Anderson was tall and of vigorous frame. His face was too long-nosed to be handsome, but there was something both fine and strong about it, making him look perhaps more intelligent than he actually was. He had fought Indians and Mexicans. He had suffered battle wounds. He had won promotion. At West Point he had served as professor of artillery, and the army still used his training manual. Kentucky-born, with a Georgia wife and slaveholding kindred, he felt considerable sympathy for the Deep South. But he was an old soldier of the United States regular army, and he proposed to uphold the Union, there behind ramparts washed by secessionist waters.

Charleston Harbor must have looked to Anderson like the harbor of New York City, reduced to half size. The town was built on a tongue of land that licked out southward from between two broad rivers, as though to taste the salty ocean. At the left of the harbor, as one gazed down across the water, Sullivan's Island held a place somewhat like that of Brooklyn in the Northern port. Morris Island was like Staten Island, farther out and to eastward. Shute's Folly Island approximated the position of Governor's Island.

Chief fortifications in the harbor were three, all in need of repair and rearmament. On Sullivan's Island stood old and semi-dilapidated Fort Moultrie, from which once a British fleet had been repulsed, where in 1828 young Edgar Allan Poe had served, under the alias of Edgar A. Perry, as an artilleryman. On Shute's Folly rose a circular turret of brick, armed with several heavy guns but not garrisoned, called Castle Pinckney. Nearly three miles out, where dumpings of granite rubble made a rocky spit above shoal waters, stood the five-sided ramparts of Fort Sumter.

Major Anderson found his junior officers seasoned and competent. The nineteen non-coms were mostly grizzled, respectable old engineers and gunners. Of the seventy-six private soldiers, eight were musicians and formed a passable little military band. More than one hundred civilian laborers were at work on the harbor's defenses, an inadequate force for the rebuilding Anderson thought immediately necessary. And the garrison itself was about one-twentieth what Anderson could wish for.

He established headquarters at Fort Moultrie, where the chief work of construction was under way. The owners of several pleasant homes at the landward end of Sullivan's Island sent cordial invitations to the major and his officers.

But South Carolina would vote on December 6 for delegates to a convention that surely would sweep the state out of the Union that Anderson served. A similar election of delegates had been called in Alabama for December 24. November 28 found Georgia's legislature passing a bill for an election of delegates, and on the day following, Mississippi's legislature passed a similar bill. On December 2, the anniversary of John Brown's death on the gallows, the Columbia *Daily South Carolinian* loudly summoned from their graves the state's Revolutionary War heroes. "They then asserted self-government as necessary to a conservation of their rights," shouted the editorial, "and we are now invoked by the same spirit of conservation to dissolve our present political Union, in order to retain that inheritance of self-government."

Congress met at Washington on December 3. It still included moderates from the Upper South. On motion of Alexander Boteler of Virginia, the House voted to appoint a Committee of Thirty-three—one representative from each state—to seek compromise. The Senate acted more slowly to organize its own Committee of Thirteen. In the Deep South, these committees were scorned as devices for evasion and time-serving. Charleston's housetops had broken out in a rash of palmetto flags, defying the Stars and Stripes that flew only over Fort Moultrie.

On December 10, before either committee for compromise could meet, Howell Cobb of Georgia offered his resignation as

Secretary of the Treasury in the form of an address, not to the nation but to the people of the South. "Equality and safety in the Union are at an end," he pronounced flatly, "and it only remains to be seen whether our manhood is equal to the task of asserting and maintaining our independence out of it." Thus renouncing the Federal government and his office therein, Cobb applied for and received his mileage allowance for the journey home. Even his fellow-Georgian Toombs chuckled derisively at so thrifty a farewell.

Mary Chesnut, back in Charleston, heard noisy eloquence in the nearby dining room. Local secessionists honored, with supper and speeches, the visit of Mayor Francis Bartow of Savannah, Georgia, who had done his eloquent best in urging secession upon his state. Ex-Senator Chesnut, just elected a delegate to the forthcoming convention, called for Mary to meet him at Kingsville Junction and return to Mulberry Plantation. "Mrs. Chesnut does not look at all resigned," she heard someone say in the depot, and forbore, with an effort, from making a stinging rejoinder.

Almost alone of the outspoken against South Carolina's gallop toward disunion was venerable James L. Petigru of Charleston, whose remarks might have brought a duel upon anyone less traditionally respected. Benjamin Franklin Perry and gigantic Wade Hampton were Unionists too, but quieter than Petigru. Talking enough for everybody was done by the other side. Cotton, felt Senator James Hammond, would settle the question. "The North, without us, would be a motherless calf, bleating about," he declared, "and [would] die of mange and starvation." And suppose the Union did try that military action which so daunted lukewarm Upper Southerners? "Two battles will close the war and our independence will be acknowledged," was the candid opinion of Governor William H. Gist, finishing his term of office in an atmosphere of pleasurable excitement. "Great Britain and France will offer their mediation and the Yankees will gladly accept it and make peace."

Francis W. Pickens, barely home from Russia, was elected to succeed Gist, and on December 14 he began his duties by expediting all approaches to secession. "I was born insensible to fear," had been his lifelong boast, and all but a few of the most clear-thinking South Carolinians, Mary Chesnut among them, believed him and honored him for the sentiment. As South Carolina's secession convention met on December 16, at the First Baptist Church in Columbia, Pickens sent commissioners to neighboring states, to ascertain their views on the issue. At the same time he welcomed John A. Elmore from Alabama and Charles E. Hooker from Mississippi, representatives of their own governors as observers and applauders of the South Carolina convention.

Confidently these envoys assured Pickens that the rest of the South would follow any move made in Columbia. Elmore displayed a telegram from Governor Andrew B. Moore in Montgomery: "Tell the convention to listen to no propositions of compromise or delay."

But delay came, the threat of a smallpox epidemic. After choosing General Daniel F. Jamison of Barnwell District president of their convention, the delegates adjourned to Charleston.

Mary Chesnut, bored almost to tears at Mulberry, was happy to hear from her husband that she might join him, but could not resist an ironic comment to her diary: ". . . the men, who are all, like Governor Pickens, 'insensible to fear', are very sensible in case of smallpox." As she wrote those words, the Camden militia mustered and drilled nearby. Blue secession cockades adorned the hats of men, the bonnets of women.

On December 18, the hundred and sixty-nine delegates crammed aboard a train and traveled slowly to Charleston. The breakfast stop at Kingsville Junction found the little railroad restaurant all too poor in chairs and tables for so much company. There was food enough, however. Grave and distinguished men, accustomed from babyhood up to being waited on, drew their own coffee from the urn and foraged buffets for hot bread and eggs. Thus sketchily supplied, they continued on to Charleston.

Artillery salutes boomed. Smart-uniformed Citadel cadets paraded. President Jamison's carriage was escorted to his hotel by one of the bands that were getting so much work as secession drew nearer and became more thrilling.

The delegates met at St. Andrew's Hall on the morning of the

19th. John A. Inglis was named chairman of a committee for the drawing up of an ordinance of secession, to be considered on the following day.

All the other states waited for news. So did the lands beyond the sea.

Edmund Ruffin, honored guest at a hotel near the hall, was almost crazy with delighted anticipation. Mary Chesnut, visiting her friends the Kirklands on a nearby plantation, felt her state was doing what should be done, but could not banish a sense of hovering doom. In his little home near the Virginia Military Institute, Professor Thomas Jonathan Jackson characteristically took his country's crisis to the Lord in prayer.

III

The Cry Rose Near and Far

THE MORNING of December 20 was mild and bright over Charleston. The rising sun enriched with its fresh glow the cobbled streets, touched warmly the brick and plaster fronts of the houses, the wrought-iron grilles and balconies and gates, the tiled roofs, the chimneys, the aspiring steeples, the subtropical green of walled gardens and pleasant parks. That day's *Mercury* advertised a performance of Christy's ever-popular minstrel troupe. The Carolina Light Infantry announced regimental parade at nine A.M. In the evening, other fashionable units would drill—the Marion Artillery, the Phoenix Rifles, the Sumter Guards, and the Charleston Riflemen.

Midmorning, and the delegates crowded again into St. Andrew's Hall on Meeting Street, the thoroughfare that ran down the peninsula of the town past white, belfry-topped St. Michael's Church toward the palmetto-grown Battery. Hosts of townsfolk swarmed along the pavements, craning for glimpses of distinguished men as they entered the hall.

Ex-Governor Gist was there. So was A. G. Magrath of Columbia, who on hearing of Lincoln's election had ripped himself out of his black robes of a Federal judge; a canvas banner, with a crudely spirited picture of Magrath in the very moment of that melodramatic action, hung yonder across the street. James Chesnut, forty days out of the United States Senate, had left Mary with

41

the William Kirklands on their Combahee plantation and sat with the other delegates. With him appeared W. Porcher Miles and Lawrence M. Keitt, late of the lower House of Congress, and, like Chesnut, authors of dignified resignations. Veterans of earlier Congresses included Robert Barnwell Rhett, silently chafing because Pickens had been elected governor instead of himself, and ex-Senators William F. deSaussure and Rhett's cousin Robert W. Barnwell. James L. Orr had been speaker of the House in Washington, and Langdon Cheves, too, had served in the House. Ex-governors like Gist included James H. Adams, John H. Means, J. P. Richardson and John L. Manning.

Of those still active in office, the most distinguished were the new lieutenant governor, W. W. Harllee, and veteran Attorney-General I. W. Hayne. Memminger, the banker who had spoken South Carolina's fighting gospel to Virginia and Maryland, was present. There were lawyers, judges, planters, merchants, ministers of the gospel. Some names harked back to German emigrant forefathers—Dozler, Geiger, Quattlebaum, Weir. Others echoed French Huguenot ancestry—deSaussure, deTreville, Manginault, Gourdin. Still others sounded Irish—Magrath, McCrady, McKee, O'Hear.

Of all those so momentously gathered and determined, the names of few indeed would be heard again in history.

General Jamison, trim-bearded, alert-eyed, sat on the platform. Behind him hung a banner, hastily worked like that streamer-portrait of Judge Magrath outside the hall. It pictured an arch built of massive blocks that bore the names of the fifteen slave states. South Carolina was the keystone, of course. Inside the arch grew a palmetto tree, its trunk coiled around with a deadly-looking serpent. At the foot of the tree were grouped cannon, cotton bales and tobacco casks. In front of the structure lay broken fragments labeled with the names of the free states and, lest anyone misunderstand all this symbolism, there was a title in huge capital letters: BUILT FROM THE RUINS.

Sergeants-at-arms closed the doors against the mob outside, but several notable visitors had been admitted. John Elmore from Alabama and C. E. Hooker of Mississippi were there, ready to pledge the prompt secessions of their own respective states. And Edmund Ruffin was escorted to a special seat of honor.

His spry little figure in coarse gray homespun, his seamed face and his tumbled locks of white hair made him look like a shrewd old farmer in a stage comedy. On his lap he held a broad soft hat, its brim caught up with a blue secession cockade.

Necessary routine matters hurried themselves along. Then, at seven minutes after one o'clock, Chairman John A. Inglis of the ordinance committee was recognized. Gravely he presented a document, its language brief and clear and unequivocal:

We, the people of South Carolina, in Convention assembled, do declare and ordain, and it is hereby declared and ordained, that the ordinance adopted by us in Convention, on the 23rd day of May, in the year of our Lord 1788, whereby the Constitution of the United States of America was ratified, and also all Acts and parts of Acts of the General Assembly of this State ratifying the amendments of the said Constitution, are hereby repealed, and that the union now subsisting between South Carolina and other states under the name of the United States of America is hereby dissolved.

Silence for a moment, more dramatic than the loudest jabber. Then began the roll call.

"James H. Adams."

"Yea," responded the ex-governor.

"R. T. Allison."

"Yea," said Allison.

"D. C. Appleby."

"Yea."

Delegate after delegate answered to his name with the same brief assent. Last of them was Henry C. Young. At a quarter after one, the verbal vote was announced as unanimously in favor of the ordinance.

Someone waved a signal from a window, and the crowd that packed the street outside voiced frantic hurrahs. The cobbles and the walls vibrated. From the Citadel echoed the boom of cannon, loaded by the cadets hours earlier. Hats and handkerchiefs flourished. From Charleston's steeples thundered out the brazen applause of bells.

Old James Petigru saw and recognized an excited young man. "Where's the fire?" growled Petigru.

"Mr. Petigru, there is no fire," replied the youngster happily. "Those are the joybells ringing in honor of the passage of the ordinance of secession."

"I tell you there is a fire," insisted Petigru, gloomily sententious. "They have this day set a blazing torch to the temple of constitutional liberty, and, please God, we shall have no more peace forever."

Petigru was virtually alone in this pessimistic mood. The streets and walks teemed with shouting, hurrying people. Old men yelled like boys, their faces bright as with triumph already achieved. Newsboys appeared on the corners, hawking an extra edition of the *Mercury* with the secession ordinance on its front page—how was that possible, within minutes of the vote that approved it? Several who knew explained to others. Barnwell Rhett had served on the ordinance committee and had supplied his paper with an advance copy of the document. More news kept leaking from inside St. Andrew's Hall.

The convention had voted to wait until evening for the ceremonial signing and sealing of the fateful ordinance. Then they had adjourned to dinner, for which they must have begun to feel hungry. Commotion reigned all afternoon until, meeting at six-thirty, the delegates prepared to march to spacious Institute Hall, three blocks away on the corner of Broad Street. There they would affix their names in public.

The early December night had fallen as the procession formed, but bonfires and torches lighted the pavements and the fronts of the buildings. Fireworks popped and blazed, crowds yelled their hysterical admiration. The delegates reached Institute Hall, to find the auditorium already jammed with three thousand Charlestonians, while outside other thousands filled Broad and Meeting Streets from curb to curb.

Mounting the rostrum, General Jamison produced a massive gold pen with his name and the date cut upon the ebony holder. It had been presented to him for the coming moment of history, by the Charleston mercantile firm of Evans and Cogswell. Again

the roll was called. One by one, to waves of applause, the delegates walked to the desk where the ordinance was spread. Each
in turn signed his name.

When Barnwell Rhett was summoned, the onlookers deafened
the triumphant militant secessionist with acclaim, all the way
down the aisle and back to his seat. Another ovation greeted ex-
Governor Gist. Two hours were consumed in the affixing of
signatures. At last General Jamison signed his own name, then
straightened up and announced that the signing and sealing was
complete, and that he proclaimed the State of South Carolina a
separate and independent nationality.

Institute Hall shuddered again with the longest and loudest
chorus of cheers heard that whole noisy day, and the night was
given over to wild celebration that savored of carnival. In the
crowd appeared many militiamen in uniform. At a score of
hotels and private homes, the joyful citizens whooped for public
men to come out and make speeches. Edmund Ruffin yearned to
join the happy riot, but his old limbs and heart were tired, and he
lay in bed, exulting himself to sleep. The racket abated only in
the early hours of Friday, December 21.

Forty miles away, at the plantation home of William Kirkland
at the mouth of the Combahee, Mary Chesnut sat that Friday
morning with Mrs. Charles Lowndes. Lovely Mary Kirkland
brought into the parlor a newspaper, with the ordinance of
secession.

Gazing at Mrs. Lowndes, Mary Chesnut wondered if her own
face had gone as sickly white as that of her friend. Rawlins,
petted son of the Lowndeses, was a volunteer in the South Carolina militia, already mobilizing. William Kirkland had joined the
Charleston Light Dragoons. Mary Chesnut wrenched her eyes
away from her miserable friend and stared out at the water. A
Yankee gunboat could come there easily, into the wide mouth of
the Combahee, to smash the gracious, hospitable mansion with
shellfire. . . .

"God help us," she heard Mrs. Lowndes murmur. "As our day
is, so shall our strength be."

That day was bright and warm, like a day in spring; but it was the shortest day of the dying year, and upon its sunset would follow the longest night.

THE SECESSION CONVENTION remained organized to act as a body of advisers to Governor Pickens, also arrived in Charleston. Pickens named General Jamison his secretary of war, and Judge Magrath his secretary of state, but still there were high hopes that no war would come—at least not before other states joined South Carolina against the overpowering Union. The best-equipped and most socially acceptable militia companies filled their ranks with new volunteers, and additional companies were quickly enlisted. Meanwhile, what about those forts in Charleston Harbor, manned by United States troops? Commissioners sped to Washington, to demand the surrender of these defenses to South Carolina. They got courteous but equivocal answers from the nonplused officers of President Buchanan's Cabinet.

Christmas was nervously gay. "These are no times for festivities," said one planter who had a son in the militia and another aboard one of the hastily armed vessels in Charleston Harbor. At Abbeville, another father named Haskell let two of his sons observe the holy day by joining a regiment being raised by Colonel Maxcy Gregg, but sternly forbade their kid brother from following them into the ranks. At Columbia, the College Cadet Company had reactivated itself, complete with muskets. Spectacled, homespun-clad Charlie Hutson, graduated and at home for Christmas at McPhersonville, prepared to join the Pocotaligo Mounted Men.

In other slave states, where secession was not a fact, Christmas came much as it had come before. A merry party gathered at Vauclose Plantation, not far across the Potomac into Virginia from Washington. These people were for the most part Unionists, like their neighbors the Robert E. Lees of Arlington, and took the news of South Carolina's withdrawal as strange and disquieting. A crew of planters' sons dragged a great Yule log into the parlor and set it upon the glowing coals. Eggnog and apple toddy, traditional refreshments for the season, were served out. Young folks and old laughed, chattered and toasted each other. Then:

"Where shall we be a year hence?" wondered someone.

Nobody ventured a reply. But guest looked at guest, and a chill which no Yule fire could banish had crept into the parlor at Vauclose.

Lees gazing into the future, even a year ahead, distinguished young South Carolinians rallying to the palmetto flag.

Major Anderson, at Fort Moultrie in Charleston Harbor, dissembled his own grave concern, avoided several holiday-week invitations, and on the evening of December 26 cut down his flagstaff and spiked the guns on Moultrie's ramparts. Then he ferried his men and their supplies across to more defensible Fort Sumter, midway of the harbor's narrowest point. The golden sunrise of December 27 found the move completed.

Fury possessed every heart in Charleston. An act of military aggression, vowed Pickens and his lieutenants, and the newspapers echoed them. Pickens ordered the immediate mobilization of the Fourth Brigade of South Carolina militia, made up of society companies in the Charleston area. These formed two regiments. The First Regiment was commanded by Colonel Johnston James Pettigrew, a kinsman of Petigru the Unionist. The Washington Light Infantry, its shakos and crossbelts decorated with badges of leopard skin, was the honor company. The Charleston Riflemen proudly headed the other regiment, the Seventeenth. Pickens also called up a regiment of artillery, three companies of cavalry, and four independent rifle units furnished by volunteer fire organizations.

Before noon, a boat tied up at Fort Sumter's narrow esplanade. Out hopped Colonel Pettigrew, accompanied by Major Ellison Capers of the First Regiment, to demand an interview with Anderson.

The commander of Fort Sumter greeted them with what he must have meant to be disarming friendliness. His move from Moultrie, he insisted, was no act of aggression; indeed, he felt that withdrawal to this new and remote position would reduce the danger of a bloody clash with excited crowds on Sullivan's Island.

"In this controversy between the North and South," he added frankly, "my sympathies are entirely with the South."

Pettigrew was not to be blandished. "Well, sir," he rejoined, "however that may be, the governor of the state directs me to say to you, courteously but peremptorily, to return to Fort Moultrie."

"Make my compliments to the governor," said Anderson, urbane as before, "and say to him that I decline to accede to his request; I cannot and will not go back."

"Then, sir, my business is done," Pettigrew rasped out. He and Capers departed without another word.

Back to the Battery went Pettigrew with his report. Pickens directed him to seize Castle Pinckney at once, while Lieutenant Colonel Wilmot Gibbes deSaussure, the ex-senator who had signed the ordinance of secession, was told to lead a hundred artillerymen into deserted Fort Moultrie. Both were enjoined to "act with the greatest discretion and prudence." As they prepared to move their men, at noon, the Stars and Stripes climbed the staff above Fort Sumter.

Pettigrew landed on Shute's Folly with three companies of infantry, and overawed the lieutenant and sergeant who were the only military men at Castle Pinckney. His troops manned the ramparts and appropriated several heavy guns, a well-stocked magazine and a large supply of provisions. That evening, deSaussure entered Fort Moultrie, where a single sergeant offered no resistance. The militia artillerists took possession of fifty-six guns but moved gingerly over ground where rumor located land mines.

At table with the Kirklands, Mary Chesnut heard a fiercely confident voice: "Anderson has united the Cotton States. Now for Virginia!" She decided that life outside Washington society circles might not be dull, after all. In Charleston that night, her husband went walking on the Battery, and was accosted by a friend.

"These are troublous times, Colonel," said the worried Charlestonian. "We are at the beginning of a terrible war."

"Not at all," Chesnut told him cheerfully. "There will be no war, it will be all arranged." Then, repeating his epigram of election eve: "I will drink all the blood shed in the war."

Chesnut may actually have believed his own comforting words. But at Fort Moultrie, work gangs of Negroes had arrived to help strengthen the tumble-down bulwarks. They were supplemented by details of the gentlemen militia, less skilled with pick and shovel than their dark comrades, but willing for all that. Artificers drilled the spikes from the touchholes of the guns and repaired smashed carriages. Powder and shot arrived to serve these recommissioned pieces.

On December 28, a detachment of the Washington Light Infantry occupied the United States arsenal and seized a rich booty of arms and munitions. Boats from Sumter were allowed to fetch from Moultrie the luggage belonging to Anderson's men, but the fifty-six guns already glared toward Sumter. Mails went to the defiant garrison, and Anderson's commissaries visited Charleston to buy fresh provisions.

On the last day of the year, Pickens heard from his envoys in Washington that a ship would head for Sumter with reinforcements and supplies. In a panic, the governor sent orders to his forts:

The authentic news from Washington not very favorable. Re-inforcements may be *on their way* . . . be careful—and intercept all re-inforcements if possible at all *hazards*.

Pickens added a code of signals—flags by day, lanterns and rockets by night—to warn the town if a hostile force approached. The sky of New Year's Eve was stormy over Charleston.

IN MONTGOMERY, capital of Alabama, Governor Moore had ordered a salute of an even hundred guns to celebrate South Carolina's departure from the Union. On December 24, the various Alabama counties had elected an even hundred delegates for a convention to set Alabama upon the same course. These delegates could not meet until January 11; but, profiting by the Fort Sumter embarrassment, Moore sent his militia to occupy the forts in Mobile Bay and the United States arsenal at Mount Vernon. Similarly anticipatory was the action of the Georgia militia, and Francis Bartow vindicated the good opinion of Charleston secessionists by commanding, as captain, troops that seized Fort Pulaski outside Savannah.

On January 6 and 7, Florida's governor ordered the capture of forts on the soil of his state. Lieutenant Adam J. Slemmer, at Pensacola Harbor, had wind of this and took a leaf from Anderson's book and withdrew his handful of troops to Fort Pickens in the harbor. At Charleston in the early gray morning of January 9, the naval supply ship *Star of the West,* with supplies and troops aboard, tried to steam in. Fort Moultrie's hastily reactivated guns roared at her, and she withdrew to open sea.

Even as the *Star of the West* was showing her heels to the South Carolina shore batteries, William S. Barry rose in the convention hall at Jackson, Mississippi, to announce that the state's delegates had voted for secession, eighty-three to fifteen.

A jammed audience freed its elbows to applaud. Crinolined ladies swept down the aisle to put a flag into Barry's hands. The device was a magnolia tree on a white ground with, in the upper left-hand corner, a blue field centered with a single white star. Barry waved the banner vigorously above his head.

"The first flag of the new republic!" he cried.

Cheers grew louder, a prolonged storm of sound, Harry McCarthy, a young Irish actor, hurried away to his lodgings and scribbled verses:

> We are a band of brothers and native to the soil,
> Fighting for the property we gained by honest toil,
> And when our rights were threatened the cry rose near and far,
> Hurrah for the Bonnie Blue Flag that bears a single star!

That night, McCarthy sang his new songs between acts at the theater where his company performed. He used a rollicking tune of his homeland, "The Irish Jaunting Car," and the refrain was one in which any audience could quickly learn to join:

> Hurrah! Hurrah! For Southern rights, hurrah!
> Hurrah for the Bonnie Blue Flag that bears a single star!

The next day Florida was out, too, by a vote of sixty-two to three. The militia companies mustered for drill. In St. Augustine another bevy of ladies sewed frantically at a huge flag. It bore a palmetto tree to honor South Carolina's leadership. An eagle supported a globe with two stars. LET US ALONE, shouted the motto. In sight of the town square where the flag went up, the Spartan widow Frances Kirby Smith wrote what she felt was cheering news to her son, Major Edmund Kirby Smith, at a Federal fort in seceded Texas:

> . . . Col [William J.] Hardee . . . says it is difficult to advise, but a *Southern Confederacy* will organize an army—*Jefferson Davis* will have much to do with this—*bear this in mind*. . . .

For Senator Davis' state, Mississippi, was out of the Union now, and Senator Davis was a friend of Major Smith, and Senator Davis would be high in the councils of the rumored new nation.

Davis—his name was an inspiration to excited Southerners. He had lived thrilling adventures, had won glittering triumphs. A West Pointer, he had shown promise as a young officer but had left the army after eloping with Zachary Taylor's daughter. She had died, and Davis had mourned for years, then had married lovely Varina Howell. He had served with distinction in Congress. During the Mexican War he had led a regiment to glory at Buena Vista, had won the grudging praise of unreconciled old Zack Taylor, had refused a brigade because it was offered by the United States government, which did not seem to Davis valid for command of state troops. After that, he had been senator from Mississippi, then Franklin Pierce's Secretary of War—the energetic best, vowed men, ever to hold that post. In 1857 he was back in the Senate, a leader of the Southern Democrats who insisted on States' rights and slaveholders' rights before all others. He had been cautious, perhaps, about advocating secession, but surely he would shine in the nation building itself in the Deep South.

In Alabama, William Lowndes Yancey was chairman of the committee that would draft a proposed ordinance of secession. He harangued his fellows in the hall at Montgomery, vowing that any opposition to his ordinance was treason against the state.

If treason it was, some tried to make the most of it. Several of the northern counties muttered about a secession of their own, to leave Alabama and form a new Unionist state with the delightful name of Nickajack. But when, on January 11, the ordinance passed by a vote of sixty-one to thirty-nine, the town of Montgomery went as wild as had Charleston on December 20. Upon the dome of the high-columned state house flew a flag, made by ladies as prettily patriotic as those of Florida and Mississippi, and as imaginative in their symbolic blazonry. One side of the flag displayed the Goddess of Liberty bearing a single-starred banner, and over her head the words *Alabama*—INDEPENDENT NOW AND FOREVER. The other side showed a cotton plant and a coiled rattlesnake with, for scholars to translate for less learned acquaintances, the legend NOLI ME TANGERE.

The convention then voted, on recommendation of South Carolina's visiting commissioner A. P. Calhoun, to invite representatives from other seceding states to a meeting on February 4:

. . . for the purpose of consulting with each other as to the most effectual mode of securing concerted and harmonious action in whatever measures may be deemed most desirable for our common peace and security.

Concerted and harmonious action—state leaders everywhere clarified the words and agreed that they portended an alliance and the formation of a government.

Militia, hastily called to active duty, went to help the Floridians glare toward defiant Fort Pickens. A few Alabamians deplored every bit of news they heard. A die-hard Unionist legislator scowled at the flag sewn by Montgomery's fairest, and wrote home to Limestone County:

. . . Here I sit & from my window see the nasty little thing flaunting in the breeze which has taken the place of that glorious banner which has been the pride of millions of Americans and the boast of freemen the wide world over. I look upon the old banner as I do or would view the dead body of a friend and I would scream one loud shout of joy could I now see it waving in the breeze although I know the scream would be my last.

No wise man would scream for Union in Alabama.

But the old banner still waved in the breeze above Fort Sumter in Charleston Harbor. On the day that Alabama left the Union, Governor Pickens sent Secretary of War Jamison and Secretary of State Magrath to demand again the fort's surrender. Jamison told Anderson, with a fine sense of the theatrical, that twenty thousand South Carolinians were eager to storm Sumter and pull the walls to pieces bare-fingered. Again Anderson refused to evacuate, but agreed to send an officer to Washington for instructions. Pickens dispatched Hayne on the same errand, and cannily improved the time of waiting by heaping up new defenses at Fort Moultrie and on Morris Island opposite, and by bringing more guns into position at both points.

On January 19, Georgia's secession convention lightheartedly voted its state out of the Union, two hundred and eight to eighty-nine. William J. Hardee left Florida to offer his military talents to his native Georgia. He spoke once more to Frances Kirby Smith, who on January 21 wrote the conversation to her soldier-son in Texas:

. . . it is *fully believed* that there will be formed a Southern Confederacy—a government and Army organized. It is said that without doubt Jefferson Davis will be the Genl in Chief or Secy. of War of this new Confederacy—may God prosper it!

That same morning, at nine o'clock, Jefferson Davis came to the Hall of the Senate in Washington to tell the Federal Union good-bye.

He had remained for nine days after Albert Brown, his colleague from Mississippi, had quietly resigned and gone home. Davis was trying to help the South Carolina commissioners to get some sort of reply from President Buchanan to their demand for Sumter's surrender. And he had been ill—frequently, when excited or depressed, Davis took to his bed. But he felt, he knew, that with Mississippi twelve days seceded he could hold his seat in the United States Senate no longer.

Everybody in Washington knew that Davis would speak, and what he would speak about. The gallery had begun to fill as early as seven o'clock that morning. By nine it was packed, and the entrances to the gallery and the floor were packed, too. Fine ladies collapsed their crinoline hoops to sit on the floor against the walls, like children at a party. Crowded, cramped newspaper correspondents poised their pencils above wadded paper. Varina Davis had been forehanded in dispatching a servant to hold a gallery seat for her, and she arrived to claim that seat just before her husband was scheduled to appear. She looked down into the hall, at the grouped faces of young women in a doorway; like a mosaic of flowers, thought Varina.

Davis entered the hall and came forward to speak. He looked frail, but he stood erect and bold. His slim tall figure was dressed in gray, far finer of weave and cut than Edmund Ruffin's now-famous homespun. His finely chiseled face, with its long straight nose and its square, beard-fringed chin, appeared to some like a more delicate version of the face of Abraham Lincoln. He swept the hall with his brilliant eyes, and only Varina and a very few others knew that one of those eyes was blind.

Quietly, clearly, he began to speak:

"I rise for the purpose of announcing to the senate that I have satisfactory evidence that the State of Mississippi, by solemn ordinance in convention assembled, has declared her separation from the United States," he said. "Under these circumstances, of course, my functions terminate here. It has seemed to me to be proper that I should appear in the senate and announce that fact, and to say something, though very little, upon it."

Raptly they listened as Jefferson Davis rehearsed his faith in a state's right to secede. His words and his delivery were restrained, but they were eloquent, even by the standards of those wordy days. Hearers in the gallery wept audibly. Senators grimaced or glared or trembled at their desks. Davis ventured, at last, a plea for peace between the divided sections.

"Whatever offense there has been to me, I leave here," he said in conclusion. "I carry no hostile feelings away. Whatever of offense I have given, which has not been redressed, I am willing to say to senators in this hour of parting, I offer you my apology for anything I have done in the senate; and I go thus released from obligation, remembering no injury I have received, and having discharged what I deem the duty of man, to offer the only reparation at this hour for every injury I have offered."

He bowed, and turned to depart. Four other senators rose to follow him—Stephen Mallory and David Yulee of Florida, Clement Clay and Benjamin Fitzpatrick of Alabama. Around the departing senators crowded Northern Democrats to say good-bye. Also to shake Davis' nervous hand came two intransigent Republican Unionists, Simon Cameron and John Parker Hale.

That night, Varina Davis heard her husband praying softly for peace between North and South. He remained in Washington for several days more, writing Governor Pickens in South Carolina to offer the benefit of what Davis considered his own great military wisdom. On or about January 26, he and Varina and the children set out for home.

THE TWO-STORY HOME of Thomas Jonathan Jackson, professor of physics and instructor in artillery at Virginia Military Institute, stood a conveniently short block away from the Lexington Presbyterian Church. That January 26, without the summer flowers Anna Jackson loved to cultivate every year, it looked plain and even austere, to match its master as he sat down in his study to take stock of his own grave opinions concerning Southern rights to slavery and secession.

Jackson never had been headlong in any pursuit, save once; as a young officer in the Mexican War he had sought glory at reckless hazard of his life, and he had found it. That had been fifteen years earlier, before he had experienced bereavement, disappointment, and a profound spiritual awakening.

Sorrow knew its way to his door. As a boy he had lost both father and mother. Relatives had reared him, and he was not always happy—indeed, he had run away once, had toiled for months as a woodcutter for Mississippi steamers before coming home to western Virginia. After West Point, hopes for military recognition and promotion had gone glimmering; nobody moved up quickly in the peacetime service; and he had resigned to teach at the Institute. His happy first marriage had ended with the death of his young wife in childbirth. Three years later he had remarried, again happily; the bride had been Mary Anna Morrison, lustrously brown-eyed daughter of a North Carolina pastor. Then tragedy again, with the death of their baby girl. But Anna had brightened the sternness of Thomas Jackson's moods, and behind the closed doors of that plain house they were true, impassioned lovers.

To almost everyone but his Anna, Jackson was a stern bearded presence, half military scholar, half Old Testament prophet. He was a deacon in the Presbyterian Church down the block, he was Sabbatarian and staid in church and out. Some of the cadets thought him amusingly eccentric, even while they profited by his thorough instruction. Jackson was an artillerist of the utmost skill and advanced theory, and under his austere guidance the young men became good gunners.

Jackson had grown up in a slaveholding family, and in his Lexington home were black Amy and Emma to do the housework, with young boys for the chores. Albert, a grown man who wanted freedom, was allowed to work in town for wages that would apply toward his own purchase. But not once had Jackson spoken publicly for secession as a safeguard of the rights of states and men.

Indeed, Anna considered her husband a Unionist, like many in western Virginia. She remembered how Jackson had enjoyed last summer's New England vacation, and the religious chat with that Yankee preacher. More recently, Jackson had written to his sister Laura Ann Arnold:

. . . I am looking forward with great interest to the 4th of January when the Christian people of this land will lift their united prayers as incense to the throne of God in supplication for our unhappy country.

He had mailed that letter on December 29, while South Carolina volunteers set their guns to cover Fort Sumter. On January 4, as Deacon Jackson and other devout men prayed for peace and conciliation, Florida and Alabama militia had moved to seize United States forts.

Again, to a beloved aunt, Jackson had written hopefully:

. . . Viewing things at Washington from human appearances, I think we have great reason for alarm, but my trust is in God, and I cannot think that He will permit the madness of men to interfere with the Christian labors of this country at home and abroad.

That letter was dated January 21, even as Jefferson Davis spoke his sad but irrevocable farewell in the United States Senate and led other Southerners with him toward the promise of a new nation.

Major Jackson's neighbors mostly spoke for preservation of the Union. Such had been his own earlier hope and speech, and he had expressed soldierly distaste for the possibility of war to follow secession. But things were not quite as simple as deciding what you wanted—there was right, and there was wrong. He sat down to write to his namesake, Sister Laura Ann's son Thomas. It was a Saturday, and he would hold the letter until Monday, lest it travel on a Sabbath-violating mail train; but now, now, he set down his views:

. . . I am in favor of making a thorough trial for peace, and if we fail in this, and the state is invaded, to defend it with a terrific resistance. . . .

Invasion had occurred already in Virginia, as Jackson well remembered, under the leadership of John Brown for whose hemp-sped soul Jackson had ventured to pray. If war came, which way would Virginia move as the colors massed and the drums beat? Jackson felt he could guess that:

. . . I desire the state to use every influence she can to procure an honorable adjustment of our troubles, but if after having done so the free states, instead of permitting us to enjoy the rights guaranteed to us by the Constitution of our country, should endeavor to subjugate us and excite our slaves to servile insurrection in which our families will be murdered without quarter of mercy, it becomes us to wage such a war as will bring hostilities to a speedy close. People who are anxious to bring on war don't know what they are bargaining for; they don't see all the horrors that must accompany such an event. . . .

Old Edmund Ruffin could not see the horrors, he who had

served in 1812 but had never heard a shot fired in anger. Exultant in the hopes of conflict that would stampede Virginia and the rest of the Upper South out of the Union, Ruffin lingered in Charleston, within sound of any gun Fort Sumter might care to touch off. He had even lent a withered hand in the shoveling of earth to strengthen Charleston's shore positions, and had thrilled like a romantic little boy to the possibility that he himself might be fired upon. Nor did William Lowndes Yancey see the horror—his experience of gunfire had been limited to the dueling ground—nor did Barnwell Rhett, who badgered Pickens to order the storming of Anderson's ramparts. Surely Jefferson Davis, gloomily departing for home, could remember the deafening volleys, the bright blood splashed on Mexican battlefields. Most certainly Jackson himself remembered. He had seen all the horrors at close quarters, on disputed stretches of earth with exotic names like Cerro Gordo and La Hoya and Contreras and Churubusco and Chapultipec. Blood flowed in wars, like smoking red rivulets on the floor of hell. And if war came, he, Thomas Jonathan Jackson, must do the fighting on fields where those who did the talking could not venture.

But these were baleful matters to write to his young nephew. In any case, Virginia's leaders still preached compromise. Major Jackson attempted a more cheerful note in closing:

. . . For myself I have never as yet been induced to believe that Virginia will even have to leave the Union. I feel pretty well satisfied that the Northern people love the Union more than they do their peculiar notions of slavery, and that they will prove it to us when satisfied that we are in earnest about leaving the Confederacy unless they do us justice.

He sealed the envelope, while down in Louisiana another state convention voted to secede, one hundred and thirteen to seven, and William Tecumseh Sherman, with unashamed tears, announced his resignation as head of the Louisiana State Seminary of Learning and Military Academy. In Mississippi, the governor signed a commission making Jefferson Davis major general in command of state troops.

TWO DAYS LATER, Texas called into session its delegates to vote on leaving the Union, despite the last-ditch opposition of sick, desperate old Governor Sam Houston. And representatives from South Carolina, Florida, Alabama, Mississippi, and Georgia began to pack their luggage for the journey to Montgomery, where they would form the Confederate States of America, adopt a constitution and elect a provisional President.

IV

A Band of Brothers

MARY CHESNUT, heading for Montgomery with her husband, knew and liked and silently criticized the others of South Carolina's delegation—Robert Barnwell, Barnwell Rhett, Lawrence Keitt, Judge Thomas J. Withers, W. Porcher Miles, William W. Boyce, and Christopher Gustavus Memminger. All but Boyce had been members of the secession convention. Miles and Keitt were graceful and handsome. Memminger and Withers were older men, but pungently individual. Rhett and Barnwell, those erstwhile estranged cousins, still harbored resentful differences of opinion. Mary's James, habitually quiet, nevertheless acted as though he bore a freight of history. Montgomery promised to be exciting.

They found the town pleasant and beautiful on the left bank of the Alabama River, almost at the geographical center of the nation they would help bring forth. Its population was less than nine thousand, but the spacious arrangement of streets, the elegance of homes and shops, the busy iron foundries, wharfs and mills, caused a Northern observer to set it down as double that size. There were many fine houses, with Georgian roofs, wrought-iron fences, pleasant gardens.

From the steamboat landing, Main Street ran a full mile to the State House Square, where the tall capitol building of brick and stone dwarfed lesser roofs around it. The portico's three-story pillars bore crowns of carved leafage, like the tops of steamboat chimneys. From terraced slopes of lawn rose a flight of wide marble steps to the front door. Halfway between wharf and capitol stood the two principal hotels, the adequate Exchange and the rather unsavory Montgomery Hall, compared by a secessionist wit to the Raven of Zurich for "uncleanliness of nest and length of bill." These, and all boardinghouses and taverns besides, filled fast with the assembling host of politicians and adventurers.

The Chesnuts were fortunate in securing apartments at the Exchange. Mary felt her spirits sink. "Everywhere political intrigue is as rife as in Washington," she said. In other ways, conditions were dolefully different. Many deputies from various states were obliged to crowd together, two and three and even more in a single bedroom.

The South Carolinians had arrived just too late to hear a notable speech by Yancey, but the town still rang with it, and Yancey's admirers felt that it would dispose of Upper Southern coyness toward secession.

"All of those States—Virginia, Maryland, Delaware, Kentucky, Missouri, North Carolina and Tennessee—are heavy grain and stock growing States," Yancey had pointed out to his hearers, "and if they get rid of their slaves, could still prosper to a large degree. If they remain in the late Union, they will be powerless to protect their slaves; and in time, the pressure will be so great on the institution that they will endeavor, by sale, to get rid of every slave as a necessity. The only place they can sell them will be the Southern Confederacy. . . . Shall they join the South and keep their slaves or sell them as they choose, or shall they join the North and lose their slaves by abolition?"

Edmund Ruffin had written to the like purport four years earlier, for *De Bow's Review;* but many Southerners listened more easily and happily than they read, and Yancey, as he spoke, felt that he was being heard beyond the reach of his voice, beyond the limits of Montgomery, of Alabama and of the states already pledged to form a new government.

"That issue," he wound up with all the triumphant confidence in the world, "will be for each of these States to decide for itself, of course; and I cannot for a moment believe but that in time, each would decide, from motives of self interest as well as from equally weighty considerations in favor of good government, to join the Cotton States, and thus present to the world the South united, prosperous and powerful for the purposes of peace or war."

War. . . . Somebody had said the word again, somebody who was unable to see the horrors war would bring. But there was hope of peace in the hearts of men with sad experience and cool heads. The delegation of nine from Alabama had rather mysteriously excluded Yancey, and Barnwell Rhett, even while he blustered in the hotel lobbies and State House offices about militant secession, had lost prestige. Ruffin was nowhere near the meeting, preferring the atmosphere of romantic danger at Charleston. Able men were present in all the state deputations. Among Georgia's ten delegates were two ex-senators, Robert Toombs and Alexander Stephens, with Howell Cobb the ex-Secretary of the Treasury and Francis Bartow of Fort Pulaski fame. Mississippi sent seven, Louisiana six and Florida three. Of the whole gathering, a majority could show past records of Union sympathy.

They met at the State House on February 4, organized themselves as the provisional Congress of the Confederate States of America, and chose Howell Cobb to preside over their deliberations. Cobb's secretary was Johnston Jones Hooper, the Alabama author of the delightful *Adventures of Simon Suggs*. The deputies wore frock coats, shirts with pleated or ruffled bosoms, great upflaring white collars, and cravats tied in broad bows. Beards or luxuriant side whiskers sprouted on many of the earnest faces. Strong upon them was the sense of history to be made by their own hands. Alexander Stephens, never prone to overstate his enthusiasms, said that here was a Congress more able and intelligent than any of the sixteen he had attended at Washington, where, as Stephens spoke, delegates from the states still in the Union strove once more for peace.

The new Confederate Congress declared, promptly and soberly, the establishment of a provisional government to continue for one year from date, or until a permanent organization could be achieved. A constitution was adopted, sounding very much like that of the forsaken Union. Departures from the pattern included specific outlawing of the foreign slave trade, guarantee of the return of fugitive slaves from one state to another, and measures to treat with the Union for settlement of public debts and title to public property.

Less quiet was debate over who should be President.

It had been agreed that four state delegations out of the six present must agree on a single candidate, and several men present had ambitions toward the presidency. Mississippi nominated Jefferson Davis, Georgia offered the name of Howell Cobb. Toombs of Georgia, who much appreciated his own gifts and who had sneered publicly at Cobb for that frugal insistence on travel pay after resigning at Washington, swallowed a private disappointment and mildly endorsed his rival. Meanwhile, several other states looked to South Carolina for a first expression of approval for a candidate, and for hours South Carolina said nothing.

Chairman Barnwell did not convene his fellow deputies for any sort of discussion. He himself felt that Davis was a better choice than Cobb, but his enthusiasm for Davis was lukewarm. Chesnut admired Davis as a statesman and liked him as a friend. Keitt and Boyce wanted Cobb. Rhett, still the fire-eater and still in some crumbling hope of his own nomination, called Davis "egotistical, arrogant and vindictive, without depth or statesmanship." Rhett harked back to a speech made by Davis to New Englanders, on July 4, 1858; had not Davis compared the secessionists of two and a half years before to "mosquitoes around the horns of an ox, who could annoy but could do no harm"? Davis had really said that about "trifling politicians in the South, or in the North, or in the West," but none to whom Rhett talked seemed to be able to correct the quotation.

Rhett's cousin Barnwell refused to be aware of these differences among his companions. He interviewed them, singly and in private. Only his cousin Rhett, argued Barnwell, actively opposed Davis. He, Barnwell, thought Davis' ability mediocre— might have hinted that his own ability was superior?—but Davis was just, honorable, experienced, and devoted to the ideal of Southern independence. Further, since it seemed to be a choice between Davis and Cobb, here was the chance to have them both in the government; Davis, as President, could be counted to give high office to Cobb and all other first-class men.

The South Carolinians agreed to vote as a bloc with the Mississippians, for Davis. Other state delegations followed their lead. When the vote was called for, all but the Georgians supported Davis. Then the Georgia delegation asked permission to change its vote so as to make election unanimous, and on February 9 Jefferson Davis was proclaimed the provisional President of the Confederate States of America, to serve one year.

Little Alexander Stephens of Georgia was elected Vice-President. He looked like a withered boy, and he had a shrill piping voice and a considerable wit. All three of these characteristics prompted admirers to liken him to John Randolph of Roanoke. Among Georgia's leaders, Stephens had most strongly deplored the departure from the Union.

Congress enacted its first legislation that day, and hurriedly expeditious that legislation was:

. . . that all laws of the United States of America in force and in use in the Confederate States of America on the first day of November last and not inconsistent with the Constitution of the Confederate States, be and the same are hereby continued until altered or repealed by the Congress.

That gave the Confederacy a temporary working program for the myriad agencies that must begin operation at once to keep the newborn government together. Then the deputies wired Davis the news of his election. They proceeded to form a committee to consider designs for a national flag, and advertised for suggestions.

In all these things they had been businesslike, even impressive. A correspondent for the New York *Herald* felt as much, and said as much, too, in a dispatch to his paper:

No one can watch the proceedings of the Southern Congress without feeling a degree of relief from the dread fears of collision and bloodshed with which the North has been afflicted for the last month or six weeks that is truly refreshing. The united front and united action of the six states that have thus leagued themselves into the pioneer guard, as it were, for the remaining nine, is an earnest that no one of them, in its sovereign capacity, will undertake a conflict with the old United States without the assent of its brethren. . . .

The old personal dissensions were fading away, because the old extremists were fading away.

At Brierfield Plantation, on its island in the Mississippi below Vicksburg, spring seemed to have come by February 10. Jefferson Davis helped Varina cut slips from the rose bushes for planting in new arrangements. A messenger hurried into the yard with a telegram.

Davis took it and read it. Varina saw his face grow drawn with sudden dismay. She wondered if some kinsman were in trouble. Davis turned and looked at her for moments of long silence. She dared not ask what distressed him. At last he spoke, in a voice of tragic emotion that to Varina seemed like the voice with which a man might say he had been sentenced to death. He had been elected the President of the Confederacy.

Hastily Davis packed. His slaves gathered to see him go, and he distributed supplies and spoke affectionate farewells. He told Varina to wait for word from him before following with six-year-old Maggie, four-year-old Jeff, and little two-year-old Joe.

His journey to Montgomery was by winding railroads that carried him through part of unseceded Tennessee and as far eastward as Georgia. His train was greeted at town after town with wild demonstrations of admiring affection. He felt weary, and sadly lonesome for Varina, but he made twenty-five speeches on the way. Eighty miles from Montgomery he was met by a committee of welcome and two companies of glittering Georgia militia. These escorted him through the afternoon of February 16, toward the Confederacy's capital and his own daunting destiny.

Rain fell that day. Davis complained of a sore throat; it may have been one of his emotional tensions. At ten P.M. the party reached Montgomery. Cannon roared salvos, militia paraded in the dark, and a crowd boiled up around the depot to follow Davis' carriage to the Exchange Hotel.

The Exchange was entered by stairs climbing above ground-floor shops, to the lobby, the bar and the drawing rooms on the second story. As Davis entered his quarters, the people called his name outside. At 10:45, William Lowndes Yancey brought Davis out upon a balcony. The rain and the clouds had vanished, and the night sky was fine.

"The hour and the man have met!" cried Yancey.

Davis bowed with dignified courtesy to the fresh applause, then cleared his sore throat and began to speak. His husky voice could be heard to the farthest fringe of the crowd:

"Fellow citizens and brethren of the Confederate States of America—for now we are brethren, not in name merely but in fact—men of one flesh, one bone, one interest, one purpose and one identity of domestic institutions. We have henceforth, I trust, a prospect of living together in peace, with our institutions a subject of protection and not of defamation. It may be that our career will be ushered in, in the midst of storms—it may be that as this morning opened with clouds, mist and rain, we shall have to encounter inconveniences at the beginning; but as the sun rose, lifted the mist, dispersed the clouds, and left a pure sunlight, heaven so will prosper the Southern Confederacy, and carry us safe from sea to the safe harbor of constitutional liberty."

He was interrupted by applause. Bowing, he waited for it to die down. Then he thanked the listeners and all the Confederacy for kindness to him, expressed his own diffidence at assuming the presidency, pledged his utmost energy and faith to service of his people. Finally and significantly:

"If in the progress of events, it shall become necessary, and my services shall be needed in another direction—if, to be plain, necessity shall require that I shall again enter the ranks as a soldier, I hope you will welcome me there."

And he said good night, and returned to his room.

To be a soldier—indeed, why not? Davis had been a soldier once, and most people had thought him a good one. The notion was not exactly original with him. The governor of Mississippi had made him a major general. Varina often had told him that his talents lay in military affairs. And many of the deputies who formed the Congress, even if skeptical of his gifts in the presidency, had wanted him as general in chief of whatever army the new nation might muster.

On February 18, six white horses drew Davis' coach to his inaugural on the porch of the capitol building. Judge Withers considered that equipage foolishly ostentatious. The congressmen assembled to hear their new President speak. Among them sat Aurelia Fitzpatrick, with a beautiful woman's confidence that she was welcome there.

"Called to the difficult and responsible station of Chief Magistrate of the provisional government which you have instituted," Davis began, "I approach the discharge of the duties with an humble distrust of my abilities, but with a sustaining confidence in the wisdom of those who are to guide and aid me in the administration of public affairs, and an abiding faith in the virtue and patriotism of the people."

That was modest and gentlemanly, and it would draw the fangs of critics who, perhaps in envious disappointment, had called Davis egotistical. The President went on to describe the separation from the Union as a peaceable achievement, a properly dignified appeal to the ballot box, a reaffirmation of the principle that proper government depended always upon the consent of the governed. The South, he said, was an agricultural nation and had no ambition to rival the industrial North. He mentioned the need for a monetary system, a postal service, an army and a navy. He expressed, once more and feelingly, his hope that the Confederacy might enjoy peace and friendship with the Union. But if the Union offered violence:

". . . a terrific responsibility will rest upon it, and the suffering of millions will bear testimony to the folly and wickedness of our aggressors."

Davis said those things quietly, restrainedly. Continuing, he pointed out that the new nation's government was a departure from that of the old in its constituent parts but not in its basic system. Traditions of the Founding Fathers would be respected and maintained. He finished:

"Reverently let us invoke the God of our fathers to guide and protect us in our efforts to perpetuate the principles which by His blessing they were able to vindicate, establish and transmit to their prosperity; and with a continuance of His favor ever gratefully acknowledged, we may hopefully look forward to success, to peace, to prosperity."

It had not been a long speech. By comparison to many delivered in that time and region, it had not been a dramatic speech. But it had moved those who heard it, and the Confederacy's great men crowded around their President to offer him their expressions of admiration and loyalty. Boldly Mrs. Fitzpatrick dug the tip of her gay parasol into Davis' straight, narrow back. When he turned, she smiled bewitchingly and gushed congratulations. Mary Chesnut was shocked, but hoped that Mrs. Fitzpatrick's familiarity might convince Judge Withers that the new Confederacy was democratic in spirit, after all.

Texans were in the provincial Congress by now, and news came from Texas that various forts had been occupied and arsenals and military stores confiscated from old General David E. Twiggs, a native of Georgia who had not much protested. Kirby Smith and several other Southern officers had sent in their resignations and headed for Montgomery to offer their services; but Lieutenant Colonel Robert E. Lee of Virginia obeyed orders to report to Washington and did so, voicing his grave concern over the future of both North and South. Lee was considered the coming man in the little United States Army, the general officers of which had grown old for active duty. And active duty might come, and Lee would have high command. For which government?

On February 21, President Davis exhibited sober political sense in distributing the Cabinet posts among the various states. Sturdy, thunder-voiced Robert Toombs would be the Secretary of State. Memminger, the German-born South Carolina banker, was Secretary of the Treasury. The War Department went to Leroy Pope Walker, a square-bearded Alabama lawyer and militia general who had paraphrased Chesnut's epigram by repeated public offers to wipe up with his handkerchief any and all blood shed in intersectional strife. Florida's Stephen Mallory would be Secretary of the Navy, and bull-faced James Regan of Texas the Postmaster General. Davis handed the Attorney General's portfolio to suave, ingratiating Judah P. Benjamin of Louisiana, with whom he once had come to the brink of a duel. All these Cabinet officers searched for headquarters space in the crowded town and hurriedly assembled staffs of assistants and clerks.

Washington's Birthday was elaborately celebrated throughout the seceded states. The Washington Light Infantry paraded in Charleston to receive a banner, then returned to garrison duty on Sullivan's Island. Pampered young privates supplemented their coarse rations with *pâté de fois gras,* with imported sardines and olives, and washed these delicacies down with champagne, sherry and madeira. Out in the harbor, Anderson fired thirty-four guns to honor the Father of his Country—a gun for every state, including newly admitted Kansas and including also the seven seceded States of the Confederacy.

"Insolent wretch!" scolded Mary to her diary at Montgomery, while the town thronged with office seekers, self-styled refugees from states still in the Union, and resigned army and navy officers seeking commissions in the Confederate services.

A military establishment was in the making. Congress had approved a regular army of 10,745 officers and men, and a provisional army with a maximum of 10,000 volunteers for twelve months' service. The first general officer to be commissioned was graceful Pierre Gustave Toutant Beauregard of Louisiana, late major of the old army's Engineer Corps, who had been relieved of the superintendency of West Point after five days in that post. His rank as Confederate brigadier dated from March 1, and Davis sent him to Charleston to command the watchers of Fort Sumter. Another brigadier from Louisiana was North Carolina-born Braxton Bragg—"A little more grape, Captain Bragg!" Zack Taylor had told him at Monterey, thereby making him a folk hero of sorts. Bragg went to Pensacola, where volunteers tried to scare the dogged Slemmer out of Fort Pickens. Samuel Cooper, a New Yorker married to a Virginian, resigned as adjutant general of the Federal army, and was given the same assignment for the Confederacy, with the rank of brigadier. Raphael

Semmes of Alabama, an ex-commander of the old navy, became a captain and was ordered North to buy machinery and munitions.

Other resigned officers got regimental commands. So did sketchily experienced political leaders and fumbling militia chieftains. From West Point, far up on the Hudson River, slipped away still ungraduated cadets from the Deep South. Reporting in Montgomery, these quickly received commissions as line officers and majors and adjutants.

There were social pleasures in Montgomery. A group of citizens presented a house to President Davis and his family, to the fresh annoyance of Judge Withers. In the modest parlor, Varina Davis welcomed her old friend Mary Chesnut. Stephen Mallory came to tell of the flirtations in Washington of Eugenia Phillips. "What a mad, bad woman she is," soliloquized Mary, shocked and perhaps ever so slightly envious. Mary did not know that the autumnally alluring Eugenia served the Confederacy as a spy.

The Montgomery Theater attracted crowds. John Wilkes Booth, lately a star there in *The Apostate,* had gone North before the assembling of the Confederate deputies, but Maggie Mitchell, golden and twenty-three, enchanted audiences in *Fanchon.* Doubling in specialty, Miss Maggie sang "The Bonnie Blue Flag" and dramatically waved that emblem over her dazzling blond head, at the same time trampling beneath her shapely little feet the Stars and Stripes. Applause and infatuation, even in high places—Governor Moore, for instance. "The old sinner has been making himself ridiculous with that little actress Maggie Mitchell," noted Mary Chesnut. But Mary herself gave dinner to the grimy-jacketed Montgomery Blues, back from a month's duty at Pensacola, and later was entertained and flattered when Mallory called and offered mannerly gallantry. In less distinguished and less circumspect quarters there were gambling and drinking, reminiscent of Alabama's flush times.

March 4, and somewhere east and north of Montgomery, in a Washington increasingly dim and blurred in the memories of the secessionists, Abraham Lincoln was being inaugurated. The Richmond *Enquirer,* Jennings Wise's paper, bordered its front page in black as though to signalize an occasion for national mourning, and Edmund Ruffin had departed from Virginia for Charleston, refusing to linger on soil that recognized Lincoln as President. But Virginia's secession convention dallied dreamily, and in North Carolina and Tennessee calls for such conventions had been voted down by the people. The Northern Congress considered measures that might bring peace, even reunion.

That other Congress, the Confederate one, approved a flag for its country, the design of an earnestly secessionist North Carolinian named Orren Randolph Smith. It looked far less ornate than those mottoed blazonries of trees, eagles, snakes and goddesses; most of it consisted of three broad horizontal bars, a white one between two of red. In a blue field in the corner shone seven stars, for the seven Confederate States. While her husband sat in deliberation over this and other measures, Mary Chesnut walked out on March 4 and felt faint and nauseated at sight of a slave auction; the mulatto girl on the block looked like her own maid Nancy. Mary returned to her apartment and read *Evan Harrington*. She missed the fashionable shops she had known in lost Washington. But that evening Mallory and Judge Withers called, to divert her with more society gossip, until James upstairs stamped in vexation, perhaps in jealousy.

On the following day, March 5, the new flag was raised to the dome of the capitol. Miss Letitia Tyler, granddaughter of a President, pulled on the halyards. Cannon boomed—there was a lot of cannonading those days, in a nation not too plentifully supplied with gunpowder—but one or two watchers felt that the onlookers were subdued in manner; maybe that was because of the song the band played, "Massa's in the Cold, Cold Ground." Secretary of War Walker brightened things by promising, from the balcony of the Exchange Hotel, to raise the flag "over Faneuil Hall in the city of Boston!"

Varina Davis received guests in her parlor, and Benjamin Fitzpatrick apologized for not inviting the Chesnuts and others to his model plantation a dozen miles away—"The roads are so bad," he said. Among the ladies ran the ever-fascinating whisper of scandal.

Of such gaieties, Jefferson Davis saw relatively little. He never had been strong of body or serene of spirit. Long hours of hard work proved the more exhausting because he made himself accessible to any and all callers. He went to his office at nine o'clock each morning and returned at six in the evening, so weary that he could not eat or sleep properly. Varina confided in Mary Chesnut that she wished Davis had been made general of the Confederate armies—that "would have suited his temperament better." A few, a very few, timidly bewailed the shattering of the old Union, and were shouted down by the scornful voices of the majority. There would be no war, said confident voices. Mary Chesnut heard someone say: "This war talk is nothing. It will soon blow over. Only a fuss gotten up by that Charleston mob." The Confederacy, protested others, was a nation risen from purity of ideals—the dignity of citizens, the sovereignty of states, the sacredness of property, even of human property. To call slavery a curse was sinful.

But Mary mused alone, trusting to her journal what she would not say to anyone, even to her husband:

I wonder if it be a sin to think slavery a curse to any land. Men and women are punished when their masters and mistresses are brutes, not when they do wrong. . . .

One charge in particular always had made Southerners white with fury, the charge that slavery meant enforced concubinage. Mary was scornfully realistic:

. . . God forgive us, but ours is a monstrous system, a wrong and an iniquity! Like the patriarchs of old, our men live all in one house with their wives and their concubines; and the mulattoes one sees in every family partly resemble the white children. Any lady is ready to tell you who is the father of all the mulatto children in everybody's household but their own. . . . Thank God for my countrywomen, but alas for the men! They are probably no worse than men everywhere, but the lower their mistresses, the more degraded they must be.

She finished, and closed the book. Writing the words comforted her, but she wondered about this diary of hers. Whatever relief it gave her, it kept her from her old pleasure in reading.

Just then she felt like a "spider spinning out its own entrails."
Was it worth while, this private record of parlous times?

Congress adjourned on March 16. Mary and her husband and
the other deputies fled home in all directions from the overcrowded lodgings and confused makeshift offices of Montgomery.

V

Into the Black Cloud

PIERRE GUSTAVE TOUTANT BEAUREGARD, mannerly descendant of French Creoles, was a handsome man in his forties. He had sweeping dark mustaches, drooping brilliant eyes and a Gallic elegance of aspect, behavior and spirit. He knew Robert Anderson of Fort Sumter well; when Anderson had taught artillery tactics at West Point, Cadet Beauregard had been one of his most promising pupils. Assuming command of the Confederate forces at Charleston in early March, Beauregard found that preparations had gone forward, soundly if amateurishly, toward the time when Fort Sumter must be assailed and taken.

Governor Pickens had labored with considerable energy to strengthen all strategic positions facing the fort. A number of wealthy South Carolinians had contributed toward the purchase of armaments, and the guns captured at Fort Moultrie, Castle Pinckney, and the arsenal were reinforced with various new pieces.

Sumter was set at the harbor's narrows to defend it from outside, well away from the Charleston Battery. Beauregard's skillful calculations made the distance three miles and 838 yards, a considerable distance for amateur bombardment. But to either side of the channel at Sumter's position stood Fort Moultrie on Sullivan's Island and Cummings Point on Morris Island, both massively earthworked and bristling with guns. Cummings Point was less than a mile from Sumter, the guns of Moultrie a trifle more than a mile. Inside the harbor next to Morris Island was Fort Johnson on James Island, and Mount Pleasant was inside Sullivan's Island. Batteries grinned at these points too; from Fort Johnson to Fort Sumter the distance to throw a shell was a mile and a half, from Mount Pleasant a mile and three-quarters. At the four armed positions, South Carolina troops had mounted a total of some sixty guns, with fourteen mortars. More than 3,000 militiamen, all of them eager for trouble and some of them beginning to act like soldiers, were garrisoned at the various posts. Their officers included several efficient veterans of the old army.

But Sumter's defenses also bristled with guns, and did not lack crews well able to serve them. Massive stone walls would baffle even a heavy bombardment. To storm the fort, landing parties must cross the harbor under heavy fire, jump out on the narrowest of wharfs, and assail a mighty door, while defenders fired at close quarters with muskets. Aware of these difficulties, the volunteers bode where they were, and their discipline impressed Beauregard as slovenly.

He issued orders to commanders at the several positions, calling for stricter and more soldierly routine. Militiamen could leave their camps only if sick or for "important and urgent business" or other "extraordinary causes." Lights along the harbor's edges must go out at dark. Reveille would sound at 6:30 in the morning, with drill to follow until breakfast at eight o'clock. Guard mount was set for nine, surgeon's call at ten, and dinner at one P.M. Dress parade, showy but sometimes tiresome, would be held at five P.M. daily. Retreat was ordered for sundown, tattoo at nine o'clock and taps half an hour later.

Beauregard further informed his subordinates that drinking at the various installations must cease, instantly and completely. The new commander expressed himself as shocked to learn that sentries had been found in drunken slumber on their posts, and that soldiers had frolicked and fought each other under the influence of liquor. These matters, elaborated Beauregard, had become particularly reprehensible among the troops on Morris Island. As of March 18, then, a guard would be maintained at Cummings Point, where all boats landed and departed. Luggage and parcels would be examined, and all liquor discovered in them poured out in the presence of the abashed possessors. Further, company officers were directed to hold frequent inspection of the quarters of their men, to arrest any who were drunken, and to empty all confiscated liquor bottles into the thirsty sand.

These and other matters depressed the hearts of those who had gone to the forts as to a holiday. "I am now experiencing a soldier's life indeed," wrote a lieutenant on Morris Island to his wife. "Sleeping in tents on the ground, my trunk for a table and otherwise suffering every inconvenience that a person that has been [used to] civilized life can well suffer in hope that things would get better." The brackish water from shore wells was a legitimate complaint; in several commands it caused dysentery. The hardier volunteers thrived, however, gaining healthy vigor by toiling with pick and spade on the defenses.

Ashore, ladies and gentlemen knew a gaiety heightened, perhaps, by a touch of nervousness. The Chesnuts reached town on March 25, after a brief visit to Mulberry Plantation. They registered at the Mills House, much preferable to the crowded Exchange in Montgomery. James Chesnut rejoined the busy convention and Mary gossiped gratefully with distinguished and witty friends—Judge Withers, Langdon Cheves, and William Henry Trescott who had been Assistant Secretary of State in Buchanan's administration. These spoke French in the hotel dining room, lest Negro waiters be Yankee spies.

Mary was charmed and excited by the situation, but the judge, slow to follow Trescott's glib French, barked out: "Your conversation reminds me of a flashy second-rate novel." Back at her room, Mary found bouquets from several gentlemen. "What a dear, delightful place is Charleston," she decided, forgetting the guns that threatened each other from island to island of the harbor.

On all sides people hoped, or said they hoped, that there would be no fighting. A visitor named Ward H. Lamon said he was from Washington and intended to arrange the peaceable evacuation of Fort Sumter. Nothing came of his effort. Rumors persisted that President Lincoln dared not withdraw Anderson against the wishes of the truculent Union Cabinet and Congress, but that he would allow the Yankee garrison to consume its provisions and come out of itself.

On March 30, a steamer prepared to carry members of the secession convention and other notables on a tour of the harbor fortifications. The Chesnuts were invited, but Mary sent James alone. "A long dusty day on those windy islands?" she cried. "Never!"

Chesnut found soldiers aboard the excursion steamer, including Beauregard himself. Edmund Ruffin, too, was of the party, basking in the admiration of Charlestonians. Here and there the steamer churned, from fort to fort. The defenses seemed sturdy, the guns well kept and numerous, the garrisons alert. At one stop Chesnut fired a gun, hit a target, and was applauded.

At noon the excursionists partook of chicken salad, cake and wine. Private Charles Hutson of the Pocotaligo Mounted Men approached Ruffin, presuming on their brief acquaintanceship at Columbia the previous November. As the young men addressed the old one, the band was playing a lively song. Many aboard knew the words:

> . . . Then I wish I was in Dixie,
> Hooray! Hooray!
> In Dixie's land I'll take my stand,
> To live and die in Dixie—

Young Hutson liked the sprightly melody and the sentiment as well. "Perhaps it will become our national air," he ventured to Ruffin, but the old secessionist scowled in distaste and shook his white mane in the ocean breeze.

"I am afraid so," he grumbled. Plainly he thought that these lyrics, straight out of a minstrel show, were undignified.

So did other Confederates. Several were already trying to rewrite the words of "Dixie," with verses and refrain more pretentious and less singable.

The troops on Morris and Sullivan's Islands made "a very imposing appearance," thought one of the convention as the steamer left Cummings Point and sailed back to the Battery. She passed within a hundred and fifty yards of Sumter's esplanade.

A number of figures could be seen on the upper works, watching. One of them, tall and militarily straight, with a spyglass to his eye, surely was Major Robert Anderson. Well, let him look his fill. He'd be forced to evacuate in a day or so—everyone knew that. The band kept on playing "Dixie."

Left behind, Mary answered a loud rapping at the door. It was ex-Governor John Manning, with an open carriage and an invitation to dinner. They made calls on the way, at the Izards', the Pringles', the Rutledges'. The dinner Manning had ordered was delicious. Mary returned home, pleasantly excited, and James was there. Jealously he scolded her for flirting with the handsome Manning.

"I do not tell you everything!" Mary defied her husband saucily, and went off to her room with a swish of crinolines. The next day would be her thirty-eighth birthday, but no point in reminding folks of that advanced age. Charleston was a dear, delightful place, and the flattering pique displayed by James added to its delights.

It was April Fool's Day, appropriately enough, that the irksome problem of liquor and rowdyism on Morris Island came to a head.

Late that afternoon, Corporal Callais of the Columbia Artillery returned from leave in town, stepping off the boat just as his unit finished dress parade without him. Callais had no liquor in his external possession, but apparently he had enjoyed himself to the hilt in Charleston barrooms. Raucously he hailed various acquaintances in the ranks.

Orderly Sergeant Leiber, elaborately uniformed and wearing white gloves and a dress sword, addressed the jolly corporal. "Do not annoy the company," he said pompously.

"Do you not like it?" demanded Callais.

Leiber did not like it in the least, and promptly said so. Several gunners of the Columbia Artillery then heard Callais invite the orderly sergeant to kiss what the corporal euphemistically called his stern. Despite this public insult, which so curiously combined defiance with mock delicacy, Leiber clung to his temper and his sergeantly dignity.

"Don't make a fool of yourself," he warned Callais bleakly, but this excellent advice fell upon the deafest of ears. Callais called Leiber a liar and a damned Dutch son of a bitch.

No South Carolinian of whatever descent could be expected to listen tamely when such epithets were applied to him. Out flashed Leiber's handsome dress sword. He charged at Callais, striking him three times. Anger made the sergeant clumsy, and none of his blows had seriously injured Callais by the time Corporal Turnbull, with praiseworthy coolness and swiftness, sprang between the two men and shoved them apart. Callais ran to a private in the ranks, snatched a musket from him and tried to aim it at Leiber. Then Turnbull was upon him again and wrested the piece away.

Both non-commissioned officers were placed in arrest, and on April 3, while Morris Island's batteries fired volleys to drive back a schooner that tried to enter the harbor under the Stars and Stripes, a court-martial humorlessly found Callais guilty of using insulting language to a superior. He was ordered reduced to the ranks and confined for a week. Leiber was officially reprimanded for his angry readiness with the sword, but the court felt that the circumstances had been trying, and he was returned to duty as orderly sergeant. Discipline improved at Morris Island and elsewhere.

Also on April 3, guests at State Attorney General Haynes' home admired the blond loveliness of Lucy Holcomb Pickens, the governor's lady. Porcher Miles could not keep his handsome eyes from the corsage of violets at her delectable bosom, and she unpinned them and gave them to him, while a dozen other gentlemen gazed in envy. Mary Chesnut was there, but her spirits had sagged again. She ate *pâté de foie gras* and champagne frappé with a heavy heart.

"And so we fool into the black cloud ahead of us," she soliloquized.

Others were aware of the black cloud, and here and there the fooling came to an end. On April 7, Beauregard sent word to Anderson that Fort Sumter's commissaries would not be allowed to make further purchases of provisions in Charleston. Governor

Pickens called up 3,000 more South Carolina militia to reinforce the shore defenses, and an ironclad floating battery, now finished and a fascination to all beholders, was towed into position at Sullivan's Island.

The reasons for all this sudden new preparation were told everywhere. Somewhere in the North, an expedition was being gathered to relieve Sumter. No question this time of a single steam vessel, cargoed with bread and bacon and a few troops. A whole fleet would come to Charleston, escorted by armed ships of war and including transports with thousands of Union soldiers.

The convention that had brought secession to South Carolina finished its deliberations and adjourned. Mary Chesnut, disconsolate at thoughts of humdrum Mulberry Plantation, was helping James pack trunks and carpetbags at the Mills House when a message came from General Beauregard. Would James Chesnut serve as a volunteer aide-de-camp on Beauregard's staff? Indeed he would. Similar honorary assignments went to John Manning and Porcher Miles. James Wigfall, the shaggy-bearded Texas senator who had been valuable to the cause of secession during the last days in Washington, also was in town and was delighted to join these aides. Ex-Governor Means found a red sash and a saber to lend James Chesnut. The streets echoed with the heavy wheels of ammunition wagons. Darkness fell, and out yonder on the ramparts of Fort Sumter burned weird blue lights. Was the Federal fleet already at hand, and was Anderson signaling it to fight its way in?

Nobody could say for sure, for up in Washington the Confederate commissioners had been handed a terse memorandum informing them that the Secretary of State would take no further notice of their pleas and queries. Only spies had anything to tell Charleston, and these said that the Federal vessels already moved down the coast, armed and manned and laden.

Some found themselves able to welcome that word. Ruffin, still eager for bloodshed, felt that violence would drive more slave states into the Confederacy, making it stronger and safer and happier. A present arrived in Charleston, sent by a South Carolina shipping magnate in Europe—a big rifled Blakely gun. It went to Cummings Point, and was mounted with the battery closest to Sumter.

Roger Pryor came and registered at the Charleston Hotel. He was a showily handsome and extravagantly militant Virginian, second only to Ruffin himself in outspoken secessionism. Pryor had refused re-election to Congress because he felt betrayed by Virginia Unionists, he had published a furiously pro-secession newspaper. Serenaded at the Charleston Hotel on April 10, he emerged upon the porch to make the expected speech.

What of his remarks could be heard for the applause and confusion were loud assurances of help coming to the Deep South. War was at hand, boomed out Pryor, tossing his long locks of hair like a matinee idol on the stage, and bloodshed would bring Virginia into the Confederacy "within an hour by Shrewsbury clock." Perhaps Pryor was unaware that he paraphrased vainglorious old John Falstaff.

"I assure you," he bugled dramatically, "that just so certain as tomorrow's sun will rise upon us, just so certain will Virginia be a member of the Southern Confederation. We will put her in if you but strike a blow."

Loud cheers, silencing him for minutes. Bowing and smiling, Pryor waited for the racket to die down. Then: "I do not say anything to produce an effect upon the military operations of your authorities, for I know no more about them than a spinster. I only repeat, if you wish Virginia to be with you, strike a blow!"

Beauregard made Pryor one of his staff of volunteer aides. Ruffin's leathery old heart would have rejoiced to hear the guarantee of his state's coming into the Confederacy; but he was nowhere near the Charleston Hotel as Pryor spoke. At sixty-seven years of age, he had enlisted.

On April 9, with a carpetbag in one hand and a borrowed musket in the other, wearing his gray homespun suit and the broad felt hat with its blue cockade, he had boarded a vessel carrying recruits for the Seventeenth Regiment on Morris Island. Stepping upon the wharf, he asked if any company would accept him as a temporary volunteer, to serve only through whatever action was surely upon the defenders of Charleston.

Loud and flattering yells greeted his offer. The Palmetto Guards invited him to join them, and strong young hands took turns in shaking his old parchment-backed one. Someone found a bright company badge to pin beside the cockade on Ruffin's hat, someone else brought white crossbelts and a bayonet to strap over his gray coat. He spread his blankets on the ground inside a tent, and on the night of April 10 turned out with the rest of the Seventeenth Regiment at rumors of the Yankee fleet steaming in.

The fleet was not yet outside the harbor bar, but plainly it was on its way.

April 11 found Beauregard worried but determined. He summoned Captain Stephen D. Lee and James Chesnut, who had been given the temporary rank of colonel on Beauregard's staff. To them he handed a written message for Anderson, that yet again demanded the prompt surrender of Fort Sumter. Beauregard addressed his old artillery professor with courtesy, even friendship:

. . . All proper facilities will be afforded for the removal of yourself and command, together with company arms and property, and all private property, to any post in the United States which you may select. The flag which you have upheld so long and with so much fortitude, under the most trying circumstances, may be saluted by you on taking it down.

It was shortly after noon of April 11 when the two aides went to the battery and found a rowboat to take them to Fort Sumter. At their summons, the heavy doors opened and they went in. After some delay, Major Anderson appeared. They presented him with Beauregard's message, and Anderson read it in grave silence. Captain Lee noticed that the time was 3:45 P.M.

Anderson consumed three quarters of an hour in drafting his reply. Chesnut and Lee accepted it, spoke courteously, and turned to seek their boat.

"Gentlemen," said Anderson in farewell, "if you do not batter the fort to pieces about us, we will be starved out in a few days."

By 5:15 P.M., the paper was in Beauregard's hands, and the

two aides, who had missed their noon dinner, hurried off in search
of food. Chesnut found Mary at table, entertaining Porcher Miles
and other witty men and women. He helped himself generously,
and parried eager questions. He would say only that his interview
with Anderson had been "deeply interesting."

Beauregard, meanwhile, studied Anderson's letter:

GENERAL: I have the honor to acknowledge the receipt of your
communication demanding the evacuation of this fort, and to say in
reply thereto, that it is a demand with which I regret that my sense of
honor, and of my obligation to my Government, prevent my compli-
ance. Thanking you for the fair, manly, and courteous terms proposed,
and for the high compliment paid me,

I am, very respectfully, your obedient servant,
ROBERT ANDERSON
Major, First Artillery, Commanding

Beauregard telegraphed the correspondence, together with a
note of Anderson's verbal remark about being starved out, to
Montgomery. Jefferson Davis assembled his Cabinet to consider
what must be done.

Davis knew and liked Anderson, and would admit that Anderson himself had been manly and courteous. As to his refusal to
get out of the fort, that could be understood; Anderson had a
duty to perform, had been left at Sumter by his government to
perform it. Apparently he would welcome a chance to eat up his
last provisions and declare himself unable to stay longer. But
what about that fleet of warships and troop transports and supply
craft, somewhere close to Charleston? The Cabinet officers felt
that, if Anderson would not leave, he must be driven out.

One of them spoke against bombardment. Surprisingly, it was
Robert Toombs, once so fire-eatingly defiant of the Union. He
paced the floor of the conference room, big hands clenched together behind his coattails, as he argued.

"Mr. President," he growled at Davis, "at this time it is suicide,
murder, and will lose us every friend at the North. You will wan-
tonly strike a hornet's nest which extends from mountains to
ocean, and legions, now quiet, will swarm out and sting us to
death. It is unnecessary; it puts us in the wrong; it is fatal."

Davis called for a vote. Everyone but Toombs voted for opening fire on Sumter. Secretary of War Walker telegraphed the decision to Beauregard:

Do not desire needlessly to bombard Fort Sumter. If Major Anderson will state the time at which, as indicated by him, he will evacuate, and agree that in the meantime he will not use his guns against us unless ours should be employed against Fort Sumter, you are authorized to avoid the effusion of blood. If this or its equivalent be refused, reduce the fort as your judgment decides to be most practicable.

Upon the heels of that wire, another arrived at Beauregard's headquarters, this time from the commissioners still in Washington:

The *Tribune* of today declares the main object of the expedition will be the relief of Sumter, and that a force will be landed which will overcome all opposition.

The expedition—how close had it come this instant, while the night of April 11, cloaked in chilly damp fog, stole down upon Charleston? Beauregard made up his mind. He sent for Chesnut and Stephen D. Lee, the two aides whose service earlier that day had pleased him. While he waited for them he wrote, without much hope of success, an ultimatum to Anderson.

As Beauregard set down his final demand for peaceable surrender, word went all along the shore batteries, ordering them to be ready for action. The signal for the bombardment to begin would be a shot fired from Fort Johnson on James Island. When that shot resounded, every gun of the other positions was to join in.

At Cummings Point, the gentlemen volunteers consulted quickly. Officers and privates heard a motion. It was seconded, voted and accepted, and someone went to fetch Volunteer Edmund Ruffin. He, said the meeting, must fire the first gun at their position. Flattered and happy, Ruffin consented. He returned to his tent and lay down without taking off so much as his shoes. He felt like a boy who waits for the dawn of Christmas Day and a shower of gay presents.

Chesnut and Lee reported at their general's headquarters.

With them came Colonel A. R. Chisholm, another honorary aide, who knew Charleston Harbor well and had provided his own barge, with six strong and loyal Negroes as oarsmen. Beauregard handed the trio his dispatch to Anderson, and gave them emphatic verbal instructions: Let Anderson state specifically the time when he would evacuate, and agree to hold his fire in the meantime unless fired upon, or take the grim consequences.

As the three sought Chisholm's boat, the flamboyant Virginian Roger Pryor ran to the dock and jumped aboard with them. The fog closed in dankly. The slaves rowed them, almost by guess, across the black waters toward Sumter. It was 12:45 A.M. of April 12.

A sentry's harsh voice challenged, then the big doors creaked open. Pryor said that he would remain in the boat; to his own embarrassment, his state still remained in the Union. Chesnut, Lee, and Chisholm walked into the fort and demanded to see Anderson.

The commander of Sumter did not appear at once. Two hours went by, deadly slow and deadly tense, and then the visitors urged that someone inform Anderson that they could wait no longer to give him a message of the utmost importance. That brought Anderson to them. He ushered them into a casemate where he maintained his headquarters.

"You have twice fired on my flag," he said, referring to the driving back of the two ships, "and if you do so again, I will open my fire on your batteries."

Without comment, they handed him Beauregard's communication. He read it, then hesitated until Lee and Chesnut called upon him for a reply. Finally he sat down at a table and quickly wrote something. As on his previous visit, Lee looked at his watch: 3:15 o'clock in the black, black morning.

Anderson handed them his note to read. It said that he would feel forced, by lack of provisions, to march out of Sumter on the 15th, and would do so without further hesitation—and then came a qualifying clause:

. . . should I not receive prior to that time controlling instructions from my Government, or additional supplies.

He was bargaining for more time, and Lee, Chesnut and Chisholm knew that no more time could be granted him. That fleet from the North was closing in, heavily freighted with controlling instructions and additional supplies, and with guns and men as well. Upon the three aides fell the responsibility of saying what Beauregard had told them to say.

They borrowed pen and paper and a corner of Anderson's table. Chesnut dictated. Lee wrote, and Chisholm made a fair copy. Within five minutes they gave Anderson what they had achieved:

By authority of Brigadier-General Beauregard, commanding the Provisional Forces of the Confederate States, we have the honor to notify you that he will open the fire of his batteries on Fort Sumter in one hour from this time.

> JAMES CHESNUT, JR.
> Aide-de-camp
> STEPHEN D. LEE
> Captain C. S. Army, Aide-de-camp

Anderson read, with visible agitation. He walked out with them, and beside their boat he shook hands with them, one after another.

"If we never meet in this world again," he said, "God grant that we meet in the next."

Out across the harbor they rowed again. They had spoken for the Confederacy, they must act for the Confederacy as well. Chisholm piloted them through the fog to James Island, and Roger Pryor disembarked with them. They sought out Captain George S. James, commanding at Fort Johnson.

Captain James listened with sober attention to the story of what had just happened at Fort Sumter. He ordered his men to form for action at the guns. A ten-inch mortar stood ready loaded with a shell to voice the harsh announcement of war. Captain James addressed Pryor, whose Shrewsbury Clock speech had been welcomed by so many Charlestonians.

"You are the only man to whom I would give up the honor of firing the first gun of the war," he said.

But diffidence still weighed Pryor down. Foggy darkness seemed to destroy the confidence he had displayed at the Charleston Hotel. He shook his handsome head.

"I could not fire the first gun of the war," he protested in a hoarse voice.

Very well, then; Captain James himself would fire it. He stepped to the side of the mortar and seized the lanyard. The party entered the boat once more, and the oarsmen pushed away. Out in the water, fog-swaddled and nervous, they ordered the men to ship their oars and wait.

It was half past four in the morning.

A flash from Fort Johnson's breastworks, a sky-scaling streamer of flame. Over Fort Sumter a ball of red burst into gorgeous radiance. The flat, dead shout of its explosion brought everyone in Charleston wide awake.

VI

Throw Away the Scabbard

MARY CHESNUT needed no awakening.

For all James' reticence, she had guessed very shrewdly as to what he was up to out there in the harbor, knew in her heart that he could tell Anderson to surrender or stand the fire of that artillery massed along the shores. Wide-eyed in her bed at the Mills House as the dark hours crawled by, she heard the chimes from the steeple of St. Michael's—four o'clock. Minute after minute ticked by in the night, a taut half hour of minutes. Suddenly, the boom of a gun, terribly shattering the stillness.

In a trice, Mary scrambled out of bed and flung herself to her knees, praying. In the hall outside her door, excited feet scurried this way and that. More guns spoke, farther away and nearer.

The second gun of the bombardment was also fired from James Island, by Lieutenant Wade Hampton Gibbes, late cadet at West Point. The artillerists at Morris Island stood to their places. Edmund Ruffin stepped to a piece ready charged and aimed, caught the lanyard in his withered fist and yanked. One Virginian, at least, would not wait an hour by Shrewsbury Clock. Fire vomited into the black damp air. The shell sprang across the water and burst at an angle of Sumter's parapet. Then the other guns of Morris Island joined in.

All Charleston was up now. Men and women climbed to the roofs. Mary Chesnut finished her frightened prayers, pulled on a robe and flung a shawl about her shoulders. She ran out of her bedroom, up a flight of stairs, and emerged upon the flat roof of the hotel in the moist darkness.

There around her, and on housetops near at hand, people gathered in half-seen knots. Fire streaked the black sky, shells burst like gay rockets.

"Waste of ammunition," complained someone, but Mary thought of James, perhaps even then in a frail open boat on the face of those bombarded waters. The glowing tracks of the shells, their sudden lurid bursts, seemed to build a roof of bright menace above the harbor where James Chesnut floated. Weakness suddenly weighed Mary down. She half-groped her way to what looked like a stool on the roof, and sank down upon it.

A stranger rushed toward her. "Get up, you foolish woman!" he roared. "Your dress is on fire."

He dragged her up violently from the chimney pot she had mistaken for a stool, and with efficiently violent hands slapped the sparks from the skirts of her robe.

All the guns seemed to be in it now, the two sides of the harbor howling at each other like strophe and antistrophe of the devil's own chorus. But the shots went too high to damage the fort that held its dark silence. Ruffin, scrambling up the parapet at Morris Island to see the effect of the fire and call it down to the gunners below, was disappointed. Would Fort Sumter take this pummeling without resistance? That would be too bad, too bad, anticlimactic. Ruffin wanted a real battle.

As dawn made the blackness gray, the six-oared boat with the aides came to the Battery. At the same time, the practice of the guns to either side of the harbor improved. Shells began to burst against the heavy walls of Sumter. At 7:30 o'clock, Anderson's own guns went into action themselves.

They were not well aimed or well served, judged Captain Stephen D. Lee, himself an artillery officer of six years' service in the old army; but admiration surged through Confederate soldiers and civilians alike. Cheers went up at the volleys from Sumter, as though for well-respected opponents in some kind of polite game.

The bright sun burned away the mist, and three tall ships

showed outside the bar of the lower harbor, in sight of both Fort Sumter and the outermost batteries. They were the relief expedition, loitering there in sudden timidity. No indication of an effort to support Anderson's defense could be discerned.

Meanwhile, more reinforcements and more gathered in Charleston. The College Cadets, the "brag" company of students from Columbia, was there to offer itself. Some of the boys reached Sullivan's Island by steamer, and in the Moultrie House behind the fortifications heard hair-raising tales of Indian warfare from gaunt thin-haired Colonel Nathan George Evans—Shanks was his nickname—as he loitered and watched militia officers commanding the bombardment. The Moultrie House had been turned into a hospital, but the only patients were volunteers sick from dysentery.

Along the shores of Sullivan's Island gathered groups of civilians, gazing with eager interest toward the beleaguered fort. Ill-tempered cannon barked at them. Two shots struck the Moultrie House, to the wrath of doctors among the cots of the ailing, and others smashed into Fort Moultrie's massive parapet of sandbags and cotton bales, and wrought havoc among the tents of the troops behind.

The civilians scuttled away like frightened chickens, but the young men of Fort Moultrie's garrison yelled in happy excitement. A cannon ball tore through a cotton bale, scattering white tufts like unseasonable snow.

"Cotton is falling!" yelled someone.

Another shot demolished the chimney of a kitchen and flung loaves of bread into the air. A cheer went up.

"Breadstuffs are rising!" a second young soldier capped his friend's joke.

Nobody was hurt there or at the other batteries, or yet among Beauregard's aides who were rowed here and there across the harbor to carry orders. Soggy swamps to landward of every shore defense made communication with headquarters possible only by boat through the fire-whipped channels. Miraculously, no shot from Fort Sumter hit these water-bourne couriers; but the Confederates were improving in marksmanship. Shellfire drove An-

derson's observers from the parapet of Sumter, and the fragments
of one bursting shell severed the halyards of the flag so that it
hung halfway down the mast like a signal of distress or mourning
for the ruptured Union. Smoke obscured the defenses of both
sides, and good aim grew difficult. From behind Sumter's massive
walls licked ruddy flames, with sooty clouds rising above them;
the wooden barracks inside must have caught fire. When Anderson's guns began to speak less frequently, the besiegers knew that
the crews had been called from their posts to fight the fire, and
Southerners cheered again.

In Charleston, the irregular racket of the cannonading disturbed ladies at their noon dinners. Some of them lay limply on
their beds, moaning in anxious expectation of disaster to husband
or son or brother. Mrs. Wigfall sought out Mary Chesnut at
the Mills House.

"God is on our side," said Mrs. Wigfall confidently.

"Why?" demanded Mary, by no means so sure of which side
God favored.

"Of course, He hates the Yankees, we are told," reminded her
friend, with a gallant effort to be funny. "You'll think that well of
Him."

Mary did not laugh with any pleasure in the joke. She wondered
about the Negro servants, her own and those at the hotel. They
were silent, respectful—studiedly so, Mary fancied. Their indiffer-
ence was too profound to be convincing. "They carry it too far,"
she wrote in her journal. "You could not tell that they even
heard the awful roar going on in the bay, though it has been
dinning in their ears night and day. . . . Are they stolidly stupid,
or wiser than we are; silent and strong, biding their time?"

Bitterly sad it was to think such things of her own Negroes, especially of James' trusted personal attendant Lawrence. But she
had learned to speak French in their presence, lest they be spies
and enemies, after all. She consulted the newspapers. "Washington and Richmond Ablaze," shouted their headlines. Ablaze with
excitement, the papers meant.

Again the night came down, and again the fire from Fort
Sumter slackened. Anderson must be getting low on ammunition,

decided the Southern gunners, and kept up their own loading and firing. Edmund Ruffin, his aged limbs tired out from a day as observer on the parapet, stretched inside the open doorway of his tent, gazing up at the glowing trails of shells against the sky.

THE DAWN brought blazes of excitement in other towns than Charleston and Washington and Richmond. The blaze gravely threatened lives and careers in Lexington, Virginia.

The Virginia Military Institute, with many Deep Southern cadets on its rolls, was largely secessionist. In the town, perhaps a majority of citizens held to the Union, and a group of these had prepared for Saturday, April 13, a parade and a flag-raising. That the National Emblem might fly higher than a certain Stars and Bars in front of the courthouse, these Unionists had cut sections from several pine trunks, ready for assembling into a towering staff. At dawn of the 13th, however, they found that someone of opposite political philosophy had bored holes in the butt piece, filled the holes with powder, and blown it to fragments.

Who, they demanded, had dared to perpetrate such an outrage? Someone spoke of cadets prowling the streets in citizens' clothes during the dark hours of the 12th. Several cadets were at hand in uniform, having ambled into town that morning. Challenges and threats assailed the boys. One traded fisticuffs with a citizen, and he and some of his mates were captured and dragged off to the Lexington town jail. Those who could get away sprinted back to the Institute and told what had happened, with exaggerations.

At once the other cadets tumbled out of their quarters, seizing and loading their muskets. By custom long become habit, they fell in as four companies of an infantry battalion, then marched in column toward the courthouse, little more than half a mile away.

As they approached, the Unionist townsfolk made ready to meet them in the same spirit. Some men fetched guns from their houses, others made hasty purchases of arms and ammunition in Lexington stores. A local milita company assembled and took cover in the courthouse and behind corners of the square. Angry fingers trembled on musket triggers.

As the cadets closed in on the courthouse square, a group of men hastened toward them.

"Here they come!" cried one lad, and brought his piece to his shoulder. His thumb drew back the hammer with a baleful click.

"Don't fire, you fool you!" scolded his chum, seizing the barrel of the musket and shoving it upward.

A moment later, Superintendent Smith ran along the flank of the battalion. He was pale and weak from a recent illness, but he panted determined orders. He did not know what was happening, he said, but if the cadets were to fight, it was for him to command and lead them.

"All right!" cried young voices.

The approaching civilians came close, and halted. Nervously they identified themselves as an impromptu committee of mediation. The captured cadets would be released, they made quick and apologetic promise. Smith loudly commanded the battalion to the rightabout, and it obeyed. He marched it back to the Institute. As it entered the grounds, some of the cadets discharged their muskets, and to the clatter of exploding cartridges Smith herded them into the lecture hall of Major Preston, then mounted the rostrum to give them a scolding.

He said nothing for or against the Union or the Confederacy, but he said much about violence, insubordination and bad examples. Other professors followed him, adding their own stern voices. While this succession of lectures went on, Thomas Jackson came into the hall, sternly bracing to attention as always.

"Major Jackson!" shouted a cadet, perhaps in no more than joking recognition. But others took up the cry, urging their artillery instructor to the platform.

"Jackson!" they chorused. "Old Jack!"

Jackson shook his brown-bearded head in austere refusal. But Smith came toward him at the side of the room. "I have driven in the nail, but it needs clinching," said Smith. "Speak with them."

Thus directed by his superior officer, Jackson mounted the stage and faced the audience of cadets. He stood straighter and taller than ever. His blue eyes gave off sparks of pale fire.

"Military men make short speeches," he began, "and as for myself I am no hand at speaking, anyhow."

That last admission was true enough. Many who listened were delightedly aware that Fool Tom Jackson had had to school himself to pray out loud in church or to lecture classes and details of cadets, that he would just as soon be shot at as called upon to make an impromptu address. He was talking today, however, and with fierce vehemence.

"The time for war has not come," he rasped out, "but it will come, and that soon; and when it comes, my advice is to draw the sword and throw away the scabbard."

He faced to the side and tramped off the stage. His remarks probably were the briefest of any made on that occasion. With equal probability, they were the most to the point, and certainly they were the most clearly remembered in after years. Somewhat dashing, it might seem, for stiff old Deacon Jackson to talk about drawing swords and throwing away scabbards. But he knew, and everybody else in the lecture hall knew, that the scabbard had already been thrown away, down yonder in Charleston.

Edmund Ruffin was back up on the ramparts at Cummings Point that morning, watching the effects of the gunfire and yelling it down to his companions at the guns. Shells burst showily against the sturdy walls and inside the open-topped enclosure. Flames kept licking their red tongues from somewhere within. Fort Sumter returned fire slowly, only a single gun every five minutes now. Plainly they must be running low on powder and shot.

At half-past twelve o'clock, the smoke cleared a trifle. From Morris and James and Sullivan's Islands, observers could see. The flagstaff of Fort Sumter showed naked. The Stars and Stripes had gone down.

At that particular moment, Chesnut, Stephen Lee, and Pryor were together in a boat again, putting out from the Battery. Beauregard had told them to offer the most gentlemanly and sportsmanlike help if Anderson's garrison was in trouble with the flames inside the fort. Closer in, on Morris Island, Ruffin gave a great shout of joy when he saw that the old flag had fallen.

Near him was Louis Wigfall, who fairly ran to a small skiff at the waterside. With him went Private Henry Gourdin Young of the Palmetto Guard, to steer the boat, and three Negro oarsmen. Like the others of Beauregard's staff of honorary aides, Wigfall wore civilian clothes, with a sash and a saber. He drew the saber now, and fastened his handkerchief to its point as a flag of truce. At his word, Young steered them for the fort, less than a mile away.

A gun boomed from the parapet, and a solid shot plumped into the water, close to the boat. The oarsmen strained for greater speed, fairly thrusting the skiff through the water. It drove its nose upon the gravelly beach below the esplanade. Wigfall leaped nimbly ashore and made for the gate.

Fire licked over the stout planks. He saw an embrasure for a gun to one side, caught its edge with his free hand, and drew himself up until he could look into the fort.

A grimy gunner stared into his face. Wigfall handed him the handkerchief-decorated sword to hold, caught the rim of the embrasure with both hands, and dragged his body the rest of the way through. Panting with the exertion, he asked for Anderson.

Anderson came toward him, his bold-featured face smudged with powder smoke, his blue uniform scorched with cinders. "To what am I indebted for this visit?" he asked, wearily urbane.

Wigfall introduced himself as a colonel on Beauregard's staff, and half-begged, half-demanded that Anderson call a halt to the artillery duel. Since Anderson had struck his colors—

Anderson denied that. His flag had been shot down, not pulled down, and even now was being raised again. Not one of his garrison had been killed yet, he told Wigfall, and Fort Sumter was still full of fight. In any case, the Confederates were continuing their rain of shells from both sides of the harbor.

"I'll soon stop that," announced Wigfall; then, to the gunner who still held the sword with the handkerchief on its blade, "Wave that out there."

The gunner, as tired as Anderson but as enduring, flatly refused to be the one who would display a flag of truce. Wigfall snatched the saber back from him, mounted to the parapet and flourished the signal above his head. Anderson watched, then called for one of his men to bring a white hospital sheet and run it up the battered flagstaff.

Wigfall scrambled down once more and urged Anderson to capitulate. Beauregard was generous and soldierly, Wigfall assured the commander of Sumter, would grant the most honorable terms. Anderson seemed to agree, and went out with him to the waiting boat.

Even as Wigfall pushed off for Morris Island, Chesnut, Lee, and Pryor landed. They climbed in at an embrasure, perhaps the same that had admitted Wigfall, and Anderson was there to greet them.

One of the three said that Beauregard had inquired about the fire in the fort and offered help in extinguishing it.

"Present my compliments to General Beauregard," said Anderson, "and say to him I thank him for his kindness, but need no assistance." Then, as though just realizing what he had heard the visitors say: "Gentlemen, do I understand you come from General Beauregard?"

They assured him that they did.

"Why!" cried Anderson, mystified. "Colonel Wigfall has just been here as an aide to, and by authority of General Beauregard, and proposed the same terms of evacuation offered on the 11th instant."

One of the aides informed Anderson that Wigfall had been absent from Beauregard's headquarters for two days, and had never been authorized to offer surrender terms. Anderson turned away.

"There was a misunderstanding on my part," he said, "and I will at once run up my flag and open fire again."

But he spoke with weary sadness. Chesnut and his companions saw that the major's heart was not strongly in any resumption of the artillery duel, and they urged him to wait until Beauregard could be notified of what had happened. Anderson was willing to listen, if not to comment, and then yet another boat tied up at the wharf. It brought Major D. R. Jones, Beauregard's chief of staff, who presented a bona fide invitation to surrender, this time from Beauregard himself.

While these matters were discussed, Roger Pryor had seated himself at a table in the casemate where Anderson's surgeon, Captain Samuel W. Crawford, had set up quarters. Before Pryor stood a bottle and a tumbler. Such an arrangement of glassware meant nothing to Pryor but liquid refreshment, and liquid refreshment, decided the Virginia secessionist, was what he needed, then and there. Uninvited, he poured himself a generous portion and flung it down his throat.

At once he realized that he had made a mistake. He hurried out to where Anderson discussed Beauregard's terms of surrender, and stammered out what he had done. Anderson sent a man to bring Crawford through the billowing smoke from inside the fort. The surgeon listened with professional gravity as Pryor told unhappily of drinking from the bottle, and how much he had poured for himself.

"If you have taken the amount of that solution you think you have," Crawford told Pryor grimly, "you have likely poisoned yourself."

"Do something for me, Doctor, right off," begged Pryor frantically, "for I would not have anything happen to me in this fort for any consideration."

Unsmilingly Crawford led the suffering Virginian to a chamber which he had fitted up as a dispensary. There he mixed an emetic, which relieved Pryor's pains and terrors in a most undignified manner.

Meanwhile, Anderson agreed to surrender, under the terms previously offered by Beauregard. He would fire no more, but would run up his flag again. On the following day he would march his men out and fire a salute of one hundred guns before lowering the Stars and Stripes once more, and permanently.

It was midafternoon as the two boats with the aides and the subdued Pryor slid back to Charleston. Silence hung heavily over the blue harbor as they approached the Battery.

As soon as they told their news, Beauregard sent fire engines from Charleston. The firemen found Fort Sumter's interior a mass of smoke and smoldering wood. The officers' quarters and the men's barracks were completely destroyed, a shell had jammed the magazine door shut, the walls were battered inside and out. Miraculously, no man of the garrison had been killed, no man even seriously hurt. Officers and men seemed ready to drop with exhaustion, and all provisions had been exhausted save a few barrels of salt pork.

Joyfully Beauregard telegraphed the news of Fort Sumter's capitulation to Montgomery. Back came Jefferson Davis' compliments, with: "If occasion offers, tender my friendly remembrances to Major Anderson." Meanwhile, yelling crowds gathered on the streets of Charleston and crowded the Battery. Telescopes and opera glasses turned toward the silent fort, to the staff of which hung again the battle-torn flag of the Union.

A glorious victory, said everybody, but thankfulness and pride were manifest rather than wild celebration. Just who, people asked each other, really was the hero?

Wryly philosophical, Mary Chesnut wrote her own answer to that into her journal:

And so we took Fort Sumter, *nous autres:* we—Mrs. Frank Hampton and others—in the passageway of the Mills House between the reception-room and the drawing-room, for there we held a sofa against all comers. . . . That was after we found that bombarding did not kill anybody. Before that, we wept and prayed and took our tea in our rooms, away from the haunts of men.

Captain Ingraham and his kind also took Fort Sumter—from the Battery with field-glasses, and figures made with their sticks in the sand to show what ought to be done.

Wigfall, Chesnut, Miles, Manning, took it rowing about the harbor in small boats from fort to fort under the enemy's guns, with bombs bursting in air.

And then the boys and men who worked those guns so faithfully at the forts—they took it, too, in their own way.

There was glory enough for everybody, at that. Beauregard's official report to Montgomery paid compliments broadcast, not overlooking "the venerable and gallant Edmund Ruffin of Virginia." Ruffin himself was lionized and paraded anew, out there on Morris Island where his young comrades said that he must lead them into the fort.

While Charleston's firemen pumped sea water against the stubborn fires of Fort Sumter, Anderson supervised the sacking of one hundred charges of powder into cartridges for the salute he would fire. On Sunday the 14th, the booming of cannon began again, ceremonially this time.

It was too bad, that saluting. As the fiftieth round was touched off, sparks ignited the pile of cartridges, and a mighty explosion shook the fort and the waters. Private Daniel Hough was killed, the sponge staff in his hand. Ed Galloway and James Fielding of the gun crew were badly hurt, and a boat hurried them to hospitals in town. Three others were singed, but not seriously. These six were the only casualties of the bombardment, unless one wanted to count Roger Pryor. The singed men marched out with their comrades, and Anderson folded the tattered flag to carry away with them. They boarded the steamer *Isabel*, which turned her nose down harbor, to carry them to that rescue fleet still huddled outside the bar. Along the beaches stood the Confederate soldiers, silent and respectful, many with their hats in their hands.

Then came barges with victorious troops, one company from each side of the harbor. The Palmetto Guards landed first, and Edmund Ruffin proudly bore their company flag. In they marched, and Fort Sumter was under Confederate occupation.

The Stars and Bars climbed the mast from which had dropped the Stars and Stripes, the halyards pulled by Captain Ferguson of Beauregard's staff. Up, too, went South Carolina's palmetto flag: Governor Pickens had sent his friend R. B. Johnson to attend to that, but at Johnson's elbow stood Franklin B. Moses, Jr., Pickens' dandified and importunate young secretary. Would Mr. Johnson do Mr. Moses a great favor—let Mr. Moses tell in town that his hands had run up the state flag? Johnson, no seeker of glory in lady-thronged drawing rooms, consented. Back to Charleston sped Moses with his glittering lie.

General Beauregard was invited to a reception at Ashley Hall, the magnificent oak-thronged estate of William Izard Bull.

Wigfall, Pryor, Ruffin, accepted the compliments of the townsfolk. Militiamen relaxed, stalwart but ill-disciplined, familiar and
even impudent in their relationships with their officers. Thomas
Clingman, the North Carolina senator, was in town, telling people
quietly that Virginia and North Carolina would secede.

Throughout the Confederacy, the sun of April 14 went down
on various expressions and moods of jubilation, and the sun of
April 15 rose on news of wrath to come.

In Washington, President Lincoln had called for some 75,000
militiamen, to serve ninety days in helping the regular army at
its assigned task of subduing armed rebellion. Each of the slave
states still remaining in the Union was called upon for its quota
of regiments, each to number 780 rank and file. Kentucky and
Missouri were ordered to muster four regiments each; Virginia,
three regiments; North Carolina, Tennessee and Arkansas, two
each; Delaware, one. The calls for troops were signed, in the
name of the President of the United States, by Simon Cameron,
his Secretary of War.

VII

So Shall Thy Strength Be

THE TELEGRAPH wires vibrated with Southern fury as they flashed answers back to Cameron:

> Frankfort, Ky., April 15, 1861
>
> . . . Your dispatch is received. For answer I will say emphatically Kentucky will furnish no troops for the wicked purpose of subduing her sister Southern States.
>
> B. MAGOFFIN
> Governor of Kentucky

> Raleigh, N. C., April 15, 1861
>
> . . . I can be no party to this wicked violation of the laws of the country and to this war upon the liberties of a free people. You can get no troops from North Carolina.
>
> JOHN W. ELLIS
> Governor of North Carolina

> Richmond, Va., April 16, 1861
>
> . . . I have only to say that the militia of Virginia will not be furnished to the powers at Washington for such use or purpose as they have in view. . . . You have chosen to inaugurate Civil War, and having done so, we will meet it in a spirit as determined as the Administration has exhibited toward the South.
>
> Respectfully,
> JOHN LETCHER
> Governor of Virginia

Nashville, Tenn., April 16, 1861

. . . Tennessee will not furnish a single man for purpose of coercion, but 50,000, if necessary, for the defense of our rights and those of our Southern brethren.

ISHAM G. HARRIS
Governor of Tennessee

Jefferson City, Mo., April 17, 1861

. . . Your requisition, in my judgment, is illegal, unconstitutional and revolutionary in its object, inhuman and diabolical, and cannot be complied with. Not one man shall Missouri furnish to carry on such an unholy crusade.

C. F. JACKSON
Governor of Missouri

'Little Rock, Ark., April 22, 1861

. . . In answer to your requisition for troops from Arkansas to subjugate the Southern States, I have to say that none will be furnished. This demand is only adding insult to injury. The people of this Commonwealth are freemen, not slaves, and will defend to the last extremity their honor, lives and property against Northern mendacity and usurpation.

H. M. RECTOR
Governor of Arkansas

Governor Thomas Hicks of Maryland, across whose state Union armies now prepared to march, hesitated only long enough to ask and receive assurance that Maryland's militia would be kept within the state borders, then complied with Cameron's order. Governor William Burton of Delaware plausibly reported that the laws of his state did not empower him to comply, but that the various militia units were free to offer their services to the Union. Later, Kentucky's governor cooled sufficiently to treat with Washington for respect of a Kentucky proclamation of neutrality.

But those other governors had meant exactly what they said in the name of their states.

The news of Fort Sumter's fall had set off demonstrations of hysterical joy in Richmond. On balconies and housetops everywhere broke out the Stars and Bars. On the evening of April 15, while Lincoln's requisition for troops came to Governor Letcher's hands, processions moved along the streets with banners and torches, pausing at every corner to utter cheers for Jefferson Davis, groans for Abraham Lincoln. Next morning found a Confederate flag at the masthead above the beautiful State House. Coolheadedly, Letcher ordered it taken down, but in its stead he raised the state flag of Virginia, not the Stars and Stripes. The secession convention was vigorously at work, and at its door stood a sergeant-at-arms with a drawn sword in his hand, like the Angel of the Lord at the gates of Eden.

On the 17th, Virginia seceded, but not by unanimous vote. Among the delegates who voted to stay in the Union was a waspish ex-officer of the army named Jubal Early. Tennessee's convention submitted secession to a vote of the people; one of the minority who marked his ballot nay was Bedford Forrest. Arkansas and North Carolina moved purposefully toward withdrawal. In Washington, more senators and representatives went home to slave states. But Senator Andrew Johnson of Tennessee, the dogged Unionist, kept his seat.

Before these new forsakers of the Union rose a prospect balefully different from that which had seemed to confront the earlier seceding states.

The Confederacy had been organized at Montgomery in the hope of peace. But the new defiers of Lincoln's requisition for troops could enter the Confederacy only to enter war, against long odds of numbers, supplies, manufactures and means of transportation. Few indeed were so craven or so foresighted as to flinch from the hazard.

Robert E. Lee had come home to Arlington, the mansion on the south bank of the Potomac inherited by his wife from George Washington Custis. Stalwart, dark-mustached, spectacularly handsome, he had been told that he might have supreme command of the Union army in the field. But Virginia was the first loyalty in his heart, and Robert E. Lee never had done, never would do, other than what his heart assured him was right. He espoused the cause that his unsurpassed military judgment assured him would be lost, and on April 22 was commissioned major general in command of all Virginia state troops.

These matters betokened war to the wise, of whom Mary Chesnut was one. She and her husband had stopped at Mulberry on their way to another session of Congress at Montgomery. Mary's dark hair was tastefully brushed by her servant Maria Whitaker and, glancing into the looking glass, Mary saw that Maria's dusky face was wet with tears.

"Maria," asked the mistress, "are you crying because all this war talk scares you?"

"No, ma'am."

"What is the matter with you?"

"Nothing more than common," fenced the servant, but Mary was becoming a trifle weary of the air of secrecy affected by family retainers.

"Now listen," said Mary, both emphatic and prophetic, "let the war end either way and you will be free. We will have to free you before we get out of this thing. Won't you be glad?"

Maria Whitaker changed the subject to a recital of her domestic troubles, while elsewhere in the South, military action of a sort took place.

On April 17, even as the Virginia delegates voted for secession, a militia force of infantry, cavalry, and artillery had moved toward Harpers Ferry and on the morning of the 18th had marched in, while forty-five United States soldiers set fire to the arsenal and retreated across the bridge into Maryland. The militia were able to save the machine shop, and posted their batteries to face possible threats from the beautiful, daunting heights across the river. On the 20th, other armed Virginians advanced on the navy yard at Norfolk, to find it, too, afire, but a number of cannon were salvaged and a great store of powder saved.

From all quarters, volunteers poured in and mobilized. The advanced cadets of the Military Institute were called up to act as drillmasters. On Sunday, April 21, Major Jackson knelt with his beloved wife to pray once more for peace, then led the cadets aboard a train for Richmond. The fair grounds there had been turned into a huge training camp, and the new drillmasters at once took charge of clumsy squads and companies. Jackson was restrained and matter-of-fact, as usual, but something about him made its impression on the wiser of Virginia's officials.

Virginia needed warriors with training and ability to make soldiers out of these green levies. They came. Jubal Early, who had wanted to stay in the Union, accepted the verdict of his state and offered his services to the Confederacy. A dashing young officer with a great plume of brown beard rode away from his cavalry post in the West and a brand-new commission as captain. Ahead of him went two letters, his resignation to Washington, and to Richmond a request for assignment to artillery or mounted infantry. The name he signed was J. E. B. Stuart. Flamboyant Captain John Bankhead Magruder bade good-bye to his beloved battery of field guns and asked for service in Virginia. Joseph Eggleston Johnston, paymaster and brevet brigadier in the United States Army, headed for Montgomery though his wife warned him against Jefferson Davis. Lieutenant Richard K. Meade, who had commanded a gun for the Union at Fort Sumter, heard the call of his native Virginia and appeared at Richmond to ask for assignment to any post where he might be useful.

There were disappointing renouncements. Lieutenant General Winfield Scott, aged and blubbery, harshly snubbed a suggestion that he owed loyalty to Virginia. Major George W. Thomas stayed with the Union, and his sisters in Southampton County never spoke to him again. Brigadier General William S. Harney turned his back on Tennessee where he had been born and reared. Philip St. George Cooke, a Virginia colonel of dragoons, kept his Federal commission, while his son John, a lieutenant, gave up his.

From another point came news of violence.

On April 19, a yelling mob of civilians had stoned the Sixth Massachusetts in its march from depot to depot in Baltimore, and a volley from the regiment's muskets killed seven and wounded many. James Ryder Randall, a Maryland schoolmaster in Louisiana, hurried into incandescent verse that became a matchless battle song:

The despot's heel is on thy shore,
Maryland!
His torch is at thy temple door,
Maryland!
Avenge the patriotic gore
That flecked the streets of Baltimore,
And be the battle queen of yore,
Maryland!

Missouri secessionists grabbed the arsenal at Liberty and armed themselves with thirteen hundred muskets and twelve cannon. Senator Andrew Johnson, hurrying home to Tennessee without resigning, escaped a violent mob at the Lynchburg railway station. Richmond was frightened, then amused, by a report that a Yankee gunboat was steaming up the James River to bombard the town.

Harpers Ferry, the most advanced and perilous of all positions occupied by Southern troops, was garrisoned by enthusiastic but salad-green and unorganized militia, under pompous political colonels and generals. On April 24, Governor Letcher had commissioned Professor Jackson colonel of volunteers and three days later sent him to take command at Harpers Ferry.

He had arrived that evening at the river town among its picturesque heights. With him as staff officers came two other professors from the Institute, J. L. T. Preston and James Massie, and two cadets to act as drillmasters. With quiet disapproval he viewed the confused and unsoldierly mob he must whip into shape.

There were some 2,000 of them, Virginians and a few Kentuckians, mostly infantry with several cavalry companies and four batteries of artillery. These served under a major general, three brigadiers and various colonels of militia. The military ineptitude of these plumed swaggerers bordered upon the fantastic.

Jackson himself was unshowy but businesslike in the worn blue blouse and forage cap he had brought from the Institute. He inspected his command's resources. The rabble had arms, at least; hundreds of muskets had been rescued from the half-destroyed arsenal, and the artillerymen had bought harness for their teams and botched up rough caissons from sturdy farm carts. As for officers, Jackson tonelessly relieved from duty most of the glittering commanders and returned their numerous incompetent aides to the ranks. Outraged protest died before his level blue stare, but steamed up again out of his presence.

Young Captain John D. Imboden refused to sympathize with a blustering militia regiment whose popular field officers had been sent back to Richmond, and harangued his own Staunton Artillery. Would they enlist for twelve months or for the war?

"For the war! For the war!" chorused the gunners, and Imboden proudly reported this reply to Jackson, who already had approved of the Staunton Artillery and the red shirts, purchased by Imboden himself, worn by its men instead of trig dress tunics. He directed the captain to serve as mustering officer for the other three batteries. When these, too, enlisted for the duration of the war, infantry and cavalry forgot their grievances and did likewise. With the mounted companies were the Ashby brothers, Turner and Richard, whom Jackson remembered from the day John Brown was hanged.

Jackson set up headquarters in a little hotel close to the bridge of the Baltimore and Ohio Railroad where it ran across the Potomac into Unionist-occupied Maryland. There he completed regimental organizations and found men to handle with some adequacy the mysterious labors of commissary, ordnance, and communications. His two cadet drillmasters and some others who had a smattering of military experience started to drill a whole universe of awkward squads.

Finding time for a love note to Anna back home in Lexington, Colonel Jackson made himself believe the optimistic things he wrote:

I am much gratified with my command, and would rather have this post than any other in the State. I am in tolerable health, probably a little better than usual if I had enough sleep. I haven't time now to do more than tell you how much I love you. . . .

As Jackson improved his position at Harpers Ferry, Jefferson Davis reassembled the provisional Congress at Montgomery.

Davis knew that full-scale war was coming, and chose to hope that his people would call him into active military command. His old sword, the one he had wielded as a Mississippi colonel in the Mexican War, he sent to be sharpened at a gunsmith's shop, and the sharpening was witnessed by droves of the admiring and the curious.

Flies and mosquitoes had come to Montgomery with the advancing spring. The officials and the citizens brushed these aside as they continued to exult over Sumter's fall; but Fort Pickens in Florida had been reinforced by Federals, and hopes of its capture sagged. The Chesnuts, checking in at the jammed Exchange, were welcomed by friends everywhere. Generals and congressmen presented bouquets to Mary, and when she fastened a sprig of violets to her bosom, John Hemphill of Texas was as gallant as a courtier.

"Oh," he cried, "if I had known how those bouquets were to be honored I would have been up by daylight seeking the sweetest flowers!"

That would have flattered even Lucy Pickens, but Governor Moore topped it. "The most comfortable chair is beside Mrs. Chesnut," he vowed, sitting down close to her. And she, able to laugh in the midst of this flattery, said in her heart: "Well done, old fogies!"

On April 28, Jefferson Davis himself made it his business to cross the aisle at church to speak cordially to Mary. Later, the Chesnuts took dinner at the President's house. Davis gave Mary his arm to escort her in, and she found his table conversation both witty and wise.

Even as Davis sparkled, however, his inner thoughts were serious ones.

On Monday, April 29, he delivered his message to Congress, announcing that the original States of the Confederacy had ratified the new constitution and that others were ready to join and to ratify also. He described Lincoln's mustering of troops as a declaration of war, called the bombardment of Fort Sumter the result of bad faith on the part of the Union, and announced that he had invited private vessels to apply for letters of marque and reprisal, to prey upon Union shipping. Commissioners would go to England, France, Russia, and Belgium. Many bureaus of the new government were functioning well, or so he assured the Congress.

As for that threat of Northern invasion, the Confederacy would meet it. Nineteen thousand men held strategic defense positions along the coast, and 16,000 more were on their way to Virginia. Fully 100,000 would be armed and organized.

"We feel that our cause is just and holy," he said; "we protest solemnly in the face of mankind that we desire peace at any sacrifice save that of honor and independence; we seek no conquest, no aggrandizement, no concession of any kind from the States with which we were lately confederated; all we ask is to be let alone; that those who never held power over us shall not now attempt our subjugation by arms. This we will, this we must, resist to the direst extremity."

High enthusiasm and confidence were expressed almost everywhere. The Montgomery *Weekly Mail* spoke for virtually everyone in its editorial on Davis' message:

It not only reflects the highest honor on the ability and the patriotism of its accomplished author, but it triumphantly vindicates the Southern people and their government against the vulgar slanders of that miserable old buffoon who, as President of the United States, is made the tool of a clan of perfidious usurpers, whose folly and malice are bringing ineffable disgrace upon themselves and ruin upon their country.

That the country of the enemy would be ruined was doubted by few indeed in Montgomery. As to the Confederacy in general, old coynesses concerning departure from the Union seemed to die in every corner, like flies in a frosty room. The *Weekly Mail* offered a heartening example in announcing how the dream of the State of Nickajack had faded:

North Alabama is in a blaze. The war fever runs high. . . . This is only worthy of remark because North Alabama has been very conservative on the secession question.

Word came from Richmond that Virginia's voters had ratified the ordinance of secession, and that the convention there cordially and respectfully invited the government of the Confederate States of America to move its capital from Montgomery to Richmond. R. M. T. Hunter, in Montgomery as an envoy for Virginia, was the more eloquent for the move because of the heat of May in the Deep South. Buzzing mosquitoes nibbled the high officials, the middle and the low. Office and hotel space could not be secured, and meals were unpalatable. But the Montgomery *Daily Advertiser* disliked the Virginia proposal, and said so editorially:

The proposition to move the Capitol of the Confederacy to Richmond, Va., has appeared to us so preposterous, so utterly at variance with the dictates of prudence and sound policy, that heretofore we have not deemed the subject worthy of the slightest consideration. It seems, however, that the idea is seriously entertained by many, of changing the seat of government from this place to Richmond, at an early day, and we therefore take occasion to enter our earnest protest against the move. . . .

The *Advertiser's* editor reflected other opinions than his own on the possible move to Richmond:

. . . That it might be necessary for President DAVIS to establish his headquarters there, should he take command of the army in person, we can very readily see, but the propriety of transferring the Vice-President, Cabinet or members of Congress to the scene of active operations, on the extreme Northern border of the South, is not so apparent. The moral effect, both upon our own soldiers and those of the enemy, of the presence of such a commander as Gen. DAVIS, cannot well be overestimated, but to our mind, the spectacle presented, of the government changing about from place to place, would be highly injurious.

Not only the *Advertiser,* nor yet Varina Davis, had visions of the President leading his army like some warrior king of ancient romance. John A. Campbell, who had resigned as associate justice of the United States Supreme Court when Virginia seceded, reported to Montgomery in a letter addressed to "General Davis, President of the Confederate States."

However many felt that Davis was the greatest military talent in the new nation, relatively few sided with the *Advertiser* in wanting to keep the capital at Montgomery. The little town was packed to overflowing, and the highest officials were forced to operate their departments in odd nooks and even on street corners. When Toombs was asked for a post in the State Department, he whipped off his hat with a fierce volley of oaths.

"There is the State Department of the Confederacy, by God!" he roared, pointing into the hat. "Jump in, sir!"

Meanwhile, you could still go from Montgomery to New York, by Mobile and Savannah steamer lines, for $25. But that was beginning to look like real money. On May 7, but seven hundred bales of cotton had been sold at New Orleans, and at Mobile but one hundred bales. The price was ten and a half cents a pound. William Russell, the London *Times* correspondent, noticed that a prime field hand sold in Montgomery for a thousand dollars, little more than half what he would have brought in 1860.

RESIGNATIONS of army and navy commissions continued, some written with regret, some with a joyous anticipation of quick advancement and distinction in the service of the new Confederacy. Old comrades in arms, separating as some went and others stayed, spoke affectionate farewells. In one case at least, tragic prophecy attended a leave-taking.

That was when Lieutenant E. Porter Alexander of Georgia, a brilliant young artillerist and communications officer, packed his kit at Fort Steilacoom on far Puget Sound to take the long, fatiguing road back home. His friend, Lieutenant James McPherson at Alcatraz in San Francisco Bay, wrote a last sad word on April 20:

. . . This war is not going to be the ninety days affair that papers and politicians are predicting. Both sides are in deadly earnest, and it is going to be fought out to the bitter end. . . . For your cause there can be but one result. *It must be lost.* Your whole population is about eight millions, while the North has twenty millions. Of your eight millions, three millions are slaves who may become an element of danger. You have no army, no navy, no treasury, and practically none of the manufactures and machine shops necessary for the support of armies, and for war on a large scale. You are but scattered agricultural communities, and you will be cut off from the rest of the world by blockade. Your cause is foredoomed to failure.

Seriously young Alexander pondered that warning, but he did not hesitate. If his South was outnumbered, the greater the need for his services.

Word came from Missouri, of gunfire and killing. The state militia had met for a two weeks' tour of training outside St. Louis, was surrounded by Unionist volunteers stiffened with regulars and made prisoner. When spectators yelled insults and threats, the Unionists opened fire, like the Massachusetts volunteers in Baltimore. Twenty-eight were killed by the volleys, to be hailed in Montgomery as Southern martyrs. Missouri secessionists flocked to the Stars and Bars. One youngster, ready to take up arms, heard his affectionate foster mother say: "If you find you must fall, fall with your face to the earth, shot through the heart."

At many other points gathered more volunteers, romantically vengeful and certain of their talents for Yankee-killing.

Infantry could be raised at every crossroads tavern. Young men who shot straight and walked vigorously as a daily way of life signed their names or made their illiterate crosses on the enlistment rolls. When there were enough for a company, they elected their captains and lieutenants and corporals, then sturdily fell in to be counted as soldiers of the Confederacy. It was slightly more difficult than that to join one of the society companies; the Crescent Rifles of New Orleans, for instance, required the signing of a formal application, as though for membership in an exclusive club:

To the officers and Members of the
                "Crescent Rifles"
GENTLEMEN:
    I hereby tender you this my petition for Membership in your Corps, and, if elected, pledge myself to conform to all the requirements of

your Constitution and By-Laws, and perform the duties of a soldier to the best of my ability.

Very respectfully. . . .

Such a request must have countersigning by two bona fide members of the Rifles as references, and an initiation fee of five dollars.

But more romantic even than such units were the cavalry companies, and more expensive. To join one of these, the recruit must bring his own saddle horse, an animal fit for gallant galloping service. Frequently these four-footed aspirants underwent a more thorough and expert examination than did their masters. Artillery batteries were recruited mostly in towns and cities, where skilled mechanics and engineers sought that service.

Those who seemed sufficiently trained were gathering in Virginia. The First South Carolina had rolled into Richmond on April 24, and the welcome of these mannerly, monied volunteers set a precedent for future contacts between soldiers and civilians. One of them wrote home:

. . . And it was the women that seemed to honor us most, and tried to outdo each other in making us comfortable. I have formed a high estimate of Virginia character and hospitality.

Another train brought the Third Alabama Volunteers up through Georgia and Tennessee toward Lynchburg in Virginia. In East Tennessee, pretty girls pelted the soldiers with bouquets. One Alabamian's heart raced as he read a note attached to the bunch of flowers he had caught in mid-air:

Hail! brave defenders of a holy cause. Our heartfelt wishes, our constant prayers, attend you whithersoever you go to search the hated foe. Let no Yankee footsteps pollute the native soil of free men and free women. Your memory will be sacred to us if you fall, our smiles shall reward you if you return victorious.

That particular soldier yearned for the sweet smile of whoever had written the promise. None but the brave deserve the fair. . . . But at Lynchburg waited more and lovelier girls still, with, as tokens of their favor, hams, tongues, turkeys and pancakes. Also dazzled by provisions and flirtations were privates of the Eleventh Mississippi, one of whom wrote home from Lynchburg:

. . . The manifest kindness of the fair ones has made a wonderful impression upon the minds of many of our boys & you must not be surprised if they bring a good many of these ladies to show their fortunes in the sunny south.

Kirby Smith commanded at Lynchburg, where the Deep Southern regiments pitched tents, bought carpets for the dirt floors, and nailed together tables and benches and gun racks. The camp served as a deploying point for troops rushed to sectors more seriously threatened. The troops, Smith felt, were "the best blood of our country . . . the youth of sixteen and the aged sire side by side." He tried not to think of them dying in battle. News that Thomas Jackson was at Harpers Ferry pleased him— he had known Jackson at West Point, felt that he was "a brave man who will defend his post to the death. . . ." Lee's command in Virginia did not strike Smith as particularly reassuring. Smith wanted Jefferson Davis to appear as military commander; failing Davis, Joe Johnston or Beauregard.

One volunteer, at least, had been mustered out of service. That was Edmund Ruffin, briefly of the Palmetto Guards. Ladies cooed over him in Charleston, men shook his hand. President Davis had written to praise Ruffin's "heroic devotion to the South . . . Truth and Constitutional Government." His photograph, showing the hat badge, the crossbelts and the borrowed musket, was on sale at the souvenir shops along with portraits of Davis and Beauregard. New companies of volunteers proudly named themselves for him: the Ruffin Rangers in Mississippi and the Ruffin Dragoons in Alabama.

He put an end to his dramatically self-imposed exile from Virginia. In Richmond, where the capital of the Confederate States would found itself anew, a committee of admirers met him at the railroad station. Sweet and heady was the taste on his triumphant lips of the words "I told you so."

A last effort to halt that move of the capital was made by the Montgomery *Weekly Mail*. Its editor was Johnson Jones Hooper, secretary of the Provisional Congress and a seasoned master of homespun sarcasm:

What would be the effect of removing the Capital? It would be said at once by our enemies: "What! Call this little *itinerating* concern a *permanent* government? It is rather like a travelling grocery, seeking custom by squatting about in various localities. Wonder if it won't go next to the next seceding State, to Maryland, or even to little Delaware, if they will come over to the grocery side? Whoever before saw a pretended government dodging about so? Where will it go next? Who bids for the next squat?

Hooper's editorial was in the *Weekly Mail* for May 17, and may have been read by Jefferson Davis. But to Davis that same day came a telegram from Richmond:

PRESIDENT DAVIS:
For the salvation of our cause come immediately and assume military command.
                    EDMUND RUFFIN

Salvation of the cause—military command. Davis wanted them both, and did not doubt his ability to procure the first, his right to assume the second. Too many people had assured him that his place was at the head of the Confederate armies. Varina thought that; so did the newspapers, in Virginia and in Montgomery; so did sound and seasoned officers like Edmund Kirby Smith, and so, as the telegram showed, did Edmund Ruffin, the apostle of secession. If Davis had not made his mind up earlier, he made it up then.

Alas for Hooper's wry lamentation. The capital would move, though not to Maryland or Delaware. Both of these slave states were full of blue-coated troops, and neither could secede if it wanted to. The Confederacy would move its seat to Richmond, and Davis would be there, too, for all the enemy guns that threatened.

His determination did not make him joyous. Aurelia Fitzpatrick thought him gloomy after his recent polished gaiety at receptions and dinners. Davis told lovely plump-cheeked Aurelia that the war would be long, with early reverses to be expected. "Men and money count so much in war," the Alabama beauty quoted Davis to Mary Chesnut on the 19th.

"As they do everywhere else," Mary made sententious rejoinder, for she thought Aurelia made too much of the President's solemnity. The two ladies went out to more parties.

At one of those parties, Mary found the food so bad that she ate only cold asparagus and blackberries. Lunch on May 20, with Varina Davis, was more palatable, and Varina was in a mood as happy as her husband's mood was gloomy. James Chesnut sided with the Montgomery papers against the move to Richmond—let the troops go, but not the government. His lady and the President's were all for Richmond. Varina, in particular, looked forward to living in Richmond. Summer would be ghastly hot in Montgomery.

"The Yankees will make it hot for us, go where we will," she commented, "and truly so if war comes."

"And it has come," reminded Mary.

"Yes," agreed Varina, "I fancy these dainty folks may live to regret losing even the fare of the Montgomery hotels."

"Never!" said Mary stoutly, for she could imagine no fare worse than that.

Congress adjourned on May 22. Back to South Carolina went the Chesnuts, to find that young Johnny Chesnut had enlisted as a private. Childless Mary worried over her husband's clever, handsome young nephew. Affectionately she reproached him for squandering money that might have helped him raise and equip a company, with himself as its glittering captain.

"We do very well in the ranks," Johnny said confidently, "men and officers alike; we know everybody."

He was on his way even then, with a regiment that would seek the enemy on Virginia's border. Mary wanted to bid him good-bye with some message of confident comfort. But all she could think of was what Mrs. Charles Lowndes had said when

South Carolina had seceded. She spoke the words to Johnny, with all the solemn meaning she could put into them:

"As thy day is, so shall thy strength be."

Impressed, Johnny went off to the war. Mary wept bitterly and alone, as though for the departure of the son she had never borne.

VIII

---◆---

Give Us a Fair Field

COLONEL THOMAS JONATHAN JACKSON was starved for sleep at Harpers Ferry. He had to steal odd moments in order to rest, to eat, to write letters to his Anna. High command was his, at a post both important and unchancy, with only raw materials at hand to shape into its defense.

Harpers Ferry lay among wildly beautiful scenery of rivers and mountains, just west of the brawling juncture of the Shenandoah and the Potomac. Eastward across the Shenandoah, northward across the Potomac, rose picturesque but threatening heights of ground, ideal for the launching of an enemy attack to seize the town and charge beyond, up the Shenandoah Valley as a natural highway of invasion. Who would say when such an attack would be? Not Jackson, though he was Presbyterianly certain that all future events, great and small, were already noted on a heavenly timetable.

His own assignment to an important command was proof of a dire need among the countless needs of the Confederacy—military leadership.

It was becoming manifest to Montgomery and to Richmond that if 100,000 Southern troops were to be enlisted, officers for them would be hard to find. The Confederacy could count on far less than half of the 1,080 colonels, majors, captains and lieutenants who had commanded the old regular army of the United States, and even these former regulars were mostly company officers, with no experience at training, supplying and marshaling

118

bodies of men even as large as the half-organized camp of recruits at Harpers Ferry.

Governor Letcher of Virginia had acted with the utmost of wisdom, or perhaps the utmost of good fortune, in putting Robert E. Lee at the head of things. Others from the old army had been gladly welcomed and given assignments, as had graduates of the Virginia Military Institute. Civilians of any military experience could ask and receive commissions; an example was Philip St. George Cocke—not to be confused with Philip St. George Cooke, Jeb Stuart's father-in-law who had remained with the Union. Cocke had been an infantry lieutenant for three years and had resigned to spend three decades more as a wealthy planter, but now he was a colonel like Jackson, trying to arm and drill militia at Alexandria, just south of the Potomac and in full sight of the domeless capitol building in Washington. The state had accepted veterans of the Mexican War, inept militia chieftains, and men with no qualifications save political or social prestige, to lead companies and regiments.

Jackson himself had not considered his regular army career a success. That was why he had resigned to be a teacher. When it came to that, he was not known for brilliance as a teacher, either, though men qualified to judge such things had approved of his artillery instruction. Now in 1861, however, he was the best Virginia could find to face Yankee threats across the Potomac and hold safe, if possible, the Shenandoah Valley where the wheat harvest ripened.

He had been doing what he could. His drillmasters, without enough level ground to maneuver a full battalion, yet managed to sweat company after company of unhandy recruits into something like properly marching units. As each batch became a regiment of sorts, other batches appeared, to be enlisted, equipped, organized and drilled.

Jackson's fifteen field guns were stationed at high points, their apprehensive muzzles trained upon the crags from which might spring invading hordes of Unionists. As the regiments came into being and efficiency, some ruffled militia feathers were smoothed by bringing back several good men at reduced rank. Major General Kenton Harper, whom Jackson had succeeded in the Harpers Ferry command, became colonel of the Fifth Virginia Volunteers. John A. Harman sloughed off a meaningless commission as a militia brigadier to be Harper's second in command. Colonel William Baylor accepted a majority.

Supplies of all sorts were badly needed, and hard to get from the poverty-stricken military depots at Richmond. Throughout Virginia, ceremonial salutes and displays of fireworks were a thing of the past. The precious store of powder from Norfolk was ordered made up into cartridges for muskets and field pieces.

On May 9, banner-bearded Jeb Stuart rode into Harpers Ferry as a lieutenant colonel, and Jackson mustered the various cavalry companies present to form a scratch regiment with Stuart in command. This did not please Turner Ashby, nor did it please the volunteers he had led out of the mountains. The swarthy captain had been doing a splendid reconnaissance job along the Potomac River and beyond in Maryland; he was older than Stuart, considerably more dignified, and he felt that he deserved any promotions going in the mounted service. Stuart impressed some of the Harpers Ferry garrison as a sort of overgrown and prankish boy, and none of them seemed to know that he had shown himself both brave and efficient in frontier campaigns against hostile Indians. Ashby told Imboden that he would resign in protest. Imboden, the diplomatic, begged him not to, then wrote to Jackson and secured detachment of the two companies commanded by the Ashby brothers to form a nucleus for a second regiment of cavalry. Mollified, Ashby proved his right to this consideration by scouting in civilian clothes all the way to Pennsylvania and bringing back word of Federal concentrations above Harpers Ferry.

To Robert E. Lee's headquarters in Richmond Jackson sent more and urgent pleas for weapons, clothes and food to furnish his growing garrison. He gave up with regret the machinery salvaged from the half-destroyed arsenal—it had been converting old flintlocks for the use of the recruits. As for rations, "the commissary department here is in a suffering condition." But Jackson proposed to seize and fortify those commanding heights in

Maryland across the Potomac, against the forces which Ashby had reported as pointing toward Harpers Ferry. He, who had not wanted the war, still felt that only the fiercest of fighting would win it. To Lee he wrote gravely:

. . . I am of the opinion that this place should be defended with the spirit which actuated the defenders of Thermopylae, and if left to myself, such is my determination.

At almost the same time, he sought to reassure his beloved Anna:

. . . I am strengthening my position, and if attacked shall, with the blessing of Providence, repel the enemy. I am in good health, considering the great amount of labor which devolves upon me, and the loss of sleep to which I am subjected. . . . Oh, how I would love to see your precious face!

Jackson's stern preparations were seen as wise by Lee and others in Richmond. Reports from elsewhere along the border showed that Virginia, soon to be the seat of the Confederate government, would be the seat of war as well.

Kentucky's formal declaration of neutrality might not keep her out of the fight forever. Even as the state's leaders spoke movingly for peace and mediation, young Kentuckians streamed across the Ohio to enlist for the North at Cincinnati and across the Tennessee border to enlist for the South at Camp Boone. Yet, for the time being, Kentucky buffered any chances of invasion by Federals of the whole middle of the Confederacy. The only way in, for the superior armament of the Union, would be through dubious Missouri or into Virginia.

The approaches to Richmond were several, and none of them too easy to defend. The Shenandoah Valley might be entered across the upper Ohio, from western Pennsylvania, or through Maryland. The Peninsula was vulnerable to invasion backed by heavy naval guns. And across the Potomac forces could move into central Virginia. In early May, the only troops standing in the way of such movements were the untested Virginia volunteers, under officers commissioned by the state. The Confederate government, packing to leave Montgomery, hastily sent its best men from the Deep South and granted commissions to Virginians who might deserve them.

On May 23, Jackson achieved something of a bloodless military triumph at Harpers Ferry.

The Baltimore and Ohio Railroad had continued to run its trains through the town and along the Virginia shore of the Potomac to the westward, fetching coal and other supplies into Maryland. Jackson had not appeared to resent this support given the Union under his very eyes; but he had complained, with prosy courtesy, to the heads of the railroad that the constant puffing and clanking around Harpers Ferry disturbed the slumbers of his 9,000 troops. As military commander at that point, Jackson must insist that the trains be so routed as to pass in either direction only between the hours of eleven A.M. and one P.M.

The railroad complied, and around noon daily the double tracks at Harpers Ferry were crowded with strings of cars. On the 23rd, Jackson stationed troops and cannon to block traffic at both ends, and captured a tremendous prey of rolling stock.

More than fifty locomotives and some three hundred cars he turned over to his government. Some of the engines were rolled from the track and along southward turnpikes behind troops of dray horses. Such freight as seemed to him military in character he also confiscated. A carload of cavalry horses was especially welcome. Jackson bought two of the beasts for his own use. One, a smallish but compact and enduring sorrel, he thought at first might be sent to Anna, lately moved to her father's North Carolina home. Fancy, he named the horse, though it was no fancier than himself. After trying it and finding its gait easy and its stamina considerable, he kept it as his own mount.

On the following day, Joe Johnston appeared, a brigadier in the provisional army of the Confederacy, to take command at Harpers Ferry. Jackson asked and received confirmation of Johnston's right to supersede him—that confirmation was an order from the office of Lee. Then he turned over the post and gratefully relaxed.

Johnston felt no impulse toward relaxation. He expressed disappointment in the half-trained, half-equipped regiments of boys and their amateur officers. He was accustomed to neat uniforms, spotless arms and accouterments, and smart drill.

Dr. Hunter McGuire, a surgeon on Jackson's staff, noticed the new commander's mournful disapproval. He called attention to the Second Virginia, just then marching past. McGuire knew many of the officers and men personally, and spoke half to comfort the general, half in loyalty to his friends.

"If these men of the Second Virginia will not fight, you have no troops that will," said McGuire.

Johnston was not impressed; quite the contrary.

"I would not give one company of regulars for the whole regiment," he snubbed McGuire.

But even with regular troops, reflected Johnston, Harpers Ferry would be impossible to hold against any determined movement from those high approaches. He would prefer to drop back up the Valley with his command, or lead it to join and strengthen the garrison of some other and safer point.

While Johnston settled into Harpers Ferry that day, Yankees crossed the bridge from Washington into Alexandria. Cocke's Virginia militia retreated before them. There was no battle, but there was bloodshed on both sides.

Elmer Ellsworth, the self-dramatizing young colonel of the New York Zouaves, tore down a Confederate flag from the roof of an Alexandria hotel. The proprietor shot him dead, and was instantly killed a moment later by some of Ellsworth's men. In a day or two, more Union troops landed at the tip of the Virginia Peninsula between the York and James Rivers, and still more crossed the Ohio into the northwestern corner of the state. These matters understandably excited the Confederate Congress, which had assembled in Richmond on May 20.

In Montgomery, Jefferson Davis told Varina to wait for word, then pack and follow. Speaking to almost nobody else, he boarded a train on May 26, accompanied by his nephew Joseph Davis, Robert Toombs, and the Wigfalls.

The President was ailing again, and would have liked to rest during his journey. But wherever the train stopped for fuel or water, crowds gathered to call for a speech. Davis appeared, to waving flags and rains of flowers, and whatever he said was thunderously applauded. At Goldsboro in North Carolina, where secession was a fact less than ten days old, Davis ate supper in the restaurant of a railside hotel. Pretty girls besieged him. Some flung garlands around his neck, as though he were a horse that had just won a fashionable race. Others fanned him. Outside, Tarheel volunteers fired guns, and bands played.

He came into Richmond on the 29th, across the high, gaunt railroad bridge that spanned the James.

There at the riverside below the wheels of his train stood warehouses, docks, factories. The Tredegar Iron Works already was busy casting cannon. Mills ground out wheat flour and corn meal. Slave markets flourished. The train ran past these enterprises and stopped at a station below the beautiful heart of the town. Flowers bloomed in the yards, flags flew at the windows and on the roofs. The state capitol looked white and classic upon its wide green lawn, with George Washington's equestrian statue prancing alongside. Virtually the whole of Richmond's 38,000 men, women and children seemed to be out, lining the streets or gathered at the railroad station.

Richmond had felt hesitant about welcoming some of those new-rich cotton barons from deep in the South, but Richmond had wanted Davis. With him, said the Virginia papers, "victory would be certain, and chance would become certainty." No doubt, those papers felt, but that Davis would lead his armies in the field. Much was hoped in Richmond, as in Montgomery, for his military genius.

He stepped down from his car in the bright May morning, again to the strident volleying of guns, the pealing of bells, the brassy melody of a band. "Dixie," sang the horns. Davis was tired, but he stood up straight in his suit of gray.

A carriage waited for his party, and they rolled toward the Spotswood Hotel between crowded sidewalks. More flowers came pelting from the hands of admirers. A little girl could not throw strongly enough, and her nosegay fell on the cobblestones. At once Davis told the driver to pull up, then sprang down, retrieved the flowers and placed them on Mrs. Wigfall's lap.

That won the last Richmond heart to him. The citizens almost rioted around the Spotswood in their enthusiasm for him, and as in Montgomery he came to a window to show himself to his people.

After that, he was able to rest briefly from the long and fatiguing journey, but at half past five in the evening he came out and mounted a horse. Cavalry escorted him to the training camp at the fair grounds, and had difficulty in keeping him from being overwhelmed by a fresh horde of admirers. He mounted a balcony and made his first speech in the new capital, addressing the soldiers.

"It may be that you have not long been trained, and that you have much to learn of the art of war," he said to the ranks of recruits, "but I know that there beats in the breast of Southern sons, a determination never to surrender—a determination never to go home but to tell a tale of honor."

"Never!" the men assured him loudly. "Never!"

"Though great be the disparity of numbers, give us a fair field and a free fight, and the Southern banner will float in triumph everywhere."

Whoops and hurrahs again. Could anyone doubt what the President said?

"The country relies upon you," Davis wound up. "Upon you rest the hopes of our people; and I have only to say, my friends, that to the last breath of my life, I am wholly your own."

In a final storm of approving commotion, he retired, and went back to the Spotswood.

The hotel was immense, built around an inner courtyard. Confederate officials were filling it up, as they had filled the Exchange at Montgomery. Davis rested again in his quarters. Down in South Carolina, Beauregard was leaving Charleston to join his President.

Davis himself had asked for Beauregard, and the hero of the cumbersome and noisy capture of Fort Sumter hurriedly gathered luggage. Already Southerners were making laudatory verses about him, though his name was a hard one to rhyme. One of the less awkward efforts, dating from the arrival of the news of Sumter at Montgomery, had been set to music, and people managed to sing it:

> Flashing, flashing along the wires,
> The glorious news each heart inspires.
> The war in Charleston has begun,
> Its smoke obscured this morning's sun,
> As with cannon, mortar and petard
> We saluted the North with our Beau-regard.

Aware of his own fame and well persuaded that he deserved it, Beauregard wrote a farewell address to the South Carolinians who had supported and admired him in the Fort Sumter affair. He proposed, he said, "to leave as strong a mark as possible on the enemies of our beloved country, should they pollute its soil with their dastardly feet. . . . We are certain to triumph at last, even if we had for arms only pitchforks and flintlock muskets, for every bush and haystack will become an ambush and every barn a fortress."

With Beauregard went Attorney General Judah P. Benjamin and John L. Manning. When, like Davis, Beauregard heard cries for speeches at the railroad depots, he sent these two abler orators to substitute for him. At the end of his journey at Richmond he was hailed by another crowd, or perhaps the same crowd, but he would not show himself at his window at the Spotswood Hotel. While people shouted his name in the street, he conferred with Davis and Robert E. Lee, on where would be the fair field on which the Confederacy sought a free fight.

Lee had been commissioned brigadier general of the regular army of the Confederate States on May 14, on the same day that Joe Johnston had been given similar rank. As he had proven industrious and sensible in command of Virginia's state forces,

Lee became Davis' military adviser for all strategy and troop movements in Virginia. No official assignment had been given him; but Davis listened to him with a degree of respect and profit which, so the Confederates began to realize, Davis accorded very few other subordinates.

Together they sat down in the hotel room and talked on that last warm, bright day of May—ascetic, assured Jefferson Davis, Gallicly mercurial Pierre Gustave Toutant Beauregard, and calmly modest Robert E. Lee. The three men had known each other well and favorably for many years. They began at once to discuss the various Federal invasions and the threats of invasions possibly to come.

Beauregard surmised at first that Davis meant to send him to Norfolk, there to organize defense against the coming enemy advance up the Virginia Peninsula toward Richmond. But Lee spoke of what he felt was a graver threat of Federal penetration of northern Virginia—"the Alexandria Line" was what Davis called the defenses there, though the Confederates had fled out of Alexandria. Lee, just back from a tour of the positions below Washington, had a specific recommendation.

Plainly a large Union army was being organized in Washington, to flow southward and seek to fight a decisive battle. Such an army must choose an approach unembarrassed by wide, deep rivers, an approach furnished with roads along which to trundle its artillery and its trains of supply and baggage wagons. Only the day before, the 30th, Lee had returned from a point where the enemy might be expected and perhaps advantageously met, a railroad junction with certain natural defenses.

Railroads, thirty-one years old in America, were going to be important in this war that was upon the three commanders and their countrymen. Thus far, the only important military action had been the capture of Fort Sumter, and that capture had been achieved by methods harking back almost to the Middle Ages— the battering of massive defenses by massive concentrations of artillery fire. But in the fighting to come, with mobility at a premium, it behooved the Confederates to fend off any Union threat from that same railroad junction. At the same time, the position would defend against an effort to circle around behind the apprehensive Johnston at Harpers Ferry.

Davis agreed wholeheartedly with Lee. He directed Beauregard to take command at the point Lee had chosen. If the Yankees wanted a fight, they would find it at Manassas Junction.

IX

Trust in God and Davis

MANASSAS JUNCTION—where and what was Manassas Junction?

Obscurely and perhaps aimlessly, a Jewish peddler had roamed through Virginia at about the turn of the century, and at last had paused in a gap of the Blue Ridge. His name was Manasseh or Manassa; that meant he looked back through millennia of ancestry to the first-born son of Joseph, deputy of the Pharaoh, and Asenath, daughter of the high priest of On. Resting beside the trail in that lonely and half-wild country, Manassa heard in his heart the command to cease from his wanderings. He built himself a modest store which would serve the scattering of countryfolk who pioneered in the region. He could not have hoped for great fortune, but he prospered enough to live; enough even, it would seem, to gain position and respect in the community. For his customers called the pass through the mountains Manassa's Gap, and by fate's whim the storekeeper's surname would endure in the land and eventually echo through other nations and other lifetimes.

Though Manassa stayed at his little store, that name of his traveled forth from the mountain pass to set itself on other places. The builders of a railway that ran through the Valley settlements and out eastward, past the old store and on through Thoroughfare Gap in the Bull Run Mountains, called their enterprise the Manassa's Gap Railroad. Forty miles from where Manassa had

129

set himself up in business, that railroad came to the southern bank of Bull Run and there joined another and busier line. This was the Alexandria and Orange, which farther south forked one way to Richmond, the other to Charlottesville. Where the two railroads joined, the name was Manassas Junction, losing its apostrophe. A small depot and one or two sheds made a tiny pretense toward being a village.

The landscape rolled into hills northward and eastward, with two miles to the east, a considerable grassy height on the farm of Josiah Willcoxson. North of the Junction crept the high-banked brown waters of Bull Run, like a lazy snake on its way to join the Occoquan River that in turn flowed into the great estuary of the Potomac. Nearer at hand stretched great properties and small.

A scant mile northeast rose Liberia, the fine gable-roofed brick home of William Weir. Two miles beyond and close to a southward curve of Bull Run was Wilmer McLean's house, Yorkshire. Some four miles northwest of Manassas Junction jutted magnificent pillared Portici, where Francis Lewis lived. And to the west of Portici a slope climbed to the pine-fringed comb of Henry Hill, with on its slope on the far side the home of Judith Henry, widow of a naval hero of the War of 1812. Just past the Henry house was the smaller comfortable log cottage of the industrious and respectable free Negro Robinson.

From Henry Hill's top, one could look down upon the hard bed of the Warrenton Turnpike, that slanted northwest to the Stone Bridge across Bull Run. The Sudley Springs-Manassas Road, not quite so good, crossed it at right angles and came eastward to the Junction along a lesser slope of Henry Hill. On the far side of the Warrenton Turnpike the hill descended to the little valley of Young's Branch, and beyond that rose Matthews Hill, with upon it another fine house called Pittsylvania. Pine thickets tufted that height, too, and beyond it were groves, woods, with distant ascents toward the Bull Run Mountains and, far beyond that, the mist-veiled Blue Ridge.

At the north of all the Manassas Junction neighborhood, fords crossed Bull Run from steep bank to steep bank. They were named for the farmers and planters who owned the homes opposite them—Lewis', Ball's, Mitchell's, Blackburn's, McLean's. Here and there below the stream could be heard intriguing place names, Bacon Race Church and Wolf Run Shoals to eastward, and to westward Sudley Springs, Haymarket, and Hopewell Gap. On the far side of the stream, nearly eight miles north of Manassas Junction, sprawled the little town of Centreville.

First of the troops to arrive at Manassas had been the First and Second South Carolina, somewhat seasoned by the Sumter campaign. To these Lee had added three freshly mustered Virginia regiments under J. F. Preston, Richard Stoddard Ewell, and Samuel Garland. Brigadier General Milledge Bonham of South Carolina turned over command to Beauregard on June 1. Near at hand, at Culpeper just below Manassas, Cocke held his troops that had retreated from Alexandria. The total was some 6,000 officers and men, and Beauregard felt that they were not enough to fight so successfully and gloriously against invasion as he had planned.

Nor was he comforted by what his engineer's eye told him of the ground; it was not as defensible as he had been led to believe. At every one of Bull Run's fords in the vicinity of Manassas Junction, the northern approach dominated the southern. To make all hands more nervous, Federal cavalry struck Confederate outposts at Fairfax Court House eight miles above Bull Run on the same day that Beauregard reached Manassas. They killed Captain John Q. Marr, first Confederate soldier to die in action.

Quickly Beauregard organized his staff. Colonel Thomas Jordan, who at Lee's direction had assembled the forces at Manassas Junction, was competent as assistant adjutant general and was learning the surrounding country. Colonel S. Jones was chief of artillery. Thomas Williamson, erstwhile state engineer for Virginia, became Beauregard's chief engineer and started work on an elaborate system of fortifications. Major W. L. Cabell, as quartermaster, gathered wagons for transporting supplies. Dr.

R. L. Brodie, the chief surgeon, was at least as good as most doctors of the region and era. There were also several South Carolina volunteer aides, socially and politically important but of scant military experience—John S. Preston, John L. Manning, Porcher Miles and A. R. Chisholm.

Beauregard wrote to Davis for more men, and prepared and caused to be printed for circulation an address to the citizens of the surrounding country. Like that other hero of Sumter, Edmund Ruffin, Beauregard wrote far more thrillingly than he spoke:

A restless and unprincipled tyrant has invaded your soil. Abraham Lincoln, regardless of all moral, legal and constitutional restraints, has thrown his abolition hosts among you, who are murdering and imprisoning your citizens, confiscating and destroying your property, and committing other acts of violence and outrage too shocking and revolting to be enumerated. All rules of civilized warfare are abandoned, and they proclaim by their acts, if not on their banners, that their warcry is "Beauty and booty." All that is dear to man, your honor, and that of your wives and daughters, your fortunes, and your lives, are involved in this momentous contest.

In the name, therefore, of the constituted authorities of the Confederate States, in the sacred cause of constitutional liberty and self-government, for which we are contending, in the behalf of civilization and humanity itself, I, P. G. T. Beauregard, brigadier-general of the Confederate States, commanding at Camp Pickens, Manassas Junction, do make this my proclamation, and write and enjoin you by every consideration dear to the hearts of freemen and patriots, by the name and memory of your Revolutionary fathers, and by the purity and sanctity of your domestic firesides, to rally to the standard of your State and country, and by every means in your power compatible with honorable warfare to drive back and expel the invaders from your land. I conjure you to be true and loyal to your country and her legal and constitutional authorities, and especially to be vigilant of the movements and acts of the enemy, so as to enable you to give the earliest authentic information to these headquarters or to the officers under my command. I desire to assure you that the utmost protection in my power will be extended to you all.

While nagging Richmond for troops, Beauregard undertook to enlist one man himself. He telegraphed James Chesnut in South Carolina to join his staff. Chesnut was not attending the third session of Congress at the new capital, and at once he began to pack trunks and to choose horses and servants at Mulberry Plantation. Mary swore in her heart that she would follow him.

At Harpers Ferry, Johnston began a correspondence with Davis, less eloquent than Beauregard's but more insistent. He, too, wanted more men—he felt that 12,000 were none too many for his perilous post, even though he did not want to hold it. Half of such a force, as he planned, would fight a delaying action against any Unionist advance. The other half would wait up the Valley as a reserve on which to fall back. Kirby Smith expressed his agreement with Johnston that Harpers Ferry was "the most perfect cul de sac which troops have ever been thrown into," and added that Johnston would "fall a victim, I fear, to the negligence & incompetency of a government whose inaction & mistakes may be more disastrous than treachery. . . ."

And out on the Peninsula at Yorktown, Magruder had begun to nag on the same subject. Only short days earlier, Magruder had boasted that with 5,000 men he would undertake to capture Washington. Now he wanted his force increased to 10,000, to hold a line extending from the York to the James. Lee, the toiling, unstampeded chief at headquarters, did not parade his worry over these demands from three fronts. If he were to meet all requests, he would be hard pushed to find the troops, the officers, and the supplies.

The government at Richmond was doing what it could in a thousand ways. A number of good departmental workers had come down from Washington and were made welcome. General Reagan studied designs for postage stamps. These would bear, for the first time in American history, the portrait of a living man —Jefferson Davis. Memminger of the Treasury planned even greater glamour for Confederate bank notes. The dollar bills would display the lovely face of Lucy Holcomb Pickens. Private printeries, more prompt than these officials, were offering stationery and envelopes blazoned with the Stars and Bars and appropriate rhymed sentiments. One in particular was liked by the soldiers in the camps:

> Stand firmly by your cannon
> Let ball and grapeshot fly,
> And trust in God and Davis,
> But keep your powder dry.

Adjutant General Cooper studied the task of uniforming the swift-growing host of Confederate troops. The militia companies appeared for enlistment in gaudy rigs of blue, gray and green, in rough butternut and jeans, in Garibaldi red shirts and Zouave fezzes and bloomers. Many had no uniforms at all. Some officers, including Johnston and Beauregard, prepared to fight against the Union in the uniforms they had worn to fight for it. On June 6, Cooper issued a general order prescribing cadet-gray pantaloons and tunics, with red facings for the artillery, yellow for the cavalry, blue for the infantry. Varying insignia distinguished the officers, who could also exhibit gold braid and patterns of gilt buttons. Headdress would be a visored cap like that worn by the French army. Generals and their staff were directed to appear in plumed cocked hats.

Richmond had dominated Virginia society since the Tidewater's decay in wealth and influence, and to dominate Virginia society was, in the viewpoint of Virginians, to dominate the world. As capital of the state, Richmond had been accustomed to see governors and legislators go to Washington for high office and high prestige in drawing room and banquet hall. As the pioneer Confederates rolled in from Montgomery, a haughty reviewing stand awaited them. It was packed with Randolphs, Carters, Taylors, Culpepers, Washingtons, Dabneys, and Venables, together with their especially observant and critical ladies.

Davis, first to arrive, had thawed the frost from these *soigné* and exclusive folk by his magnificent presence and address. Judah P. Benjamin, keeping bachelor hall with his brother-in-law, proved exactly the plumply ready wit to become welcome every-

where. And the South Carolinians, themselves formidably proud
and mannered, seemed to be all right. But what about Robert
Toombs, that growling bear of a secretary of state, his heavy
hard lips stained with oaths and tobacco juice? What about
Stephen Mallory, prone to tell shocking stories? And Regan the
tough Texan, Walker the Alabama militiaman, and all those
other rugged provincials who, for all Richmond knew, might start
to pick their teeth with bowie knives?

The ladies helped. Mrs. Mallory was Spanish-born and of a
winning beauty and grace. Mrs. Toombs was a special favorite
of the Davises, which recommended her to Richmond. Mrs.
Walker, of a wealthy Alabama family, set off her spectacular
good looks with dazzling dresses. And Varina Davis was called
a "Western belle" by the influential Mrs. Joseph E. Johnston.

While teacups clinked and fans fluttered in a score of drawing
rooms, the fighting began again. It flared up on June 10, down
on the Peninsula, where some 7,000 Federals under squint-eyed,
self-important General Ben Butler advanced from their base at
Hampton. They were met in the marshy environs of an old white-
painted church called Big Bethel, by some 1,500 defenders under
Magruder and Colonel D. H. Hill, and were clumsily but thor-
oughly beaten and driven back. A single Confederate was killed
in the battle, a thoughtful young private of the First North Carolina named Joseph Lawson Wyatt. His burial in Hollywood
Cemetery, with the fullest of military honors, provided Richmond with emotions of sentimental sorrow that brave young lives
must be sacrificed. Ben Butler's routed forces had lost heavily,
said the flood of rumors; as many, perhaps, as three hundred.

James Chesnut, with four Negro servants to wait on him, came
into Richmond on the night of June 11, in time to hear the happy
news of the Big Bethel victory. The new capital was hot, dusty
and crowded. His horses had not arrived with him, and he went
on to Manassas without waiting for them to catch up. Beauregard
welcomed him cordially and mounted him on a cavalry charger
captured from a Yankee scouting party. Chesnut rode out with

his general to survey the country where, Beauregard felt increasingly sure, a big battle was coming.

These things Chesnut wrote home to Mary, with matter-of-fact messages of affection. Mary felt worried, even ill. Her ailment, she decided, was a burning wish to follow her James to Richmond. She heard scolding criticism of Southern officers who had stayed with the Union, and expressions of good-humored tolerance for the old Unionist Petigru, who in church at Charleston had risen from his knees when the minister read the prayer for the President of the Confederate States. She also heard, with shocked amazement, a shallow-minded South Carolina planter accuse Robert E. Lee of treasonable impulses toward the Confederacy. And she was amused at the story of how Colonel Joseph Kershaw, with Beauregard at Manassas, had complained that Bull Run was a highly unrefined name.

"Let us try and make it as great a name as your South Carolina Cowpens," Beauregard had disarmed Kershaw's prudery.

All around Mary a vast military camp seemed to extend. Every race track, every fair grounds, had become a training field. That June, special interest throughout the state attended the development of Hampton's Legion at Columbia. Wade Hampton was its colonel. He had no military experience, but his natural gifts for command and organization were instantly manifest. He rode and shot as well, perhaps, as any young man who sought to enlist under him. His Legion was a combination of all the services —six companies of infantry, four of cavalry, and a battery of artillery for which Hampton had bought with his own money six rifled Blakely guns.

The best blood of South Carolina swarmed to the Legion. Its honor company was made up of volunteers from the Washington Light Infantry of Charleston. James Conner, who had resigned as United States Attorney for South Carolina and who had emerged as an efficient infantry officer during the siege of Sumter, was captain of the company. Charles Hutson happily transferred into it from the Pocotaligo Mounted Men, and to be more soldierly bought himself cheap shoes and a cherrywood pipe, and had his fuzzy young mustache shaved off.

Other veterans of the Sumter campaign had joined to be drillmasters, and drill was constant and good in the Legion. Hampton's second in command was Lieutenant Colonel B. J. Johnson, who had almost been elected governor instead of Pickens. Captain of those fine Blakely guns was Stephen D. Lee. The Legionnaires hoped earnestly to be ordered into Virginia and active conflict.

Every unit hoped for that. The ill-supplied capital could accept only those who had their own proper arms and other equipment. A happily greeted reinforcement was the Washington Artillery of New Orleans.

That fine volunteer battalion had left its home town on May 27. At Christ Church there had been prayers, and at City Hall an address. The loveliest ladies of New Orleans had belabored the artillerists with flowers, had tingled them with kisses. A special train of twenty-one cars had fetched them across Alabama and Tennessee and Virginia, nearly three hundred officers and men with their own fine horses and gleaming brass field pieces, their sophisticated Negro servants with Creole accents, their French chef Edouard recruited from a glittering New Orleans restaurant, their pert little vivandière Madame Bahr. Richmond buzzed with tales of how, leaving the cars in the early morning, these trig soldiers had spent $250 in gold for a magnificent breakfast. How were such luxurious fellows doing in camp at the fair grounds?

They were doing very well, it turned out. They knew their drill and their duties. Jefferson Davis himself, accompanied by Louis Wigfall, came to visit the camp, and the pair tried to ride in from one side. Private P. Von Colln, on sentry duty, crisply ordered them to halt.

Wigfall was outraged. "Don't you know the President?" he roared, but Von Colln was equal to the occasion.

"No," he replied above the slope of his musket. "I know no one. I only know my orders. Go round by the guard tent; you can't pass here."

Davis calmed Wigfall and gravely complimented Von Colln. The President, too, was taking the war seriously. He issued a formal proclamation that June 13 would be observed throughout the land as a day of fasting and prayer.

The religionistic South heard him with approval, and for the most part prepared to spend June 13 devoutly. There were exceptions, however. Young Dr. Robert D. Bone was a regimental surgeon in Texas, and no admirer of his President. He wrote home to his lovely wife Minerva in Nacogdoches County: "I see by a recent proclamation that Jeff Davis is still not buried—the Davis family seem to be unfortunate in that enterprize."

To fast and pray was no extraordinary behavior for Davis himself; he prayed much and ate little as a general way of life. Others observed the occasion in their own various ways.

Edmund Ruffin stayed quietly at Marlbourne, envying his son who did scouting duty on the Peninsula. Ruffin fatigued easily that June. To God as well as to man, he may have said, "I told you so."

Adjutant General Samuel Cooper at last approved the suggestion of Joe Johnston that the Harpers Ferry garrison fall back to more defensible ground up the Valley. A force of Federals under old Robert Petterson, who had been one of the four brigadiers of the line in the old army, moved fast toward Maryland Heights across the Potomac, and on the 13th Johnston told his men to prepare to evacuate.

Colonel Thomas Jackson, acting as a brigade commander under Johnston, made his own regiments ready for the march. While he waited he prayed; like Davis he needed no formally appointed occasion for his devotions. He felt special gratitude to the Almighty that Anna was out of the Valley, and safe with her father in North Carolina.

In Talladega, Alabama, Mrs. Louisiana Bradford thought the solemnity of the occasion appropriate for writing a letter to Mary Chesnut, whose character and accomplishments she much admired:

DEAR MADAM:

This being the day set apart by our noble President for prayer for our Southern Confederacy, the interest of our section has come up before my mind in all its bearings, and although I am utterly opposed to women taking any part in affairs publicly, I am a great advocate for their influence in the right time and right direction.

That Mary Chesnut could exert great influence was a certainty to Mrs. Bradford; and what that influence should be the lady proceeded to set down:

Occupying the position you do, you and the other ladies of the Congress and of the Cabinet have it in your power to give tone to society for all time to come. I trust in God, you will exert it in the right way, and I believe you will. The ladies of your State I have always admired. There is a well assured confidence of position about them, and therefore, they are plain and unassuming. This elegant simplicity is so desirable, that I trust it will be kept up in our higher fashionable circles. . . .

Much more Mrs. Bradford wrote, underscoring for the sake of earnest emphasis. At the same time, another Southerner committed to paper his own notion of what thoughts the day's spirit made obvious.

This was I. A. Randall, overseer of spacious Magnolia Plantation, the fine estate owned by Effingham Lawrence in Louisiana. That same day had begun sadly for Overseer Randall, for a valued mule had died at the dark hour of two A.M. It may be that his unhappiness over this bereavement informed the words he set down in the plantation record book, along with notes on work to be done and expenses to be met:

This day is set a part by presedent Jefferson Davis for fasting and praying owing to the Deplorable condishion ower Southern country is In My Prayer Sincerely to God is that every Black Republican in the Hole combined whorl Either man woman o chile that is opposed to negro slavery as it existed in the Souther confederacy shal be trubled with pestilents & calamitys of all Kinds & Dragout the Balance of there existence in misray & Degradation with scarsly food & rayment to keep sole & Body togeather and O God I pray the to Direct a bullet or a bayonet to pirce the Hart of every northern soldier that invades southern Soile & after the Body has Rendered up its Traterish Sole give it a trators reward a Birth in the Lake of Fires & Brimstone my honest convickshion is that Every man wome & chile that has gave aide to the abolishionist are fit Subjects for Hell I also ask the to aide the Sothern Confedercy in maintaining Ower rights & establishing the confederate Government Believing in this case the prayes from the wicked will prevailith much Amen.

X

Now That We Have Stung Their Pride

INTO Richmond they poured, the splendid young men who thought that they were already soldiers and capable of whipping anybody.

Southern rhetoric, at least, remained plentiful in the Confederacy, and sonorous names were spoken for the arriving units. There were fencibles, hussars, voltigeurs, dragoons, guards, Zouaves, rangers, and flying artillery. These wore all sorts and colors of uniforms, or no uniforms at all.

From its depot of mobilization at Corinth in Mississippi, the Sixth Alabama Regiment rode across country in boxcars. Its field officers had donned frock coats of green cloth, as though they meant to march in a St. Patrick's Day parade. There were frequent stops in West Tennessee, where townsfolk proved admiring and hospitable. The soldiers got out of the cars to sample corn whiskey offered in jugs, then climbed aboard again. Some of them rode in boozy high spirits on top. In the mountains of East Tennessee, stamping grounds of Unionist leaders like Andrew Johnson and Parson William Gannoway Brownlow, the people scowled and sneered. The Sixth Alabama wanted to jump off the train again, to pull down United States flags on display at certain depots. Their officers sternly forbade them to start their own war. They reached Manassas, and became part of a new brigade in Beauregard's growing command.

Up from South Carolina puffed another train, with Hampton's Legion. The Legionnaires, like every other body of heroes, had

141

been addressed, prayed over, lauded and kissed. A certain dash was given the Legion infantry by capelike white havelocks that descended from the backs of their forage caps to drape over necks and shoulders. Private Charles Hutson had learned to eat fat bacon and patch his own pants. He and his comrades stared from the slow, hot cars as they trundled through North Carolina. Thankfully they accepted food and water brought to their windows at various stations, but they were tired and hungry when, three days later, they reached Petersburg below Richmond. The Petersburgers welcomed them with palmetto flags and a wondrous meal of ham, cabbage, Irish potatoes, and raw onions. They boarded another train that took them to Richmond, where they arrived after midnight in a pounding rainstorm. They slept exhaustedly on the floor of a tobacco factory.

Such hardships evoked only a few complaints—"a certain amount of grumbling is necessary," wrote home Captain Conner, gaining wisdom in military matters. Camped at Rocketts, east of Richmond on the James, they began at once to drill, briskly and well. Richmond sightseers were impressed, and invited the gentlemen volunteers to tea and dinner. The officers engaged ladies' sewing circles to make gray field jackets and pantaloons to replace the dressy but impractical uniforms of the various companies.

The elite Legion and the rustic Sixth Alabama were but two of many shipments of soldiers. All of these men were green, but they had known all their lives how to ride and shoot. Such volunteers, in their new uniforms of gray homespun, marched through the capital by company or regiment, their bucolic eyes wide at the glory they found. A North Carolina youth, shaky in naught save spelling, scrawled a letter to the folks back on the farm:

Make your self well satisfied about me for I am doing what is right for my country. I have learned more since I left home than I did in all the rest of my life. You never saw anything in your life. I have seen more than my pour tongue can ever tell. Richmond is a site to see more than you can think. . . . We have a plenty to eat, though we have to cook and wash for our selves and we have to work mity hard.

Whole armies imbued with a spirit so venturesome and confident would be needed. For the bluecoats of the Union, beaten at Big Bethel and resolutely faced below Alexandria, were threatening at another corner.

In late May, some 9,000 Federals had moved slowly but purposefully through the western Virginia counties below the Ohio, some of the same counties that had voted strongly against secession and, more recently, had talked of secession on their own part to rejoin the Union. The commander of this army, Brigadier General George Brinton McClellan, was much admired in the North. He drove a small Confederate force out of Grafton, then followed it to Phillipi and drove it from there as well. Equally disquieting was the news that Patterson's force approached the heights across the Potomac from Harpers Ferry, threatening Johnston. Beauregard, at Manassas Junction, badgered his subordinates for a system of ramparts to defend the position.

Beauregard had set up his headquarters at William Weir's Liberia. A road ran past to Bull Run, across Blackburn's Ford, and on to join the Warrenton Turnpike at Centreville. Into the big front room of Liberia Beauregard's clerks moved their desks, and upon the walls they fixed all maps of the region the engineering staff could find. The upper floor became living quarters for Beauregard and his aides, and the great pillared portico swarmed with couriers.

The general and the high-toned South Carolina gentlemen who did rather fumbling volunteer duty at various staff posts ate simply, of provisions purchased at neighboring farms, with plenty of rice from South Carolina plantations. The surrounding mass of tents and horse lines, named Camp Pickens in honor of the governor of the first seceding state, was the main base of troops. Beauregard put a strong detachment across Bull Run in Centreville, with his most experienced regiments, the South Carolinians, at Fairfax Court House.

With Colonel Williamson, the chief engineer, Colonel George H. Terrett supervised the construction of defenses. Terrett had been a major of Marines and had drawn the first plans for the breastworks. The volunteers at Camp Pickens grumbled and threatened mutiny when told to ply picks and shovels, and Beauregard, well aware of what might seem degrading labor to a Southern gentleman, hired slaves from the surrounding plantations to throw up the earth and shape it into redoubts. Naval guns captured at Norfolk were trundled in and set up. Meanwhile, Beauregard fretted over shortages of rations and ammunition. To Wigfall, his comrade of the Sumter bombardment, he wrote that he expected an attack by 40,000 Federals, but: "My troops are in fine spirits and anxious for a fight," he added proudly. "They seem to have the most unbounded confidence in me.

"Oh, that I had the genius of a Napoleon, to be more worthy of our cause and their confidence!"

His own genius might not be Napoleonic but, decided Beauregard, it might be adequate for the problem at hand. News of Patterson's move toward Johnston's lines at Harpers Ferry inspired the Creole to draw up a plan of counterattack, which he addressed directly to Davis, ignoring his superiors Cooper and Lee. The letter was handed to the President by Lieutenant Colonel Sam Jones of Beauregard's staff, on June 13, and may have disturbed prayer on that day officially dedicated to devout address to heaven.

Beauregard's plan of campaign, said the message rather flatly, "should be acted upon at once." It elaborated:

The enemy seem to be taking the offensive toward Harper's Ferry, and a few days hence may find General J. E. Johnston in such a critical condition as to render it impossible to relieve him. If he were ordered to abandon forthwith his present position and concentrate suddenly his forces with mine . . . we could, by a bold and rapid movement forward, retake Arlington Heights and Alexandria, if not too strongly fortified and garrisoned, which would have the effect of recalling all the enemy's forces from northern Virginia, for the protection of Washington. But should General Johnston be unable to unite his forces with mine, then he ought to be instructed to retreat at the proper time towards Richmond, through the valley of Virginia, checking the enemy wherever and whenever he can. When compelled to abandon my present position, I will fall back also on Richmond;

the forces along the lower Potomac, on the Peninsula, and at Norfolk, may have to do likewise. Then, acting on interior lines, from Richmond as a centre (our forces being increased by the reserves at that point) we could crush, in rapid succession and in detail, the several columns of the enemy, which I have supposed, would move on three or four different lines.

This unasked advice by a brigadier to his President, involving what amounted to instructions to that brigadier's superior officer at another point, may have seemed extraordinary to Davis, whose prompt reply, however, was courteous and moderate.

"I do not perceive why General Johnston should be unable, even before overwhelming numbers, to retire behind the positions where the enemy would approach in reverse," Davis wrote, and added: "Concurring fully with you in the effect which would be produced by the possession of Arlington Heights and Alexandria, if your rear is at the same time sufficiently covered, it is quite clear that if the case be otherwise, your possession, if acquired, would be both brief and fruitless." But, Davis concluded as though to comfort the apprehensive Beauregard, four more regiments were on their way to Manassas.

On June 15, some 4,000 Confederate troops marched northwestward to face McClellan. They were led by Robert Garnett, a sane and sober-minded brigadier of wide experience in the old army. And on the following day, Johnston's troops withdrew from Harpers Ferry, unmolested by Patterson. Johnston concentrated at Winchester, prepared to offer battle, but none came. Jackson, with the First Brigade, would have liked to fight. He wrote to Anna: "I trust that through the blessing of God we shall soon be given an opportunity of driving the invaders from this region."

However God might will such an opportunity, Patterson did not. He occupied Harpers Ferry and stayed there in all caution. The Yankees at Alexandria proved themselves more daring, and on the 17th a regiment of them rode a train of cars, with rather careless confidence, along the Alexandria, Loudon and Hampshire Railroad toward Vienna.

Colonel Maxcy Gregg was at Fairfax Court House with the First South Carolina. His aristocratic regiment had been in service

since Christmastide of 1860, first at the siege of Sumter, then in
Virginia, where it had come on April 24. Many of its private
soldiers were men of wealth and position, with good chances of
receiving commissions if they were discharged, and others had
had enough service at any rank; as a result, almost the entire
regiment looked hopefully toward disbanding at the close of its
six months' service on June 25. But a week would pass before that
date, and out came the First South Carolina, 575 strong, to join
some cavalry patrols and two field guns in the way of the trainload of bluecoats.

Shells from the two guns struck and stopped the train, and
then a volley from the muskets of the South Carolinians stam-
peded the Union soldiers. They sprang out of the cars and fled
into the forest. The triumphant Confederates found six dead and
one wounded enemy, and gathered a trove of weapons dropped
on what, for brief moments, had been the field of battle.

Two days later, some 200 Virginians and Tennesseeans drove
a Federal force across the Potomac at the bridge near New Creek,
burned the bridge to its piers and brought back two captured
cannon. Newspapers and tea parties in Richmond squealed with
delight over the reports of these victorious skirmishes; but the
news that Johnston had abandoned Harpers Ferry without a
similar glorious exchange of shots was not so pleasing. For the
first time in the Confederacy's brief history, citizens murmured
disparagingly about Jefferson Davis.

Meanwhile, the armies grew, and leadership must grow with
them.

Samuel Cooper was already a full general of the regular army
of the Confederate States, his commission dating from May 16.
On June 14 Robert E. Lee had been given a promotion to like
rank, but senior to him, as of May 30, would be his old colonel
Albert Sidney Johnston, just then on the overland route home
from California. Joe Johnston, who considered that his brevet
staff rank of brigadier in the old army established his seniority
over all these comrades in arms, began to sulk at Winchester
because he remained at brigade rank—higher in seniority, but not

in grade, than the eleven erstwhile colonels who also got their brigadiers' stars on June 17.

Several such promotions went to colonels already commanding brigades. Jackson, who led five Virginia regiments with Johnston's force at Winchester—the Army of the Shenandoah, Richmond headquarters called that force—was on the list. Barnard Bee of South Carolina also got a brigade under Johnston, and so did Kirby Smith. Out on the Peninsula, a star seemed proper recognition for Magruder's Big Bethel triumph. Two more promotions went to colonels with Beauregard.

These were Dick Ewell, a bald, popeyed ex-captain of dragoons who piped shrill blasphemies, and David R. Jones, who had borne the surrender terms to Anderson at Fort Sumter. With Milledge Bonham, Beauregard thus had general officers for three of the six brigades he had formed with the nineteen regiments then at and near Manassas. The other three he gave to colonels he considered most trustworthy—Cocke, Jubal Early, and G. H. Terrett who had helped fortify the junction. Yet another brigadier, a bulky, self-assured Alabamian named James Longstreet who had been a United States Army paymaster, was coming up from the Deep South to report at Manassas.

Beauregard was able to marshal some 20,000 men in these six brigades, and they were no more than he felt he needed at Manassas. That was, however, the largest concentration of troops in Virginia. Some twenty-five miles southward, on Aquia Creek near Fredericksburg, 3,000 more were commanded by deaf old Theophilus Holmes, a brigadier highly esteemed by Davis. Johnston, with 10,000, was nearly sixty miles to west of Manassas, with mountains between. Garnett bored resolutely toward McClellan's invaders in western Virginia, with 4,000 more. These separated commands added up to less than 40,000 officers and men between Richmond and the Potomac, most of them untried and unpredictable, against a reported 75,000 Yankees on the way. Soldiers and civilians speculated loudly and uninformedly on what would happen.

But Thomas Jackson, whose brigade had been sent north of

Martinsburg by Johnston on June 20, was characteristically restrained and thoughtful. Without any of Beauregard's flamboyance, Jackson felt that aggressive and wholehearted military action was the Confederacy's only hope: ". . . to wage such a war as will bring hostilities to a speedy close." That was what he had said six long, long months ago while peace seemed still to be upon his world, and he still meant it. But an enemy reconnaissance had withdrawn across the Potomac above him, out of his reach. Regretfully, he destroyed locomotives and cars on the Baltimore and Ohio Railroad at Martinsburg, and the fire of their burning was lurid for miles. "If the cost of the property could only have been expended in disseminating the gospel of the Prince of Peace," he pondered, "how much good might have been expected!" Destruction of Northern invaders was not so mournful a prospect to his stern, devout soul. Another venture of Yankees across the river at Williamsport caused him to march against them on Sunday, but again they retreated before him.

Ladies of the region admired Jackson. No less than three presented him with havelocks, to wear at the rear of the shabby forage cap he had brought from the Military Institute. Such gifts he accepted with grave courtesy, but with no intention of wearing them. However graceful a havelock might look draped at the nape of a dandy soldier such as might be found in Hampton's Legion, Jackson did not consider them a necessary protection in the summer sun of northern Virginia. He wished that the ladies would sew instead on haversacks, that soldiers might properly carry their rations on such marches as he, Jackson, wanted to lead.

Men were fighting not far from where Jackson fretted to get into action. On a reconnaissance upriver, above Romney, eleven gray cavalrymen ran into a patrol of Northern cavalry and infantry on June 25. Richard Ashby, who had been at Charlestown to witness the death of John Brown, fell sprawling when his horse went down. The others fell back, leaving their comrade surrounded by the enemy, then found reinforcements under Richard's brother, Colonel Turner Ashby. Charging back to the scene of the clash, they found Richard dying, pierced by bullet holes and the gorings of bayonets. They rode after the enemy, caught up at the edge of the river, and exacted revenge. Turner Ashby became a grim-faced thirster for Yankee blood.

Down in Camden, South Carolina, Mary Chesnut boarded a train for Richmond. With her went her pretty young kinswoman Mary Hammy, whose fiancé was with the South Carolina troops in Virginia. Lawrence Keitt and a minister named Meynardie escorted the two ladies, and the rest of the car seemed crowded with soldiers. Every railway station was besieged by girls who waved handkerchiefs and raised melodious cheers for the warriors.

Two more women entered the car. They told Mary that they were schoolteachers from the North, trying to find their way home again. As Keitt began to bluster criticisms of President Davis and his Cabinet, Mary felt obliged to scribble a note and pass it to him:

Do not abuse our home and house so before those Yankee strangers going North.

Unabashed, Keitt told the new joke about trying Confederate recruits with splashes of water. If they did not "sizz," vowed Keitt, their patriotism was too cool.

Stephen Mallory and Louis Wigfall met the party at the Richmond depot and led the way to the Spotswood Hotel. Passing the capitol grounds, Mary Chesnut reflected that the array of statues, with Washington on horseback among them, looked like a stand of cruets—"vinegar cruet, pepper pot, all that!"

The hotel itself proved as crowded as had been the inadequate hostelries in Montgomery, and the room the ladies had reserved was not vacant. They borrowed a room belonging to their old friend Mrs. John S. Preston and, when that lady returned from visiting her volunteer colonel at Manassas, Mary Chesnut and Mary Hammy moved into a cheerless little cell of a chamber, jammed with a double bed, a chair and a washstand. They hung their dresses on nails behind the door. Out in the corridor, Varina Davis greeted them cordially and insisted that they take their meals at the President's table.

Someone else hurried to knock at the door of the tiny room. It

was James Chesnut, down from Manassas to bear a request from
Beauregard for more ammunition. His reunion with Mary was
affectionate, but she winced as he sat on that single chair and
puffed clouds of pipe smoke toward her clothes on the nails.

"Wartimes," James reminded her, affectionately but crisply.
"Nobody is fussy now. When I go back to Manassas tomorrow,
you will be awfully sorry you snubbed me about those things up
there."

That was true, Mary scolded herself; she would miss James
terribly, would fear for him at Manassas, toward which hordes of
hostile Yankees set their faces. They headed for supper with the
Davises in the Spotswood dining room.

Chesnut was not alone in asking for ammunition. Joe Johnston,
too, had sent word that he could not conduct a proper fire fight
should the invaders advance upon him at Winchester. Jefferson
Davis was grave about the shortage of powder, but at table he
made himself josh James Chesnut about the ex-governors and ex-
congressmen who surrounded Beauregard in the mansion at
Liberia. "Whoever is too fine," the President chuckled, "that is,
so fine that we do not know what to do with him—we send him to
Beauregard's staff!"

After supper, James and Mary joined a throng in the President's drawing room. Officers and politicians were present with
their ladies, and the air throbbed with gossip, mostly about the
war. Davis sat on a sofa with Mary, and was the fascinating companion that he could be when he wished; but he stunned her by
saying that only fools doubted the courage of the Yankees.

"Now that we have stung their pride," he said, "we have roused
them until they will fight like devils." The war would be a long
one, he felt. And, perhaps remembering his jibe about Beauregard's elegant amateur aides, he added that it had been a mistake
to give James Chesnut a staff appointment; James was officer
material, and should raise and command a regiment in the field.

Mary trembled apprehensively at the suggestion. A gay tale
came, just in time to cheer her up. It concerned an adventure of
one of those frantic ladies' sewing circles—it had cut out only the
right legs of trousers to uniform a regiment of Maryland volun-

teers. The embarrassed seamstresses had had to scramble for more gray cloth, to make the left legs and complete the garments.

On June 29, James hurried back to Manassas to report on his errand after ammunition, and Mary drove out in an open carriage with Mrs. Wigfall, Mrs. Preston, and Mary Hammy to see the troops at the fair grounds. *Champ de Mars*, Richmond liked to call the training camp. Jefferson Davis rode past the carriage on a superb gray horse, looking every inch the strong, able chieftain. At his side cantered his nephew Joe Davis, Louis Wigfall, and General Robert E. Lee, black-mustached, strikingly handsome, nobly sure in the saddle. The ladies chattered about volunteering as nurses.

The streets of Richmond were crowded those days. Others besides generals and Presidents proved themselves expert riders. The Black Horse Cavalry, made up of Virginia's elite of beasts and men, dazzled the watchers—even a New York schoolteacher trying to find her way home and furious because a bystander had spat tobacco juice upon her silk dress. More thrilling than the Black Horse, in its own way, was an exhibition of mounted Texas Rangers, who sprang on and off their galloping horses, dropped their pistols and wheeled to race back and swoop down from the saddle to snatch them up.

On the hot first day of July, Edmund Ruffin was in Richmond. He bought blankets, a round cheese, and a small keg of hard crackers. The next morning he would board the train for Manassas, again to offer his services to the Palmetto Guard that had welcomed him to the storming of Sumter and now made part of the Second South Carolina at Fairfax Court House.

The sun went down, and the sky blazed with a comet. Like a hoary-bearded prophet of doom it crawled northwestward across the black heavens, toward two hosts of armed men, blue and gray, that faced each other across the upper reaches of the Potomac.

Under that comet-patrolled sky on the night of July 1, Thomas Jonathan Jackson spread his blankets on the ground north of Martinsburg.

XI

Battle Summer

As JACKSON lay down, some 2,200 soldiers camped around him. They were Virginians like himself, the four regiments of his brigade and the Rockbridge Artillery.

Jackson knew most of the Rockbridges by name. They came from Lexington, one of those elite volunteer units, made up of students, lawyers and other young men of money. Their captain, William Nelson Pendleton, was a handsome and polished man of fifty-one, who had been brilliant in classes at West Point but who had resigned after three years of army life. He had taught in various colleges and then, taking orders, had become rector of the Episcopal Church at Lexington. Pendleton was an old friend of Jackson's; other old friends were the six bronze cannon of the Rockbridge Artillery—they had come from the Military Institute, where Jackson had used them in past years to instruct class after class. He was well acquainted with the powers and peculiarities of each piece.

Good acquaintanceship extended throughout the command. Some early complaints of Jackson's strict discipline had vanished as the men became soldiers. "Old Jack," the infantrymen called their brigadier, and few remembered that his nickname had been Fool Tom at the Military Institute. His shabby uniform, his slouching but assured figure on the horse they knew as Little Sorrel, were viewed with affectionate understanding. Let others sing those painfully rhymed praises to Beauregard; Old Jack and his men did well together.

A number of officers and privates had pitched tents, but Jackson disdained to spread shelter above or mattress beneath. A soldier's bed was the ground, in the open. He rejoiced that he slept well, that he became inured to rough military life in the presence of the enemy. If only the enemy would come . . .

The enemy came in the dawn of July 2, thousands upon thousands of the enemy.

Jeb Stuart's cavalry, on watch between Jackson's camp and the Potomac, saw blue regiments splashing across the ford at Falling Waters, and a courier galloped to Jackson with the news, at half past seven. It looked like invasion in far greater numbers than Jackson had; perhaps greater numbers than Johnston's main Army of the Shenandoah could marshal at Winchester.

Promptly the bearded commander issued his orders. Kenton Harper, who had doffed the gay plumes of a militia general to develop into a competent colonel for the Fifth Virginia, moved along the road toward the ford with the 380 muskets he could employ that morning. Two more regiments formed to follow Harper as a reserve. Jackson rode swiftly to join Stuart, and after him Pendleton brought two guns of the Rockbridges. The rest of the camp struck its tents and loaded its baggage wagons to make ready for retirement.

The bluecoats were across the river, and formed line of battle as Jackson came in sight of them. They advanced along the Valley Turnpike, slowly but with confidence. Jackson, exultantly steady of voice and manner, told Harper to open fire.

Harper's first volley struck down some of the Federal skirmishers in advance of the main formation, and the others halted. Studying the enemy front, Jackson saw that there were thousands of infantry, with cavalry massed on the road at the very center of the formation. While he estimated the situation, the blue line moved forward again.

Harper's Virginians took cover behind a roadside house and barn and in the trees to right and left. Another fusillade of musket balls slowed up the onslaught. Jackson saw the flanks of the enemy curling in, right and left, as though to trap his little force, and sent orders for Harper to drop back. Then Jackson rode to where Pendleton waited beside one of the bronze guns, and told him to cover the retreat that now became necessary in the face of such overwhelming numbers.

Yankee guns were already barking, but Pendleton gave his orders coolly. His crew moved the gun into position. Private J. L. Massie rammed home a charge, and Pendleton himself aimed the piece into the center of what seemed to be a squadron of cavalry preparing to charge along the Turnpike. The preacher-captain glanced up to the summer sky and muttered something. Later, some of the Rockbridges would swear that he prayed: "Lord, have mercy on their souls!" More loudly and unmistakably, he gave the command: "Fire!"

David Moore pulled the lanyard. The gun roared, and the ball seemed to sweep the horsemen out of the way, like paper cutouts in a sudden gust of wind. Instantly Pendleton ordered the gun's muzzle moved leftward, to glare at a Federal cannon. Another shot, and the blue gun crew scattered away from its station.

This excellent marksmanship gave Harper a chance to fall back in good order, keeping up the fire of his muskets. The Yankee guns, big and small, dropped men in the ranks but did not break the formation. Again Pendleton's gun fired, and again—eight times in all, while Jackson cautioned Pendleton to conserve the ammunition in his cart. Stuart's cavalry, fanned out on the flanks of the retiring Fifth Virginia, scooped up overconfident Federals who got ahead of their main advance. Forty-nine prisoners in all were hustled rearward. Apparently a number of the invaders had been killed or wounded.

Jackson retired through the region where he had camped the night before, then through Martinsburg. Stuart's horsemen continued to screen him properly. At Big Spring Jackson halted his men and made ready to fight, but the superior numbers of the invaders had stopped at Martinsburg. It was noon, and Jackson took time to reckon his losses.

Twelve of the Fifth Virginia had been wounded, and their re-treating comrades had carried them along. Thirteen others were missing—killed, or left wounded on the field and captured. But

Jackson saw that the spirits of his men were excellent as they went into camp for the night.

The following day another retirement, to a beautiful meadow near Darkesville. Jackson wrote his report and sent it on to headquarters at Winchester. Back came direction to bring in his command, and on July 4, to the echoes of a noisy holiday celebration from the Federal lines at Martinsburg, Jackson obeyed.

Less celebration of America's Independence Day occurred in the South. The date was barely noticed in Charleston, and in Richmond observation took the form of parades by the troops in training and an artillery salute at sunset. Mary Chesnut was packing again, to go to Fauquier White Sulphur Springs with Mrs. John S. Preston—both the ladies' colonels felt that they might slip away to the White Sulphur between tours of duty. Again came rumors that Johnston, waiting for Patterson to move against him from Martinsburg, lacked ammunition for a real battle.

"If my Joseph is defeated, I will die!" wailed Mrs. Johnston.

"Lydia, beware of ambition!" Varina Davis reproved her.

Johnston, naturally cautious, was watchful but by no means thinking of defeat. As Jackson came into Winchester, Johnston handed him a letter from Richmond. It was brief but cordial:

My dear general, I have the pleasure of sending you a commission of brigadier-general in the Provisional Army, and to feel that you merit it. May your advancement increase your usefulness to the State.

Very truly,

R. E. LEE

Enclosed was the commission, dated June 17. Jackson was happy as he wrote a letter himself, to Anna in North Carolina:

. . . One of my greatest desires for advancement is the gratitude it will give my darling, and [the opportunity] of serving my country more efficiently. I have all that I ought to desire in the line of promotion. I should be ungrateful if I were not contented, and exceedingly thankful to our kind Heavenly Father. May His blessing ever rest on you is my fervent prayer. Try to live near to Jesus, and secure that peace which flows like a river.

But war flowed like a river into Virginia.

The men of Beauregard's forward elements gazed, with a fascination that included something of awe, toward a blob in the sky above the northern horizon. That was a Yankee observation balloon, the more knowing of the troops said. It hung there, tethered by a long cable, and in its swaying basket perched observers who trained powerful glasses to spy out the numbers and positions about Manassas. War in the sky . . . something out of the Book of Revelations.

Not so lofty was the observation point chosen by Captain Porter Alexander, reporting to Beauregard as signal officer. He set up his signal station on that highest hill east of the Junction, the hill on Willcoxson's Farm. From various nearby regiments he drafted intelligent privates who quickly learned the system of flag signals which Alexander himself had helped perfect for the United States Army in 1859.

This involved the use of a single bright-patterned flag on a long staff, and was based upon the Baines telegraphic alphabet. A sweeping wave of the flag to the signaler's left meant a dot, a similar motion to the right meant a dash. Letters spelled out words and messages. Alexander felled woods to give two clear six-mile lanes across the land, one beyond Bull Run to Centreville, the other westward to a hill by the Van Pelt house at the stone bridge that took the Warrenton Turnpike over the Run. All around him, as he drilled his signalmen, mumbled the rumors of imminent invasion.

Jefferson Davis heard such rumors all the way to Richmond, and his grave disapproval of the expedition of Mary Chesnut and Mrs. Preston to the Springs made the ladies feel both furtive and daring. Mary determined to go, however. Perhaps her spirits rose with her temper on the night of July 4, when in the drawing room of the Davises she heard a Virginian say: "Mrs. Davis' ladies are not young, are not pretty."

Mary was one of those ladies, and, while she would say of herself that she was neither young nor pretty, she did not welcome the opinion from someone else, particularly from a spiteful someone. Mary Hammy and Varina's lovely sister Maggie Howell must be sent into the foreground like shock troops of glamour—but she would marshal her forces later. She and her friends set off for the Springs and got there by July 6, delighted at another brief glimpse of her husband.

At the Fauquier White Sulphur, too, the talk was of war. Beauregard, said James Chesnut and others, could stop 60,000 Yankees at Manassas. Beauregard knew all about Federal plans —lovely ladies rode into Camp Pickens, with thrillingly important letters of information hidden in their hair or clothing.

"They are spies," offered Mary, aware in her heart that she was jealous of such adventuresses. "They are for sale. Maybe they are fooling you. Seward can outbid you."

"Never," came the shocked protest of the gentlemen. "These are patriotic creatures, risking everything for their country."

"For men," flashed back Mary.

On July 7, she went with her husband on his way to Manassas, as far as Warrenton. She shuddered at more rumors that Johnston was fleeing from Winchester as he had fled from Harpers Ferry, and that hordes of Federals came to threaten Beauregard. If Beauregard should be beaten, James might be captured. Would he be treated as a prisoner of war or a trapped traitor? Mary carried the baleful question back to the Springs with her. That night she fancied she heard guns, rumbling far off. Where? Fauquier White Sulphur Springs was fifty miles from Washington, twenty from Harpers Ferry, twenty-five from Manassas.

But the night also brought the comet, a fuzzy blur of light high in the roof of darkness. A few young men were at the hotel, ready to escort the prettiest ladies out upon the shadowed piazza to see the wonder, perhaps to hear romantic whispers about volunteering for combat service, about devoted memories beside bivouac fires. Mary Hammy was promenaded a number of times to the piazza with the comet blazing overhead, but she wept for worry over her true love at the wars.

"Our battle summer, so called," wrote Mary Chesnut in her faithful diary. "May it be our first and our last." Again, in the dining room, she heard mockery of "Mrs. Davis' ladies" for their age and their poor taste in dress.

No more chances on James Chesnut's part to come visiting his wife. He wrote that it looked like action coming at Manassas: ". . . The enemy is advancing slowly on our front, and we are preparing to receive him. He comes in great force, being more than three times our number." Would Mary please return to Richmond? "Don't stay longer than Saturday. The enemy might make a flank movement and cut you off, by taking the railroad."

Another fancied cannonade, somewhere in the disputed distance, hastened Mary's obedience to her husband's urgings. On July 11 she, Mrs. Preston, and Mary Hammy took the train. "To tell the truth," Mary confessed to her diary, "we are terrified women and children. . . ." Arriving in Richmond, they fluttered unhappily at the sight of sick soldiers, lying in close rows on the depot platform. President Davis made them welcome at the Spotswood.

Whether Mary Chesnut had heard cannon in reality or only in fancy on July 11, cannon actually boomed that day, at Rich Mountain sixty miles west of Fauquier White Sulphur Springs.

Through a beautiful but difficult land of high tree-tufted ridges and plunging valleys, with a population for the most part scowlingly Unionist, Robert Garnett had led his troops to Buckhannon Pass beyond Beverly, and had arranged them in hopes of launching a surprise attack on McClellan's superior force. On the slopes of Rich Mountain, Garnett stationed a regiment with guns, under Colonel John Peagram, and he himself fortified nearby Laurel Hill. The Federals had come close, and advance elements of both forces had skirmished on July 6 and 8. Then, on the 11th, Peagram's force was flanked and badly beaten. McClellan seized a road that cut off Peagram's line of retreat and threatened Garnett's.

On July 12, Garnett tried to get away. Rain fell as his men forded tumbling mountain streams. McClellan pursued Peagram and surrounded him on the 13th. Peagram's entire command, 553 officers and men, was captured. Giving up his sword, Peagram was reminded that his former service as an officer of the United

States Army might be made the basis for charges of treason against him.

That same day, Garnett commanded a thin line of crack marksmen that covered the retreat of the troops that remained to him. The blue infantry charged stubbornly, firing as it came. A bullet slapped Garnett out of his saddle, and his rear guard fled, all save one who sought to lift his general's prone body. This unknown soldier, too, fell under Yankee fire. The brief time gained by the sacrifice of those two lives let the others draw ahead of pursuit. Leaderless, they stumbled at last into the mountain village of Monterey. Garnett had been the first general officer of the war to be killed in action, and the Confederate loss of some 700 killed, wounded and captured banished all Southern exultation over Fort Sumter and Big Bethel. McClellan triumphantly held western Virginia, where the inhabitants loudly proclaimed their intention of forming a Unionist state of their own.

Before the bad news reached Beauregard, he had written new suggestions for sweeping troop movements against the Federals. A lady named Rose Greenhow had sent him news of an imminent move by a large Federal army, under Beauregard's West Point classmate Irvin McDowell, upon Manassas Junction. On July 11, Beauregard had drafted a letter to President Davis, including this daunting information. On the 13th, while Garnett died fighting and Peagram surrendered, Beauregard sent another message to Johnston at Winchester.

Beauregard's suggestion was that Johnston would leave "four or five thousand men to guard the passes of the Blue Ridge," and join Beauregard with the rest of his force, to meet and smash McDowell. "Then," went on Beauregard, afire with the dream of victory, "we could go back with as many men as necessary to attack and disperse General Patterson's army, before he could know positively what had become of you. We could then proceed to General McClellan's theatre of war, treat him likewise, after which we could pass over into Maryland, to operate in rear of Washington. I think this whole campaign could be completed in from fifteen to twenty-five days. Oh, that we had but one good head to conduct all our operations!"

Johnston, who had only a few more than 8,000 troops of all arms and was beginning just then to get proper supplies for them, made no reply. Beauregard, however, did not wait for one.

James Chesnut, who continued to serve well as a volunteer aide at Manassas, brought someone to Liberia for his general to meet. This acquaintance turned out to be a former departmental clerk at Washington and, by Chesnut's assurance, a trustworthy, intelligent and discreet Confederate into the bargain. Chesnut felt that here was an ideal secret messenger to send through the Federal lines into Washington.

Beauregard accepted Chesnut's recommendation, and gave the ex-clerk a message to Mrs. Greenhow. "Trust the bearer," said the message in code, and nothing more. The fellow went away to northward, and Beauregard held another conference with Chesnut, at the dramatic hour of midnight, July 13.

To his aide Beauregard handed a memorandum of his radiant plan for the Napoleonic defeat, in detail, of one Federal army after another. Chesnut must seek out Jefferson Davis and, from that memorandum, describe Beauregard's strategy verbally.

Chesnut left headquarters at six o'clock on the morning of Sunday the 14th, and was on the train for Richmond shortly after seven. He arrived in the capital at half past three that afternoon and went promptly to the Spotswood.

Mary sat in the President's drawing room, in conversation with Judge Robert Ould. As they talked, Mary glanced toward the door into the corridor that led to Davis' private quarters. There stood her James, looking at her silently, his face tender with a smile.

Like a girl at sight of her sweetheart, Mary sprang from her chair. She left the judge and flew across the room, her ample skirts fluttering, toward where James waited; but, before Mary could reach and embrace him, Varina Davis appeared. She touched Chesnut's shoulder and gestured him through the inner door, into Davis' room.

To Mary, her husband's sudden appearance and equally sudden snatching away must have had the quality of a frustrating dream about an absent loved one. "Army business," Varina explained to Mary, and Mary sat down again and waited.

As the door closed behind him, Chesnut found himself standing beside a bed. Davis lay there, ill but immediately interested. He heard Chesnut's errand, then asked if he would return at seven o'clock that evening. By that time, the President would have found Adjutant General Samuel Cooper and Robert E. Lee, to listen with him. Chesnut asked if he might bring along Colonel John S. Preston, also of Beauregard's staff, who was in town. Davis gave him permission, and Chesnut departed to send for Preston and to greet Mary properly.

By evening the President felt better, or said that he did, and rose from his sickbed. He sat with Lee and Cooper, at a table spread with maps, when Chesnut and Preston appeared. To this council of war, Chesnut presented Beauregard's recommendations in detail.

Those recommendations called for the junction of 20,000 men under Johnston with Beauregard's forces at Manassas, a counterattack as McDowell came within reach and then, after the obliteration of that invading army, a return of Johnston with his own troops and 10,000 of Beauregard's to "attack and destroy Patterson, at Winchester, or wherever he might be." The following week, as Chesnut quoted his commander, would find Beauregard advancing to threaten Washington while Johnston hurried headlong to finish McClellan in western Virginia. After that additional victory, both armies would reunite, to cross the Potomac and attack the Federal capital.

Davis, Lee, and Cooper heard Chesnut's explanation with the most respectful of attention. When he had finished reciting his general's message, all three chieftains agreed that the plan was "brilliant and comprehensive," and added to this judgment a request that their personal compliments be carried to Beauregard. There were, however, objections.

For one thing, Johnston did not have 20,000 men to send to Beauregard, nor half that many. For another—Lee reminded the meeting of this—the Federals still held various strong points just within the borders of Virginia, and could not easily be cut off from supporting troops and bases of supply. Beauregard's plan might be followed later, agreed Davis and his two advisers; but not just now.

Chesnut was disappointed, but this first close contact with Lee impressed him greatly. He bowed himself out of the President's chamber and hurried back to Mary.

His lady wanted to know what had happened behind the President's closed door, and was maddened by James' lofty air of official mystery. He refused to tell her anything of what had been said and decided—only that Robert E. Lee impressed him as "sensible and soldierly."

Unable to wring from James any word about the conference with the President, Mary changed the subject. She expressed anxiety because James had traveled without his Negro servant. James replied that Lawrence was at Manassas, guarding a trunk that held James' watch, his best clothes and two or three hundred gold pieces.

"Maybe he will pack off to the Yankees and freedom, with all that money," Mary scolded, but her husband lightly shrugged away any doubts of Lawrence's affection and loyalty.

"Fiddlesticks," laughed James. "After all, what can he ever be better than he is now, a gentleman's gentleman?"

James had leave to stay another night in Richmond, and Mary gleaned a few bits of news from him, to scribble into her journal:

As far as I can make out, Beauregard sent Mr. Chesnut to the President to gain permission for the forces of Joe Johnston and Beauregard to join, and unite to push the enemy, if possible, over the Potomac. Now every day we grow weaker and they stronger; so we had better give a telling blow at once.

Early on the morning of the 16th, James Chesnut kissed Mary good-bye and took the train back to Manassas. She stifled her sadness at this latest parting, and that day she took dinner at the table of the Davises. The President's handsome nephew Joe asked her if she took "white port wine," and poured her out a glass of some clear liquor.

It burned Mary's mouth and throat like fire, but she refused to look startled or pained, and made herself empty the glass. Indeed, a sense of flattered pleasure stole over her; a dashing young man thought her attractive enough to play a practical joke upon her.

Chesnut arrived at Beauregard's headquarters by midafternoon and made a verbal report, then wrote a confirmatory account of the conference with Davis. Beauregard filed this with his papers. After supper that night, a letter at once briefer and more interesting than Chesnut's report came to Beauregard's hand.

That ex-clerk sent spying to Washington had been able to smuggle a note from Rose Greenhow back across the Potomac. Quickly Beauregard decoded the single sentence:

McDowell has been ordered to advance tonight.

Indeed, McDowell was already advancing. Even as Beauregard read that warning message, the blue divisions were on their way to find and fight him.

XII

Send Forward Any Reinforcements

THE Federal army that climbed out of the trenches at Alexandria and Arlington and formed on the Warrenton Turnpike was thirty thousand strong, splendidly armed and equipped, and light-heartedly hopeful for a chance to do some rebel-killing.

McDowell, a seasoned and capable soldier, would have liked to train his ninety-day volunteers longer and harder, but his government and his people had insisted on immediate action. He was glad he could stiffen those untested troops with hard-faced cavalry, artillery, and infantry regulars, and he knew that his commanders were almost all good professional officers, veterans of the wars against Mexico and the Indian tribes.

His five divisions were led by Daniel Tyler, David Hunter, Samuel P. Heintzelman, D. S. Miles and Theodore Runyan, all but the last of them West Point graduates and grizzled in the service. The commanders of the eleven brigades included others whose names would be remembered—Ambrose E. Burnside, whisker-jowled and moonfaced; William Tecumseh Sherman, who had wept as he gave up the superintendency of the Louisiana Military Academy but who now looked tearlessly toward punishing the South for daring to secede; O. O. Howard, William B. Franklin, Erasmus D. Keys, Andrew Porter. Brigadier General R. C. Schenck, whose train-borne troops had been driven pell-mell from their cars at that Vienna skirmish a month before, was with the army and thirsting for vengeance. Among McDowell's twelve fine batteries of guns were no less than nine units of regular artillery. The best of these were two batteries of new rifled pieces, commanded by two splendid captains, James B. Ricketts and Charles Griffin. The cavalry rode under Major I. N. Palmer, a Mexican War veteran of fifteen years' service. One of the last junior officers to join Palmer was a brand-new lieutenant just graduated at West Point, bottom of his class and happy for the war that had kept him from being dismissed for inefficiency. He was George Armstrong Custer.

The infantry that made up the five divisions included volunteers from thirteen states of the Union. New York furnished eighteen of the fifty regiments, including the "Highlander" Seventy-ninth that had grudgingly exchanged its waggling kilts for blue pantaloons, a gaudy rooster-plumed outfit called the Garibaldi Guards, and two fez-wearing Zouave commands. New Jersey had sent eight regiments, and Maine and Massachusetts four each. Every soldier carried in his haversack three days' rations of cooked pork or beef, hardtack, coffee and sugar. In the wake of the marching columns rumbled more than 250 big laden supply wagons, and details of drovers prodded along hundreds of beef cattle. There were trains of ordnance carts and ambulances.

Spies and scouts galloped to Beauregard with vivid descriptions of this army. Most such reports exaggerated the numbers of the willing but awkward marchers who followed McDowell for ten hot, dusty miles on the afternoon of July 16 and bivouacked not far above Fairfax Court House. At early dawn of July 17 the menacing roll of drums alerted the Southern troops in their barricaded camp among the beautiful groves of the town's environs.

With the disbanding of the First South Carolina, the Eighth South Carolina had been sent to replace it beside the Second. These two regiments had happily consumed most of the chickens and eggs in the Fairfax Court House region, and Edmund Ruffin, gay among his friends of the Palmetto Guard with the Second South Carolina, had been playing soldier for fully two weeks. Now he turned out with the others as Colonel Kershaw hastily formed line of battle. The advancing Federals looked overwhelmingly strong, and Kershaw retreated toward Centreville, ten miles southwest, while a battery of artillery under Captain Del Kemper fired to halt the head of the Federal column.

Poor old Ruffin, his feet tortured by those new shoes he had bought in Richmond, could stagger only two miles. He was forced to drop his luggage, most of which fell into Yankee hands along with rations, entrenching tools and hospital supplies that could not be brought away. As Ruffin collapsed at the roadside, Kemper's limbered guns also retreated and some of the gunners recognized the white-haired hero of Sumter. They hoisted him to a seat on a caisson. He clung as the caisson bumped springlessly all the way to Centreville, where Ruffin rejoined the Palmettos. The stop was not a long one; another retreat was ordered as McDowell pressed inexorably toward Centreville.

On the southern bank of Bull Run, Beauregard marshaled his brigades. He gave orders to destroy the bridge of the Orange and Alexandria Railroad, and concentrated troops to defend six of the fords—Lewis', Ball's, Mitchell's, Blackburn's, McLean's, and Union Mills. Guns and men also hurried to command the approach to the Stone Bridge over which came the Warrenton Turnpike from Centreville. In all these dispositions, Beauregard impressed his subordinates as inspiringly energetic and intelligent; but there was a frantic note in the telegram he sent to Richmond:

The enemy has assailed my outposts in heavy force. I have fallen back on the line of Bull Run and will make a stand at Mitchell's Ford. If his force is overwhelming I shall retire to the Rappahannock railroad bridge, saving my command for defence there and future operations. Please inform Johnston of this, *via* Stanton, and also Holmes. Send forward any reinforcements, at the earliest possible instant, and by every possible means.

This appeal came direct to Jefferson Davis, along with confirmation of the depressing rumors that Garnett had been killed and his force defeated in the western Virginia mountains. At the same time and not far from the scene of Garnett's disaster, Confederates along a watercourse with the happily appropriate name of Scarey Creek were beating back a Federal assault and capturing no less than three blue-coated colonels, but nobody in

Richmond could know this on the 17th. Well, at least Beauregard had recently received sufficient ammunition for muskets and cannon. The President replied that fresh troops would be rushed to Manassas, though it was utterly impossible to get them there that very day. General Cooper, though he had not been consulted by Beauregard, also sent a wire to say that Johnston was being told to come and help if he could. To Johnston, Cooper dispatched another message:

General Beauregard is attacked. To strike the enemy a decisive blow a junction of all your effective force will be needed. If practicable, make the movement, sending all your sick and baggage to Culpeper Court-House either by railroad or by Warrenton. In all the arrangements exercise your discretion.

Then Cooper's officers hastened to the Richmond training camps, to gather up and send away any regiments that seemed ready for combat service.

Hampton's Legion was selected. It had drilled and toughened itself into an efficient, disciplined force, with officers as good as eight weeks or so of field training could make them. Two more regiments, from Mississippi and Alabama, were told to prepare for a prompt move to the front, and the Fifth North Carolina, previously ordered to report to Johnston, was ordered to head for Manassas instead.

No particular assistance in the emergency was afforded by the action of Robert Toombs who, tired of having his unasked advice ignored, was resigning as Secretary of State. His native Georgia would give him a brigade, and he entertained no doubts of his own ability to lead it in battle.

Davis and his officers kept as much as possible of this news to themselves. Nervous Richmond was better off in ignorance. Mary Chesnut, nervous and headachy, was visited by Varina Davis, who struck the ailing Mary as strangely preoccupied. "I am sure something is going wrong," Mary wrote in her diary as she lay in bed.

Something was going wrong indeed. Beauregard had sent yet another call for help to Johnston, both by telegraph and by a galloping South Carolina aide, Colonel Chisholm; but McDowell had flowed on to the outskirts of Centreville. In something of tragic triumph at sense of disaster foretold by himself, Beauregard dashed off another wire to Cooper in Richmond:

I believe this proposed movement of Johnston is too late. Enemy will attack me in force tomorrow morning.

Rain fell, chill and dreary as the mournful tears of preordained defeat, on the troops at Manassas. The fight was trickling out of wretched old Edmund Ruffin. He had lost his blankets, his cheese and crackers, and his spare clothing up yonder at Fairfax Court House. One of the Palmetto Guard lent him an overcoat, and he wrapped this around his scrawny old body and managed to sleep a few hours. At midnight he wakened, and munched some ginger-bread nuts, the only provisions he could find. His young comrades begged him to go to the rear, find there a comfortable bed and proper food for an aged stomach. Stubbornly he shook his frowzy white head. He had come to where the fighting was. He wanted to fight, and if he must die, he would accomplish that duty also.

Shortly after Ruffin woke on the banks of Bull Run, Joe Johnston woke at Winchester. An aide brought Cooper's telegram to Johnston's headquarters. The general read it, and looked at his watch: one A.M. on July 18. He dressed, and about the time he stood up in full uniform, another telegram came in. This was from Beauregard:

War Department has ordered you to join me; do so immediately, if possible, and we will crush the enemy.

Things were not quite like that, Johnston must have reflected. Cooper's orders gave Johnston discretion—"If practicable, make the movement. . . ." And Beauregard had been urging a junction of forces again and again. Well, this time it looked like business.

Johnston sent word to Stuart's cavalry headquarters to observe old Patterson, who had come down toward Winchester as far as Bunker Hill—any chance of slipping away from that threat unobserved? Then Johnston summoned his brigadiers to discuss the chances of getting to Manassas in time.

"If practicable . . ." They wanted to go if they could, they wanted to be in on any of the fighting. Cooper had said to send the sick and the baggage to Culpeper, but Johnston had a considerable number of sick—some 1,700, most of them victims of a measles epidemic. To carry them would take all of Johnston's wagons, and wagons would be needed for the march, to carry ammunition and four days' rations. Let the hospitable citizens of Winchester care for those measles patients, and let two lately mustered brigades of militia guard the town. The army itself would move, as soon as Stuart sent word that it was safe to do so.

Sixty-five miles or so to Manassas; but there was a railroad, and Johnston would operate history's first rail movement of troops in the face of an enemy, after he got to Piedmont Station some thirty miles away. Word came back from Stuart. Patterson was moving, all right, but he seemed to be heading eastward, toward Charlestown where John Brown had been hanged. Very well, Johnston would send his army through Ashby's Gap, get high, rugged mountains between himself and Patterson, and let that old fogy study his own methods of pursuit, if and when he found that Johnston had slipped away.

The brigadiers were told to strike and roll their tents, and leave them on the camp sites. The infantry would head for Piedmont Station and the cars that would assemble there to carry them. Cavalry and artillery must march all the way to Manassas.

This decided, Johnston replied to Cooper that he would head for the junction with Beauregard if Patterson permitted him, and upon the heels of this sent an inquiry to Davis.

Beauregard, a brigadier in the provisional army, had been commissioned before Johnston had become a brigadier in the regular army, and, it may have been, thus felt himself at least on an equal footing of rank with Johnston. But Johnston had heard that he had been recommended on July 4 for a commission as full general. No official confirmation had as yet reached him. He wanted to know if he or Beauregard would have supreme command in the coming fight at Manassas.

Stuart's patrols brought back word that Patterson plainly was headed eastward as of nine A.M., and Johnston told Stuart to fall back and prepare to bring his cavalry into column for the move. The first infantry brigade to leave would be that of Thomas Jackson, best trained of Johnston's units and, by virtue of its sharp skirmishing at Falling Waters, the only brigade of the Army of the Shenandoah that could lay claim to anything like battle experience. Jackson's men quickly struck camp, happy at the prospect of doing more fighting on the banks of Bull Run.

FIGHTING ALREADY had begun there, on the morning of the 18th.

Beauregard had moved his headquarters from Liberia Plantation to Yorkshire, the pleasant home of Wilmer McLean, close to the fords at the right of his line of defense. From right to left, Beauregard had marshaled his troops as follows:

Ewell's brigade, with four twelve-pound howitzers and three companies of cavalry, held Union Mills Ford. D. R. Jones' brigade, with two brass six-pounders and a company of cavalry, was at McLean's Ford, close to the new headquarters. Longstreet held Blackburn's Ford, with the brigade formerly commanded by Terrett, and two more six-pounders. At Mitchell's Ford, which Beauregard continued to feel would be the point of Federal attack, Bonham's big brigade of four South Carolina regiments was drawn up, with two batteries of guns and five companies of Virginia cavalry. Cocke spread his men to cover both Ball's and Lewis' Fords. Shanks Evans, at the extreme left, held Stone Bridge with a scratch brigade formed from the Fourth South Carolina and a rowdy battalion of Louisiana Zouaves called the Tigers, led by big blond Major Roberdeau Wheat.

Behind Bonham, Beauregard stationed, as a reserve, the Fifth North Carolina and six companies of Louisianians, who had arrived at Manassas Junction the night before. Behind Ewell at the right, Beauregard placed Jubal Early's brigade.

Pickets lay on the far side of Bull Run at every ford, and some of these discovered, as early as 8:30 on the morning of the

18th, indications of enemy approaching through the woods between the stream and Centreville.

Federal artillery opened fire across Bull Run, and Kemper's guns replied from the flank of Bonham's position. But meanwhile, at about eleven o'clock, Longstreet's pickets scuttled back across Blackburn's Ford with the news that a strong mass of infantry, with cavalry and big guns, crowded close at their heels.

Blackburn's Ford looked awkward to defend. Bull Run cut deeply between the wooded banks at that point, and the northern slope rose abruptly to a thicketed height of some fifty feet above the southern bank opposite. There the slope was gradual, with only light timber as cover. The rifled guns that had opened opposite Bonham's position now changed their direction of fire and began to thresh Longstreet's front. Then infantry advanced to the cover at the top of the bluff on the northern bank and fired volleys of musketry.

Longstreet directed his two six-pounders, manned by gunners of the Washington Artillery from New Orleans, to reply to this bombardment. When, after half an hour of the artillery duel, the blue infantry poised as though to try a crossing, Longstreet sent a courier to Early to ask for help, then advanced his own troops to the water's edge. His Virginia riflemen began a brisk fire fight of their own, and with telling effect.

Though plainly superior in numbers, and well supported by their artillery, the Federals did not seem able to face direct volleys, and fell back up the slope. A second advance was attempted, and driven back in its turn. Two of Early's regiments, with two additional field pieces, arrived just in time to meet a third charge, more determined than either of the two previous attempts.

Some Confederates actually crossed Bull Run, met enemies with the bayonet and chased them back. Forced to retreat once more, the Federals remained on top of the bluff and kept up a scattering fire of big guns and small until Longstreet, aware that his own artillery was outmatched, withdrew it to safety a piece at a time. No further effort was made that day to force a way across Blackburn's Ford.

The defenders listed sixty-eight killed and wounded, and reckoned that they had taken a heavy toll of the bluecoats on the far side of the stream. Several Yankee prisoners, scooped in during the brief hand-to-hand fighting, told lurid tales of overwhelming forces poised to strike. Returning to McLean's home, Beauregard and his staff found that a Yankee shell had burst in the chimney of the kitchen, destroying their dinner. Hungry but tingling with exultation over the preliminary success at Blackburn's Ford, Beauregard telegraphed a happy report of victory to President Davis.

The wounded were sent away southward, to hospitals made ready at Culpeper. Through Bristoe Station just below Manassas Junction ambled a walking casualty, smoke-grimed and with his arm in a romantic sling. Out of the railroad hotel rushed a wave of ladies fairly smothering the hero with washcloths and platters of bread and meat. Munching, he assured every fair questioner that he knew her friends and relatives, had with his own eyes seen those friends and relatives do deeds of classic bravery. Two wagonloads of slightly wounded followed this imaginative messenger into Bristoe, with soberer accounts of the fight at Blackburn's Ford. By evening came a train with stretcher cases, and the novelty of caring for wounded departed from the ladies of Bristoe Station, with anxious worries greatening instead.

Back to Beauregard came assurance of more reinforcements from Richmond, and: "God be praised for your successful beginning," wired Davis. "I have tried to join you, but remain to serve you here as most useful to the times."

Still sang the bugles, then, in the ears of the President of the Confederate States, calling him to take command in the first major battle. Much more gladly would Beauregard have welcomed Joe Johnston and all of Joe Johnston's brigades. Where were they? Would they never come?

XIII

Step Out Like Men

WHILE Longstreet's infantry staved off the threat at Blackburn's Ford under the blazing noonday sun of July 18, Thomas Jackson's brigade marched through Winchester and away to the east. At almost the last moment a new regiment had been added, the hastily organized Thirty-third Virginia, which gave Jackson five regiments in all. On the far side of town, Old Jack reined in his chunky sorrel, halted his men in line, and told them to listen to special orders from General Johnston.

"Our gallant army under General Beauregard is now attacked by overwhelming numbers," the regimental adjutants read aloud to their various organizations. "The commanding general hopes that his troops will step out like men, and make a forced march to save the country."

A thundering chorus of whoops and yells assured Jackson of his men's eagerness to march and give battle. Few of them had felt at all satisfied with having to retreat before Patterson two weeks earlier. Grimly pleased, Jackson rode to the head of his brigade and started it east again. The soldiers slogged vigorously after him—they had learned how to march enduringly these past three months. The rookies of the Thirty-third brought up the rear of the column. Over their shoulders they could see more troops following them.

All of the Army of the Shenandoah was on its way, all of the infantry at least. Stuart and Ashby would remain strung from side to side of the valley, making sure that no observers from

173

Patterson's force drifted down and found out what was happening at Winchester. When Johnston's rear guard was safely away, Stuart would start his own march, leaving only a thin line of mounted pickets under Ashby between Patterson and the shaky militia in Winchester.

The wagons, laden with four days' rations for 8,000 men, trundled along with the infantry. Behind Jackson's Virginians came Francis Bartow, with his efficient Georgia brigade. In Bartow's dusty wake followed Bee, with the Fourth Alabama, the Second and Eleventh Mississippi, and the newly joined Sixth North Carolina. Last of the infantry brigades was Edmund Kirby Smith's, the Third Tennessee, the Tenth and Thirteenth Virginia, and a battalion of Marylanders under bluff Colonel Arnold Elzey.

The artillery would leave Winchester when the last foot soldier had departed, and must seek rough side roads that would let it pull ahead and roll all the way to Manassas. Stuart intended to ride across country.

By late afternoon, Jackson had brought his command fourteen miles to the village of Millwood, and there let them rest for a full hour. Citizens turned out and brought food to supplement the rough rations of the troops. When the men had eaten and filled their canteens, Jackson brought them to their feet and into formation again. He led them eastward and ever eastward, while the other brigades came to Millwood behind them. At sundown, Jackson's advance reached Berry's Ferry on the Shenandoah River.

The swift water ran waist-deep, but the men doffed their gray pants and their shoes and splashed across in high good humor. On the far side opened Ashby's Gap in the Blue Ridge, a bleak ascent from the far bank of the Shenandoah to the height of full seven hundred feet, with the darkness gathering on the jagged heights to either side.

But a moon had risen, three-quarters full, to afford them pale light on the way they must go. Jackson waited at the riverside only long enough to make sure that the Thirty-third Virginia had successfully made its crossing at the tail of the brigade. Then the heels of his big boots nudged Old Sorrel's flanks and he rode up and into Ashby's Gap, beckoning his men after him.

More miles, slower and more wearing with the climb and the death of the daylight. Midnight came and passed before the leading regiment had emerged from the rocky pass and upon the plain beyond. At two o'clock on the morning of July 19, the moon had set and deep blackness dropped around them like a cloak. At the little mountain hamlet of Paris in Fauquier County, Jackson passed along the welcome order to halt.

Worn-out soldiers flung themselves down anywhere and slept almost at once. Not so Jackson, despite his lifelong dependency on plenty of rest. He stayed awake for perhaps two hours longer. At last one of his staff officers badgered him into lying down on a matted pile of last autumn's leaves in the corner of a rail fence. Closing his pale blue eyes, Jackson, too, fell asleep. In twelve straining hours, he and his troops had accomplished twenty miles over streams and mountains.

Joe Johnston had stayed awake since Beauregard's latest appeal for help had roused him at one o'clock on the morning of the 18th, but as soon as he made sure that his army's move was properly started and masked he rode swiftly past the brigades and reached Paris where Jackson had camped. To the westward behind Johnston was strung out the rest of the Army of the Shenandoah, bivouacked along the way.

Kirby Smith had brought the infantry rear guard out of Winchester at five o'clock on the evening of the 18th. Girls crowded the porches and windows to raise sweet-voiced cheers for the marching men. Behind Smith came the artillery, with Imboden in charge—his own battery, Pendleton's, Stanard's, Alburtis', Beckham's. The guns and caissons sought out bypasses to rougher side roads, in order to get them quickly ahead of the infantry. Nightfall brought silence to Kirby Smith's tramping regiments, perhaps not as seasoned to sustained marching as were Jackson's. Past them, through the fields beside the road, came Stuart's cavalry, shadowy riders on shadowy horses, sure at last that Patterson did not threaten Winchester, knew nothing of what the

Army of the Shenandoah sought to do. By moonlight the splendid Virginia horses leaped farmyard rail fences, sprang across ditches, on their way to Manassas Junction.

The setting of the moon at two A.M. found Kirby Smith on the bank of the Shenandoah, seven miles behind Jackson and the head of the column at Paris. Smith's men slept before trying to cross.

Jackson woke as the dawn grayed the skies to eastward. It was not yet five o'clock. Line officers and sergeants stirred the men out of their drugged slumber, got them up on their feet, made them strap on their knapsacks and shoulder their muskets. Forward march again, and march for two hours more, to Piedmont Station on the Manassas Gap Railroad.

The citizens of that little community were wide awake to greet the soldiers, and fetched out tempting breakfasts on trays and platters and in baskets. With loud cries of gratitude, Jackson's famished soldiers gulped the good things, then sprawled among shocks of new-harvested wheat.

Joe Johnston was there. He had not slept all night. Under direction of Johnston's chief engineer, Major W. H. C. Whiting, a string of cars was made up, boxcars and flatcars and a few passenger cars. The little funnel-stacked engine puffed importantly as it got up steam. By eight o'clock, all of Jackson's brigade had been entrained except for the Thirty-third Virginia— that untoughened regiment had lagged behind and was lost. Every car was jammed without the Thirty-third, and many soldiers rode on top. The engine started and rumbled away with them. Another train was made ready to carry Bartow's brigade when it arrived. Johnston fretted. His volunteers did not march like regulars, not yet.

Jackson reached Manassas at about four o'clock that afternoon, his men dusty and tired but in good spirits. Somewhat the same description applied to the troops that welcomed them as they came from the Junction.

Beauregard's regiments still savored yesterday's repulse of the enemy at Blackburn's Ford, and already had been heartened by the arrival, on the morning of the 19th, of Theophilus Holmes

with two regiments. More troops had come from Richmond, and
the authorities there promised that still others would follow.
Beauregard, in particular, felt confident and aggressive again. He
read a telegram from Adjutant General Cooper:

We have no intelligence from General Johnston. If the enemy in
front of you has abandoned an immediate attack, and General Johnston has not moved, you had better withdraw the call upon him so
that he may be left to his full discretion. All the troops arriving at
Lynchburg are ordered to join you. From this place we will send as
fast as transportation permits. . . .

"You had better withdraw the call," Cooper had said, and the
words impressed Beauregard as offering advice only, not giving
a flat order. He, Beauregard, felt his head humming with new
and increasingly brilliant projects. He would not withdraw that
call on Johnston. Let Johnston come along and help, and that
swiftly. Even as these thoughts were his, here came the first of
Johnston's transferred troops.

Beauregard placed Holmes' force, some 1,265 rank and file,
in support of Ewell's brigade at the right of the line. Jackson's
four regiments went to back up Longstreet at Blackburn's Ford,
which still impressed Beauregard as the point where Bull Run
might best be jumped over, northward or southward. Other new
arrivals would similarly strengthen the position as they came to
hand. Then, decided Beauregard, he would wait no longer for
McDowell to attack.

That huge Federal army in the woods around Centreville yonder impressed Beauregard as unwieldy and nervous. A fierce
counterattack, by men familiar with the terrain and led by a
brilliant and inspiring commander of the stuff of Napoleonic
marshals . . . glory awaited that counterattack, seemed assured.

A second train puffed in after dark. It bore Jackson's missing
Thirty-third Virginia and Bartow with two of his regiments, the
Seventh and Eighth Georgia. The Thirty-third camped at the
Junction, deferring until the morrow its rejoining of Jackson.
Bartow's men went into camp at the edge of a pine thicket not
far from Beauregard's new headquarters at Yorkshire, at a point

where Bartow could move either to support D. R. Jones at McLean's Ford to the right or Longstreet at Blackburn's Ford to the left.

None of these new placements were achieved in complete peace and quiet. The bright day long, and on into the night of the 19th, patrols in blue were reconnoitering the northern bank of Bull Run. Clouds blurred the moonlight that had shone to help Jackson's forced march from Winchester, and brilliant orange flashes of musket fire winked here and there, where pickets squibbed nervously at each other from bank to bank. Colonel Jordan, Beauregard's chief of staff, moved constantly between the various points where disturbance might presage a threat of attack.

Nobody slept particularly well that night of the 19th, and on the morning of the 20th Beauregard's staff officers peered in vain along the Manassas Gap Railroad track for trains bringing more of Johnston's troops. With the Palmetto Guards at Mitchell's Ford, one of the men looked pitifully haggard and sick.

For days Edmund Ruffin had brushed aside the sympathy of his young and more vigorous comrades. He had insisted that, even if he could neither charge nor flee in those torturing shoes, at least he could stand at his place in line. But in the gray dawn of July 20 he was so miserable that he allowed himself to be begged into withdrawal. He crept away toward Manassas Junction four miles to the rear, where he might find a comfortable bed on which to stretch his old bones. Past him marched the Thirty-third Virginia, on its way to report to Jackson.

Some thirty-five miles to westward, at Piedmont Station, Joe Johnston talked to Colonel Chisholm, Beauregard's aide who had ridden to meet him. Chisholm offered another of Beauregard's daring suggestions for surprise of the Yankees—let some of Johnston's troops go by way of Aldie, north of the railroad, and burst in unheralded fury upon McDowell's unsuspecting right. This plan Johnston gestured away with a weary hand. In the brightening sun of the morning he saw to the entraining of more troops.

These included three regiments of Bee's Brigade, two of them from Mississippi and one from Alabama. Bee's fourth regiment, the Sixth North Carolina, was lost somewhere between Winchester and the railroad. Johnston himself boarded a car, leaving word for Kirby Smith, still coming from Winchester, to take charge of the final loading and dispatch of troop trains.

Johnston and Bee arrived at Manassas Junction at noon, and Beauregard welcomed Johnston with eager explanations of what he intended to do with all the troops on hand.

Something else waited at the Junction, a telegram sent by President Davis to answer the query Johnston had addressed to Richmond before he left Winchester:

You are a general in the Confederate Army, possessed of the power attached to that rank. You will know how to make the exact knowledge of Brigadier-General Beauregard, as well of the ground as of the troops and preparation, avail for the success of the object in which you cooperate. The zeal of both assures me of harmonious action.

That left no mystery as to who would exercise command; but it did not relegate Beauregard to the position of silent subordinate. Johnston himself could not but be well aware of his own ignorance of the situation, and the zeal of Beauregard, so clearly noticed by Davis, expressed itself in eloquent advice on how to marshal and launch a movement against the enemy.

Beauregard had maps, and confidently insisted that he and his staff knew the country those maps depicted. Johnston looked and listened as intelligently as his utter exhaustion allowed him. He had been awake for sixty hours, a considerable part of it in the saddle, and not once since early on the morning of the 17th had he so much as taken off his boots or lain down. Saggingly he tried to understand Beauregard's offered plan.

The main body of the invading Federals was at Centreville, said Beauregard. The maps showed that this placed them two miles and a half on the far side of Bull Run, measured to the point where the stream flung a curve northward at Blackburn's Ford. Beauregard's finger slid from point to point on the chart, describing the routes by which he felt a stunningly successful assault could be made. The Federal left was vulnerable, Beauregard kept saying, and could be struck by forces moving resolutely across those fords.

Johnston had neither the knowledge of the terrain nor the energy to ask really intelligent questions about this proposal. None of Beauregard's maps showed him the heights beyond those fords—only the course of Bull Run and its little tributary streams, and the roads and some of the houses. But Johnston did recognize the danger that Patterson, left back there in the mountains, might at any moment discover how the Army of the Shenandoah had slipped away from Winchester. Once aware of that move, Patterson would immediately follow to join McDowell. Indeed, that additional force might well be expected at Centreville by July 22. Therefore, since Beauregard was so sanguine of success, the Confederates had best attack with every man and gun, on the 21st.

Johnston yawningly endorsed Beauregard's plan of battle, told him to draw it up in writing and put it into execution, then sought a place to fling himself down and sleep.

Evening came down again upon Manassas Junction, upon anxious Richmond, and upon Piedmont Station. To the railroad tracks at the latter point wandered at last the errant Sixth North Carolina of Bee's Brigade, with Kirby Smith's leading regiment at its heels. Rain began to fall as these troops fell out and relaxed among the wheat shocks. Cars came to take them away, but the railroaders announced an emergency.

Rails had come loose from the ties just east of Piedmont Station, and a train was partially derailed and its engine damaged. Some three thousand infantry seemed cut off from the battle that surely was ready to begin, yonder on the banks of Bull Run. Concerned officers blustered. Some of them accused the engineers of sabotage.

But one colonel came forward to speak sensibly and constructively.

He was Charles Fisher, commander of the Sixth North Carolina, a fierce, aggressive man with lean shaven cheeks and a bristling tuft of chin beard. In civilian life he had been president of the North Carolina Railroad, and when he had organized the Sixth North Carolina a number of track layers and locomotive mechanics had enlisted with him. These things he told his fellow officers, and added that his men could get the train back on the track in short order; but he would summon them to do so only if they were allowed to leave on the very first cars, ahead of Kirby Smith's regiments.

Because they must, Smith and the others accepted the offer. The Sixth North Carolina went to work with professional assurance, spiking the rails back to the ties and hoisting and shoving the cars back upon them. The stubborn engine, too, was tinkered back into running order. In the small hours of the night of the 20th, the Manassas Gap Railroad was ready for business again. Happily the Tarheels scrambled into the cars and were off, while Smith's men sulked in the rain, unable to start campfires to fry that cheerless leathery concoction of meal and water the Confederates called putty-cake.

Riding ahead of the delayed trains, Stuart's regiment of cavalry reached Manassas Junction, unsaddled its sweaty horses, and lay down under the trees. The artillery came in, too, at one A.M. The gunners fairly collapsed under the caissons. But Johnston forced himself awake again, his head cleared but his nerves tingling. He asked Beauregard to show him that written order of battle.

Beauregard had not yet accomplished the task. His adjutant, Jordan, was worn out by the labors of the previous night and had collapsed among the papers that strewed his desk at Yorkshire. Beauregard had given him a sedative and sent him to sleep. Johnston offered his engineering officer, Major Whiting, as temporary chief of staff, and to Whiting Beauregard dictated his plan.

"The following order," began Beauregard, "is published for the information of division and brigade commanders. . . ."

It was all plain in the Creole's head. He had lived for seven weeks just below the sprawl of Bull Run; he could have jumped on his horse in that very hour of darkness, to lead Johnston and Whiting to any one of the crossings. They ranged themselves in his mind, those crossings at which his troops kept vigil:

Union Mills Ford was at the right of his troops, two miles southeast from where Beauregard sat with Whiting at the desk in Yorkshire's parlor. Next to the left was McLean's Ford, only a few hundred feet from headquarters. Then came Blackburn's where the battle of the 18th had been hottest, and then Mitchell's. Where Bull Run lapped southward, nearly two miles from Mitchell's, was Island Ford, crossed by a mere trail instead of a road. Another mile or so, and there was Ball's Ford, then Lewis', and finally, where the right of Beauregard's line rested on the Warrenton Turnpike, was the principal crossing of the whole series, Stone Bridge. The whole line, following the turns of the stream, measured full eight miles in length.

Here and there behind his own brigades, Beauregard had stationed Johnston's troops as they arrived. He had achieved no divisional organization, but now, as he dictated to Whiting, he decided on temporary groupings of two brigades each.

Ewell, with his brigade and that of Holmes, would move as the First Division, across Union Mills Ford and along the road just beyond that led to Centreville. Jones, supported by Early, would advance as the Second Division across McLean's Ford on Early's left. Longstreet, who with Jackson made up the Third Division, would ford at Blackburn's, keeping pace at the left of Jones. Bonham, supported by the troops under Bartow as the Fourth Division, would cross at Mitchell's Ford. Cocke and Evans, with Kirby Smith if he arrived in time, would take their regiments across Stone Bridge and Lewis' and Ball's Fords to the right, ready to move along the Warrenton Turnpike to Centreville as the attack on McDowell's left developed. Bee, with other late-arriving units, would form the reserve and follow as the battle moved north of Bull Run.

Most of the artillery Beauregard assigned to the three divisions at his right. Stuart's cavalry regiment was ordered to the reserve, and another mounted regiment was divided into details for reconnaissance and courier duty.

Brigadier General Holmes, gray in the old regular army service, was named by Beauregard as commander of the three divisions on the right. The Fourth and Fifth Divisions would be under "the second in command"—who he would be, Beauregard's order did not specify. But the Fourth Division apparently would move with the three under Holmes.

The whole plan of battle provided for the action of separated forces, at different times and in different sectors, over an eight-mile front of dubious woods and trails and heights. The troops of those hastily organized divisions were new to warfare, and most of them utterly green. Among the officers who would lead them, only Jackson, Longstreet, and Bonham had even the sketchiest of experience in battle command of more than a company. Yet Beauregard envisioned his attacking line of the first four divisions as swinging leftward like a scythe blade, with Bonham's crossing at Mitchell's Ford as the pivot. He expected McDowell to be surprised, demoralized, and routed. He fully intended to destroy that entire invading army, and go on to the framing and carrying out of new plans that would establish by glorious force of arms the independence of the Confederacy.

For each division, specific directions wound up with: "The order to advance will be given by the commander-in-chief." The watchword was "Sumter," a word that remembered Confederate victory under the leadership of Pierre Gustave Toutant Beauregard.

XIV

Soldier, I Stay to Pray for Thee

NEWS of the skirmish at Blackburn's Ford had trickled southward to Richmond and the towns below, and rumors magnified it into a triumphant major action. In Charleston, the morning papers of July 19 spoke vaguely but encouragingly of "an engagement at Bull's Run," with "decided success" for the defenders. In rumor-vibrating Richmond, much more than this was deduced.

J. B. Jones, chief clerk at the office of the War Department, felt that the affair at Blackburn's Ford had been an important battle. "That *was* fighting," he wrote in the diary he meant some day to publish, "and we shall have more of it." Adjutant General Cooper, too, thought the action a "capital thing," and so informed Mary Chesnut when she made herself able to leave her hotel room after a siege of nervous headaches. Cooper felt happy enough to attempt a pun on Bonham's name.

"Your South Carolina man, *bon homme,* has done a capital thing at Bull's Run," announced Cooper, "driven back the enemy if not defeated him."

He went on to talk about killed and captured Federals. Mary still grieved over the news of Garnett's death, and found herself disposed to listen more seriously to her friend Mrs. Eugene McLean, who dismissed Cooper's tales of glory with shrugs of her shapely shoulders.

"A great battle fought," the lady mimicked the gossipers to Mary. "Not one Confederate killed; enemy's loss in killed, wounded and prisoners taken by us immense!" No other reports

184

would Richmond permit itself to believe, vowed Mrs. McLean. But Lawrence Keitt proved himself an exception. He called the fight of the 18th a "skirmish of outposts." When Joe Davis sighed, "Would Heaven only send us a Napoleon!" Keitt rejoined mordantly, "Not one bit of use. If Heaven did, Walker would not give him a commission."

More troops were leaving for Manassas, and more all the time, hampered by contradictory orders, confusion of trains overladen with supplies and men, incessantly flying rumors. Hampton's Legion, for instance, found itself moving before it knew where or why.

Handsomely drilled at its camp at Rocketts, praised and petted by the ladies of Richmond, the Legionnaires had come to fancy themselves as good soldiers as ever stepped. Their latest flattering recognition had come on July 16, when Jefferson Davis in person had presented them with a magnificent palmetto flag sewn by their kinswomen and sweethearts at home in South Carolina. "A real fighting speech," one of the Legion characterized Davis' remarks, and Colonel Wade Hampton, that reserved and business-like giant, had made himself able to offer "a pretty response." Bright-eyed girls had watched, two Blakely guns of the Legion's artillery had burned precious gunpowder in a salute.

Then, on the 18th, had come orders to Rocketts that the six companies of the Legion's infantry must make ready to go to the front, where other South Carolinians already had seen action.

Officers got permission to delay until shoes could be found— Hampton wanted two pairs apiece for his infantrymen. Grumbling company color bearers rolled up their militia flags and left them with friends in Richmond. Charles Hutson closed the first volume of Macaulay's *History of England*—he hoped to be spared death in battle, if only long enough to finish that fascinating work. Captain James Conner wrote home, in an effort to reassure his terrified mother:

. . . Just you be easy about me. I shall take good care of myself, and if you don't get letters, just recollect it is because they can't come, and don't fancy that I am sick or shot or something dreadful. Recollect that we, on Morris Island, only one mile from the batteries, were told and believed that 30 of our men were killed, and never knew any better until the fight was over, so learn from that to distrust all war rumors.

The shoes had arrived by noon of the 19th, and Hampton supervised the striking of tents, the rolling of blankets, among his companies of infantrymen. At six o'clock the Legionnaires marched into town, but no train was ready at the depot. They stacked arms, ate supper, and lay down on the cobblestoned streets, feeling very much like old soldiers. Not until midnight did the cars arrive. Hampton wakened his men and marched them aboard, and they rolled slowly away. Again and again the train crawled or stopped altogether in the great mass of rail traffic that crowded the tracks to Manassas.

Everywhere, it seemed, the country had been stripped of soldiers that Beauregard might be reinforced. Winchester trembled, with no more than militia to defend its earthworks. Judith Maguire gazed around the town, lately so filled with regiments of the Army of the Shenandoah. By this time, she and her neighbors knew where those regiments had gone, and why. Anxiously, Judith Maguire wrote in her diary:

. . . Tomorrow will be a bloody Sabbath. Oh, that Providence would now interpose and prevent further bloodshed! Oh, that strength may be given to our men. Let not the enemy overcome them. Oh, God of Nations! Have mercy on the South!

Considerably brighter-spirited was another and younger diarist that day, sixteen-year-old Betty Maury at Fredericksburg. Her father and brothers were all in the Confederate service, and Betty believed them capable of whipping any enemy, anywhere and on any day. Of Blackburn's Ford she exulted:

Hurrah! We have beat the Yankees. The enemy was repulsed three times.

And at Bristoe Station, just below Manassas where warriors gathered, ladies at the railroad hotel were told that Beauregard would send an engine and a car to remove them southward to safety. With what they felt sure was womanly pluck, they declined courteously any move to take them away from where the excitement was.

Mary Chesnut, having again taken to her bed at the Spotswood in Richmond, was visited by friends. From time to time other ladies came to chat, while she jotted brief notes of what happened around her. Mrs. McLean brought her sister's baby into the room with her, and Mary, the disconsolately childless, reflected, "Women need maternity to bring out their best and true loveliness." Outside in the street, more newly arrived South Carolina troops were passing. Mary dragged herself to the window and recognized officers bowing to her from their saddles—Tom Taylor, John Rhett, the sons of families she knew. She and the other ladies waved handkerchiefs.

Ah, but the ladies had been waving handkerchiefs, as it seemed to them, almost constantly during the past three months. Troops had arrived, had camped at the fair grounds or at Howard's Hill or at Rocketts, and every true Southern woman had waved her handkerchief, had gone out to watch the infantry marching and the cavalry cantering, to see the flags presented and hear the cannon fire salutes. Patriotic sewing circles had toiled to make shirts and gray coats and pantaloons. They had knitted socks. They had fabricated those extraordinary havelocks and the abdominal bands that were supposed to protect against camp illnesses. They had scraped lint and had folded bandages for the hospitals that, very soon now, would be filled with wounded. Preparation for battle had been gay and romantic, at least the ladies had thought so. The men under arms had seemed so handsome and mannerly.

Where tonight would be the handsome and mannerly young men from every state in the Confederacy, who had shone with gray-coated valor at the parties and balls and dinners of other nights in Richmond, who had eaten the delicate sandwiches and sweet cakes, had sipped the tea or the lemonade or the wine, who had given smile for smile? Under what grim-starred sky would those young men lie down or stand waiting, those cavaliers who had lingered on shadowed piazzas and under spring arbors to point out to Richmond girls the comet of a fortnight ago? How faint had grown the echo in Richmond of the whispered compliments, the husky-voiced vows, the pleas for love! They were loved and adored, those young men strung along the banks of a creek called Bull Run, peering across it toward other young men who had come, hating and threatening them.

On to Richmond! So, in the flat, strange accents of the North, had rung the chorused cry of the invaders. It had been heard and repeated, that slogan. What was that other war cry ascribed to them in Beauregard's printed warning? . . . *Beauty and booty,* that was it, and much of both commodities waited in Richmond should the invaders triumph. How many invaders were there? Enough to sweep aside or charge over that massing of Confederate troops, enough to stamp into Richmond the day after tomorrow? It was said that behind the blue host of McDowell moved another host of Northern civilians—politicians, holidaying sparks, great ladies and gay ladies; that these had brought picnic hampers and baskets of champagne, that in their luggage were dancing shoes for the victory ball in Richmond.

Those who wanted war must be exulting now. Jeff Davis had not wanted it, nor had Robert E. Lee, nor had Thomas Jonathan Jackson. Very few of the soldiers had wanted it. Very few of them had said much about secession or war, which phenomena had been procured by the fire-eaters, the orators like Yancey and the prophets like Ruffin. Now the quiet ones, the calm men who knew the horrors of conflict, were out there standing in the way of invasion. How many of them would fall where they stood?

Poignantly, the ladies remembered a certain new Confederate song, already establishing its special legend that an actual conversation between a departing volunteer and a belle of Montgomery had inspired it. Antiphonally sung, the first verse by a baritone and the second by a soprano, it had enchanted many a social group around a parlor piano. Now it shrugged off its flavor of sugary melodrama, it sounded fiercely true:

> Lady, I go to fight for thee,
> Where gory banners wave,
> To fight for thee, and, oh, perchance,
> To find a soldier's grave.

Many soldiers' graves might be dug and filled along the banks of Bull Run. From Richmond on July 20 the ladies looked away northward, listening for what message might drift down. But only the wind blew, hot and voiceless. The wind had been sown, and now, now, the whirlwind must be reaped, with swords for sickles, volleying guns for flails. All that Richmond could do was wait for the news, be it comforting or heartbreaking. How did the second verse of the song go, the verse in which the lady made reply?

> Soldier, I stay to pray for thee,
> A harder task is mine,
> To wish and long in lonely grief
> That victory may be thine.

All right, tomorrow was Sunday, and prayer was indicated.

The mood of depression had closed down upon the War Office, too. Secretary Walker growled to Chief Clerk Jones that no gentleman should hold public appointment. Jones, swamped with paper work, complained about the delay in granting commissions. "We have talent enough in the South to officer millions of men," he felt. "Mr. Walker is a man of capacity, and has a most extraordinary recollection of details. But I fear, he is too finely strung for the official treadmill."

Did Walker toil so frantically in hopes of being President some day? Jones suspected so, but decided that future Presidents of the Confederate States would be heroic generals; that is, if the Confederate States managed to survive the war and elect future Presidents.

Trains seemed running only to bear troops away to the north, but one puffed into Richmond and unloaded men. These wore dingy blue uniforms, and armed men in gray shepherded them. They were glum-faced prisoners, fifty of them, the trophies of Jackson's adroit skirmishing with Patterson in the Falling Waters affair. They had been shipped down from Winchester, now that the Army of the Shenandoah had departed. Crowds gathered to stare, as though the circus had come to town. Mrs. Wigfall found it in her heart to pity those melancholy captives. Hers was a naturally gentle soul, and she was the first to admit that she lacked the militant assurance of, say, Mary Chesnut.

Just then, Mary knew her own dauntings and doubtings. Lying in bed, refusing drugs lest they blur her wits at this tremendous moment of history, she wondered how soon a report from Manassas would reach the President's quarters there at the Spotswood. Such a report might include some mention of James, aide to Beauregard and stationed where everybody knew the battle was to be. If Beauregard led his troops sword in hand, hero fashion, must not James be at his side, a prime mark for enemy bullets? She wished that James had given up that volunteer post, to be in Richmond. Congress was opening its third session, in the beautiful white capitol building—if only James were present to take his seat, far beyond the range of the most terrible gun in all the artillery fetched down from Washington by Irvin McDowell . . .

The Congress heard the reading of Jefferson Davis' message. The President made no specific reference to the gray army that stood its ground at Manassas Junction, or to the blue army that shoved menacingly close. Seemingly he had drafted the message in what he hoped would sound like encouraging periods. With eloquence and cordiality he offered welcome to Virginia, North Carolina, Tennessee, and Arkansas, new states of the Confederacy since last the Congress had met. He expressed happy admiration of the bountiful crops now ripe for harvest. He accused the Federal invaders of atrocities in northern Virginia, and spoke with disdain of Yankee anticipations that the South would be frightened into submission:

. . . To speak of subjugating such a people, so united and determined, is to speak a language incomprehensible to them. To resist attacks on their rights or their liberties is with them an instinct. Whether this war will last one, or three, or five years, is a problem they leave to be solved by the enemy alone; it will last till the enemy shall have withdrawn from their borders—till their political rights, their altars and their homes are free from invasion. Then, and then only, will they rest from this struggle, to enjoy in peace the blessings which with the favor of Providence they have secured by the aid of their own strong hearts and sturdy arms.

Less ringingly and more practically, President Davis addressed to Governor Joseph E. Brown of Georgia a personal appeal for twenty-five tons of saltpeter, with which to manufacture ammunition. The powder captured at Norfolk Navy Yard had almost all been made into cartridges for the guns, great and small, of Johnston and Beauregard.

The rest of July 20 seemed to many residents of Richmond to have assumed an atmosphere of stealth. Doctors were hurrying away toward Manassas, by train, by carriage and on horseback, to prepare for the treatment of heavy casualties. As evening drew near, the drawing rooms of hotels filled with whispering groups, sitting together on sofas or standing huddled in corners. Crowds paced the sidewalks, oppressed by nervous fears like herds of milling cattle before a tempest. Some found themselves able to joke. The laughter must have had its element of hysteria.

That night, men and women in Richmond slept and dreamed troubled dreams, or lay awake wondering and hoping and despairing. Sunday, July 21, dawned dry and bitterly hot.

Worshipers thronged to gray St. Paul's Church. Many looked forward to a glimpse of Jefferson Davis and his lady. Perhaps their faces would give some hint of what was happening at Manassas.

Varina was in her pew, but not the President. From mouth to mouth flew the report—Davis and several of his personal staff had boarded a train for Manassas shortly after seven A.M. Only Louis Wigfall had not been told, had been left behind. That meant his friendship and influence with Davis had come to an end.

After some excitement, the people at church and at the Spotswood accepted the news of the President's departure with returning calm. It may be that they had worn themselves out with tense anticipation during the past several days. But War Clerk Jones, close to the facts, knew that Davis intended to lead his troops in the crisis, even as so many had urged him to do. Jones wrote down his reaction:

I have always felt that he would avail himself of his prerogative as commander-in-chief, and direct in person the most important operations in the field; and, indeed, I have always supposed he was selected to be the Chief of the Confederacy, mainly with a view to this object, as it was generally believed he possessed military genius of a high order. In revolutions like the present, the chief executive occupies a most perilous and precarious position, if he be not a military chieftain, and present on every battle field of great magnitude.

Noon came, without word or warning of action up there on the banks of Bull Run. If Varina Davis knew or guessed anything, she did not tell her friends. With Mrs. McLean and Mrs. Joe Johnston, she entered a carriage on a melancholy errand; they planned to attend the funeral of the child of a couple they knew.

As they drove along the street, they were aware of excited, milling crowds. Varina told the driver to stop the carriage, and leaned out to ask a passing man what had happened.

"Yes, madam," he told her eagerly, "they have been fighting at Manassas since six o'clock this morning."

XV

Like a Stone Wall

> Manassas Junction, Va., July 21, 1861
> Sent at 5½ h. A.M.

GENERAL,—You will hold yourself in readiness to take the offensive on Centreville at a moment's notice, to make a diversion against the enemy's intended attack on Mitchell's Ford and, probably, Stone Bridge. You will protect well your right flank against any attack from the eastward.

General Holmes's brigade will support your movement.

If the enemy be prepared to attack in front of your left, leave it (said Brigade) in proper position, with orders to take the offensive when it hears your engagement on the other side of the Run. I intend to take the offensive throughout my front as soon as possible.

> Respectfully, your obedient servant,
> G. T. BEAUREGARD, Brig.-Genl. Cmdg.

Genl. R. S. Ewell, Union Mills, Va.

Dick Ewell snorted like the eager war horse described by the prophet Job. His would be the honor of opening offensive action from the right of the line, according to Beauregard's plan of battle, and he was confidently sure of his ability to do so successfully. In the hot light of the rising sun he addressed Major John B. Gordon of the Sixth Alabama, to whom he had entrusted the line of skirmishers that would first approach the ford and make ready to lead the advance in force.

"Come and eat a cracker with me," invited Ewell. "We will breakfast here together, and dine in hell together."

Such rough soldierly pleasantry took young Gordon somewhat aback: he had never seen a battle, and had no reason to think battles funny. But he stood straight as a ramrod as he munched the hardtack, then saluted and set out toward Union Mills Ford, with his line of riflemen in open order.

Among the trees on the Run's north side lurked Yankees. Some of these began to fire across the crawling brown stream, and Gordon's skirmishers replied. Even as these first musket balls whined back and forth, a courier came from Ewell to bid Gordon fall back. Gordon did so, hurried to report, and found Ewell stamping his booted feet in frustration.

"No orders, no orders," he shrilled angrily. And no orders came. Ewell held his brigade where it was, because "The order to advance will be given by the commander-in-chief."

To Ewell's left, Longstreet had moved across Blackburn's Ford, taking along two of Jackson's regiments. Then he, too, was forced to wait because no orders came from Beauregard. Bonham, poised at Mitchell's Ford, had learned from his scouts that in the hours after midnight they had heard ominous rumbling, as of many artillery wheels, beyond Bull Run. Before sunrise Bonham had sent some of the Eleventh North Carolina to investigate further, and now these came to say that regiments of blue troops were moving along the Warrenton Turnpike toward Stone Bridge, where was posted only Evans' little scratch brigade.

McDowell, to whom Beauregard's elaborate plan of battle had assigned a role of limp confusion, apparently was very much on the way somewhere, and in a menacingly purposeful manner. Bonham rushed this news to Beauregard.

At Stone Bridge, at about the same time Ewell offered Gordon that breakfast of hardtack, black-mustached Shanks Evans prepared for battle.

He commanded the Fourth South Carolina and Wheat's battalion of raffish Louisiana Tigers, some 1,100 infantry in all, with a company of cavalry and two smoothbore six-pound howitzers. Peering past the clutter of obstructions heaped upon Stone Bridge, Evans could see massive Federal formations on the Turnpike, and at about six o'clock artillery opened on him from afar. His own howitzers had not the range to answer, and coolly he kept his men and guns under cover, but ready to meet and resist any attempt to charge across the bridge. Shortly afterward, Bonham's position was shelled from the wooded heights beyond Bull Run.

Beauregard took note of these matters, but did not seem vexed or greatly concerned. Plainly, McDowell threatened the troops at Stone Bridge and nearby; he, Beauregard, would use Johnston's troops to strengthen his own left. Then, while McDowell's attention was fixed on Stone Bridge, the Confederate right—Ewell, Jones, Longstreet and Bonham—would still launch that surprise attack.

Beauregard ordered Jackson to leave his position behind Longstreet and move upstream to the vicinity of Island Ford, from which point he might support either Cocke or Bonham. Another message went to Barnard Bee, directing him to take his brigade and Bartow's two regiments still farther to the left.

Bee had set up headquarters at a farmer's modest cabin somewhat to eastward of Manassas Junction. Along a fence just outside the front yard sprawled the sleeping gunners and drivers of the Staunton Artillery. The first shots from across the Run did not disturb these men, worn out from the long forced march of the 20th, but then came a shell, screeching above the treetops close at hand to explode loudly almost at the Junction. Captain Imboden sat up against the fence rails.

His men, too, were getting up. They had slept in the rumpled, dirty shirts of red flannel he had bought for them at Harpers Ferry. Imboden directed them to harness and hitch the teams, and they did so, wondering where they would get breakfast. Bee came out upon the cabin porch in his shirt sleeves. He had just received Beauregard's orders to move to the left, and he told Imboden to bring along those four brass guns of his.

Imboden, grown practical since first taking the field in mid-April, pointed out that his battery had traveled without stopping all the previous day and night until one o'clock that morning, and that both his men and his horses were famished. Bee, who probably had eaten, waved the protest aside. He would order rations to be brought along.

"You will have plenty of time to cook and eat," he promised, "to the music of a battle in which we shall probably take little or no part."

Edmund Ruffin, too, was wakened from comfortable slumber at Manassas Junction, perhaps by the same exploding shell that had yanked Imboden to his feet. The old man scrambled out of his blankets and began once more to drag on those agonizing shoes. He heard more booming blasts from the direction of Bull Run, and he told himself that he must hurry back to his place in the rank of the Palmetto Guard. Dressed in homespun again, his musket in his skinny hands, he tottered away.

Bee drew his regiments into column and started them for the high ground near Portici, just behind Cocke's main position. Imboden limbered up his guns and directed them toward the same point. He and Bee rode together, not at any great speed, in advance of the guns and men.

They trotted their horses up the hill behind Portici, and Bee gazed away over fields and groves to where his friend Evans held Stone Bridge, then beyond Evans at the wooded course of Bull Run. On the far side, two miles past the position of Evans, rose a long cloud of dust, as though above a concealed road. Steel flashed in it. Men marched there, thousands of men.

At once Bee knew that McDowell was trying to flank the Confederate left with a strong force. He pointed to where, a mile west of Portici, rose the pine-thicketed plateau of Henry Hill.

"There is where the battle will be fought, and we are in for it!" he told Imboden excitedly. "Go and bring your guns, and I will find a place for them."

Imboden spurred away, found his battery and brought it back at as swift a gallop as the tired, hungry teams could achieve. It was nine o'clock, or nearly.

At about that time, someone else watched the movement beyond and up Bull Run.

Captain Porter Alexander stood on top of the hill on Willcox-

son's Farm, with signalmen and a mounted courier beside him.
Through his powerful glasses he peered along a lane he had cut
through the trees to his signal station beside Stone Bridge. Evans
waited near that station. Beyond Evans, a winding stretch of Bull
Run could be seen, with Sudley Springs Ford, undefended and
unguarded, more than two miles to the west of the bridge.

There at Sudley Springs, a long column of men crept across
the water like a monstrous blue snake. Already its head was
mounting Bull Run's south bank, and along the open ground
north of the ford Anderson could see at least half a mile of solidly
massed troops. Bayonets and cannon flashed in the morning sunlight.

At once Alexander dictated to one of his men the first flag
message of American wartime experience:

LOOK OUT FOR YOUR LEFT   YOU ARE TURNED

While the signalman wagged this way to his mate at Evans'
post, Alexander scribbled a more comprehensive warning, and
sent his courier off with it, to find Beauregard.

Evans had kept his attention fixed at the Federals on the
Warrenton Pike beyond the Run, refusing to answer their guns
but ready to oppose them if they tried to rush him. Horatius once
had held a bridge successfully, and with fewer men against longer
odds. Not until Alexander's message was handed him did he look
upstream. Then he, too, made out the telltale dust cloud raised by
the attacking force.

Like Bee, Evans at once grasped the implications. That impressive lathering of shellfire from up the Turnpike was designed
to pin him, Evans, helplessly at the bridge while the Yankees
forded at Sudley Springs, then came on and swallowed him and
the troops below him. As instantly as Evans grasped the enemy's
logic, so instantly he declined to go along with it.

He sent Roberdeau Wheat with a scouting party to make sure
that no other column poked toward a masked farm ford half a
mile upstream. While he waited for Wheat's report, he strung out
two companies of the Fourth South Carolina as skirmishers
below the bridge, with two more companies as a skimpy reserve.

Let these men fire fast and continuously, he directed, to keep the host opposite them in the delusion that Evans' entire force was staying where it was supposed to stay. Then he prepared to fall back with the rest of his men along the far side of the Warrenton Turnpike, to face that stronger threat halfway.

Wheat crossed the ford with his scouts. In the woods on the other bank they neither saw nor heard any frightening evidence of an approach in force, only a small patrol. They returned quickly, but not before some of the Tigers shouted defiance, couched in the choicest invective of the New Orleans river front. As soon as Wheat assured Evans that no second body of troops drove at this nearest ford, Evans led his main force at a vigorous pace a full mile across the Turnpike. At last he could see the approaching bluecoats.

There were regiments of them, and they did not come along the southern bank of Bull Run, but held to the Sudley Springs-Manassas Road, that crossed the Warrenton Turnpike more than a mile below Stone Bridge. Promptly Evans changed direction, mounted Matthews Hill, and there strung out his 800 infantry in a thin line of battle. His left rested on the road and most of his men had the cover of a brushy belt of trees on top of the hill. He posted his two howitzers at the two ends of his line, and waited.

He had not long to wait. Shortly after ten o'clock, the head of the approaching column peered through the clumps of trees that grew on either side of the road. It had no skirmishers in front; apparently it expected no trouble at this point. When it had come within 600 yards of Matthews Hill, Evans opened fire with howitzers and muskets.

With fierce joy, the South Carolinians and Louisianians saw the column halt and waver. Then a brigade trotted into view, its four regiments forming in line of battle, with a row of cannon to its front. Evans increased his fire to its utmost, and seemed to hold that greater force where it stood. Another regiment formed to the left of the brigade and attempted to advance, but Roberdeau Wheat led a yelling countercharge. Before the advance fire of his Zouaves that regiment broke and fled. Wheat fell even as he exulted in a sense of victory. A bullet had pierced his lungs, and his aides bore him to the rear. Ahead of the stretcher party spurred a courier, with a call for help.

On the western slope of Henry Hill, a hundred yards northeast of the Widow Henry's house, Bee was ordering Imboden's guns into a hollow of ground. The four pieces went into action, their charges of shrapnel clearing the rise of ground to their front by but a few inches, then flying over the heads of Evans' men to belabor the Union line of battle. Bee proposed to form his own infantry, some 2,800 muskets including Bartow's two regiments of Georgians, in support of Imboden's battery so as to hold the strategic plateau of Henry Hill as the battle moved toward it.

But then Evans' courier arrived, with the plea for support to hold Matthews Hill. Bee and Evans were both South Carolinians, and they had been friends at West Point, in the old army, and as officers during the siege of Sumter. Bee could not ignore Evans' plight, and ordered his men across the Turnpike and beyond, into position with Evans.

They arrived just as Evans' badly outnumbered little force began to waver under the raking fire of two batteries and thousands of muskets. Bartow formed the Seventh and Eighth Georgia at Evans' left, and Bee strengthened the line to the right. The augmented defenders fired into the close-drawn ranks opposite, and over their heads Imboden kept lobbing his shells and shrapnel. The bright blue sky clouded with powder smoke, the air shook with explosions. But more Federals came up behind the first line, then moved to extend it. A battery of rifled guns appeared at the left of the Sudley Springs-Manassas Road and began to batter the infantry of Bee and Evans, also to fire into Imboden's position on Henry Hill.

Again the blue regiments came inexorably forward, threatening to flank both ends of the smaller line that challenged them. A greater bluster of cannon, a sharper rattle of muskets, seemed to rock the grassy meadow, the tufts of brush and the clumps of trees. Again the Confederate line wavered. Mounted field officers exposed themselves recklessly to encourage their men, and were notable targets for marksmen in the Federal ranks. Down those officers went, one after another.

Still the defenders clung to the top of Matthews Hill, for almost an hour after the arrival of Bee. Then, from the direction of Bull Run at their right, appeared another solid mass of bluecoats, fanning out as it came.

It was unfortunate that Wheat's scouts had felt impelled to howl curses at the Yankee patrol and betray the presence of that ford just above Stone Bridge. The insulted observers had fetched a whole brigade of their friends across, to make a fitting rejoinder.

Hopelessly outnumbered, in mortal danger of being outflanked from both sides, Bee's and Evans' men began to drop back. Then they broke from their ranks and ran. Despite the commands and appeals of their officers, they raced down the eastern slope of Matthews Hill, floundered through Young's Branch below, then fled up and across Henry Hill looking for somewhere to hide.

Over their heads the sky rocked with the scream of shells, under their feet rustled bushes heavy with ripe berries. Some of them ran toward, then past, a line of Confederates who were not running, Hampton's Legionnaires.

The Legion had spent thirty hot, cramped hours en route from Richmond to Manassas, with cooked food for but a single meal in its haversacks. When it had reached Manassas Junction at six o'clock that morning, the guns were already blazing at Evans and Bonham, but sounded far away. Gratefully free from those jammed cars, the men of the Legion began frying bacon for breakfast. But even as they took their first mouthfuls, orders came from Beauregard to pick up their muskets and march westward toward the sound of the firing.

Hampton mounted his big black horse and led his column away. It was a five-mile march after those thirty hours in the crowded troop train, and the hastily bolted rations made undigested lumps in the stomachs of Private Charles Hutson and his comrades. The farther they tramped, the louder snarled and crashed the guns, in deadly promise of what waited just ahead.

Hampton brought them upon the northeastern spur of Henry Hill, north of the Robinson house, and to a deep-worn lane with a stone wall just above the Warrenton Turnpike. Across the pike and Young's Branch beyond appeared the massive approaching line of Federals, flung wide to right and left, bristling with field guns, backed up by huge blocks of reserves. Against this immense charging force Hampton strung out his six hundred men, fewer than Evans had first marshaled to defend Matthews Hill.

Young Hutson tingled with excitement, but felt that his comrades held themselves steady even in their tense awareness of dire peril. He found himself classifying his own emotions as though they were the emotions of another person, dispassionately observed. He felt surprisingly cool and confident, sure of his duty and of his willingness to perform that duty at all hazards. He had trust in Colonel Wade Hampton and in Captain James Conner, there in the forefront of the Washington Light Infantry.

The Legionnaires crouched behind the stone wall, while the retreating regiments of Bee and Evans rushed past them and bullets began to hiss and yelp around them. Then they were all alone facing the Federals, and the full advance fire, grapeshot, canister and musket balls, struck them like a sudden summer cloudburst.

Almost at once, Lieutenant Colonel Johnson fell from his saddle, shot through the head. Hampton's black horse was shot under him, but the big colonel cleared his feet from the stirrups, rolled free and caught up a rifle dropped by a collapsing infantryman. He fired expertly into the charging Union line.

Bullets chipped flint flakes from the wall, slapped the ground murderously. Charles Hutson found himself urging his mates to stand their ground and keep their formation. Straightening his spectacles he aimed and fired his first shot at an enemy, then hastily bit a cartridge and rammed it down.

Even as he drove the ramrod into the barrel, he felt a smashing blow as of a club. Down he floundered, half-stunned but able to realize that he had been shot in the head and that, luckier than Lieutenant Colonel Johnson, he still lived. He pulled off his spectacles as blood fountained his face from a gash on his brow. Rising shakily, he fished out a handkerchief and mopped the blood from his eyes. As he did so, the Legion started to retreat after Bee and Evans.

But their brief stand had checked that enemy rush, and even

now the Legionnaires did not break as had the others. They kept
their line and fired as they fell back.

At the Robinson house they tried to stand again, firing from the
shelter of the house, the outbuildings and other bits of cover.
Charles Hutson freed his eyes of blood and tried to finish reload-
ing. But a flying bullet smashed his musket in his hands. His head
throbbed, he heard as in a dream of Armageddon the hail-clatter of
balls striking around him. Then, somehow, he was flat on his back
behind the house. A surgeon patched the wound on his forehead
and told him to get away to the rear if he could.

Hampton held at the Robinson house under a racking crossfire
from both flanks of the slowly advancing Federal line. At last he
ordered another retirement, and again his Legion kept its formation as it retreated. It brought along Hutson and its other
wounded, and kept up musketry fire to slow the pursuit.

Imboden's guns still barked from the gulley east of the Turnpike, but Imboden saw no infantry support anywhere. Bee and
Evans had rushed away out of sight, and the artillery captain felt
utterly alone with his guns and the tide of Federals that flowed up
the hill toward him. It was past eleven o'clock. Half the horses
of his teams were down. Someone yelled that only three rounds
remained in the caissons—when those were fired, the battery
would be silent in the face of the Yankee advance.

In desperate, angry shame, Imboden hitched up what horses
remained and wallowed the guns out of their positions, then
started away from that roar of imminent destruction. Federal
cannon balls pelted him along. One smashed the axle of a rolling
six-pounder, and Imboden's gunners dropped it to save the
limber.

He fled before the enemy, up across the plateau. Past the house
of the Widow Henry he galloped his guns and carts. As the last of
them won beyond the yard, Imboden heard shells ripping the
clapboards and shingles into shreds. On he ran, toward the rear
of the plateau and the highest point of Henry Hill. Pines strung
the horizon.

As he approached the pines, he saw more men in gray uniform,
a whole brigade of them hastening into line from right to left. In

front was a familiar brown-bearded figure in a shabby forage cap, slouched on a close-coupled sorrel horse.

BRIGADIER GENERAL Thomas Jonathan Jackson had risen early that morning. He was well aware that it was Sunday, a singularly beautiful Sunday. Too, it was the birthday of Mary Anna Jackson, so far away in Lexington and so much missed by her devoted soldier-husband.

At four o'clock, Longstreet had sent to him for two regiments and Jackson had ordered them to Blackburn's Ford. The rest of the brigade cooked and ate its breakfast. At that point of Bull Run, the stream curved to northeast, with forested high ground on the far side and, not far away, Island Ford with its skimpy-trailed excuse for a crossing. Behind Jackson's position was open country, and away to the left were gentle slopes upward toward Portici.

Scant promise of action here, even when that raucous choir of cannon greeted the Sunday sun. Jackson's subordinates thought that their general acted gruff and subdued. He might deplore fighting on the Sabbath; but if fighting was to come, Old Jack wanted to do his share of it.

Time came and went, and it was nine o'clock. Then it was ten, and suddenly, there beyond Henry Hill to westward, broke out the unmistakable clamor of massed artillery. Battle—it had broken out there, bigger and noisier than the volleys across Bull Run.

At once Jackson's mood was transformed to one of brisk energy. He waited for no orders. A courier went flying to get his regiments back from Longstreet, and the brigade fell into column for a march toward that conflict there in the west. As Jackson started, one of the detached regiments caught up. The other, that lagging Thirty-third Virginia, had been partially deployed as skirmishers at Blackburn's Ford, and would need time to reassemble and follow. Jackson marched off without the Thirty-third, over knolls and little trickling streams toward the near slope of Henry Hill. After him came two batteries of field guns.

At half past eleven, or nearly, Jackson rode Old Sorrel to the eastern edge of the plateau, the loftiest point on Henry Hill. He saw the broken fragments of the earlier defending force seeking the shelter of ravines and gullies, while Hampton's Legion sought to cover the retreat. He saw also, as had Bee two hours earlier, that here was the ideal place for a stubborn stand.

From where he sat his saddle, the plateau sloped gently but steadily westward for some three hundred yards of almost clear ground. Behind him grew a grove of pines, affording cover and a possible hampering to any movement against his rear. If the enemy tried to charge from in front, that enemy must move upward against all the fire Jackson could command from his brigade.

Jackson's face hardened, his eyes flashed blue fire as he snapped out his orders to deploy for action.

Imboden's guns trundled toward him, the inadequate teams almost at their last gasp. Imboden rode close to Jackson. Loudly the captain complained that Bee had deserted him, and garnished his words with angry oaths.

Jackson scowled. He did not like profane language, and usually he rebuked it when heard. But now he did not take the time.

"I'll support your battery," he told Imboden. "Unlimber here."

He gestured to where, just in front of the plateau's eastward comb, the ground dipped into a saucerlike depression, ideal for the placing of guns. Imboden shouted his own orders, and the three brass smoothbores again glared toward the enemy, ready to launch the three last charges left in the carts. But the advance had paused, unaccountably and mercifully. Jackson completed the arrangement of his line of battle. At the right he placed the Fifth Virginia that had fought so well at Falling Waters, then the Fourth, then the Twenty-seventh, and at the left the Second, the regiment which Joe Johnston once had said was not worth a single company of regulars. He told the men to lie prone under the pines, taking advantage of what shelter was afforded by the trees and the ridge.

Now another man came riding. It was Bee, dusty and dismayed, his saber drawn, his horse caked with foam and staggering under him. Over yonder, Bee thought, the Federals tightened their sinews to charge again.

"General, they are beating us back!" he called to Jackson.

He spoke for his own troops, battered and driven because so greatly outnumbered, now taking cover in hollows and thickets to the right; and Jackson, replying, spoke for his.

"Then, sir," he rasped, "we will give them the bayonet."

His hard bearded lips snapped shut on those words, and Bee felt his own valor flowing back into him. He wheeled his jaded horse and spurred back to the right.

Alone of all the regiments that had tried to stand on Matthews Hill the Fourth Alabama seemed to have hung together. Every field officer had been shot down, but the Alabamians had reassembled somehow into companies, and looked as though they still had fighting heart. Here and there, other scraps of regiments slumped or milled. Bee rode in among his men.

"There is Jackson standing like a stone wall!" he roared out. "Let us determine to die here, and we will conquer. Follow me!"

XVI

Live and Die for Dixie

AMONG all the thousands of officers and men stirred into confused action along Bull Run's south bank that Sunday morning, Joseph Eggleston Johnston, full general in the regular army of the Confederate States of America, remained mute and motionless.

At dawn he had joined Beauregard, on high ground to the left and rear of Bonham's position at Mitchell's Ford. With the two generals were staff officers and details of couriers. Once on the hill, Johnston had dismounted and stood beside his horse, silent if chafing. Beauregard had done the talking, had made the dispositions of troops.

Bad dispositions those were, and they appeared worse as the morning wore on. Orders went astray, movements were delayed there at the right. Then to the left rose and greatened the commotion of an unexpected engagement. Beauregard had sent reinforcements that way, out of sight beyond Henry Hill—Bee, Bartow, Hampton, and Jackson—but prolonged gunfire rang all the way to Mitchell's Ford, and Johnston saw rising clouds of dirty gray smoke, the smoke of whole wagonloads of exploding gunpowder.

What news came back was disquieting in the extreme. At eleven o'clock, Beauregard sent an officer toward that fight at the left, with six couriers to rush back with reports at ten-minute intervals. Johnston, however, was through with standing still. He did not wait for the first courier to come back. At half past eleven, or a few minutes later, he pulled rank on Beauregard.

Speaking as senior officer to junior, Johnston directed Beauregard to get all available forces headed to the left. "The battle is there," he wound up sternly. "I am going!"

He mounted and rode after the troops already sent to Henry Hill. Beauregard remained only long enough to send word for Holmes and Early to come along, with two regiments from Bonham's command. Ewell, Jones, and Longstreet were left, with orders to demonstrate against the Federals across Bull Run. These dispositions made, Beauregard spurred after Johnston and caught up as his superior shouted for two batteries of artillery to follow along.

As Johnston and Beauregard rode to the foot of Henry Hill and up its slope, they heard the noise of firing, louder and more angry than before. Then they ran into fleeing infantrymen. It looked like the warning of a rout just beyond, but the two generals and their staffs hurried through the demoralized fugitives and came to the edge of the Henry Hill plateau.

It was past noon. Hampton's Legion still tried to fight, there at its second stand beside the Robinson house. The Fourth Alabama was drawn up, leaderless but ready to do what it could. The brigade of Jackson—Stonewall Jackson he would be, from that hour on and forever—had been strengthened by the arrival of Stanard's and Pendleton's batteries, and held its strategic position. Over yonder, on the slope across the Warrenton Turnpike, the long array of Union regiments was reopening fire with muskets and big guns.

The frazzled remains of the commands of Bee, Evans, and Bartow had plunged into pine thickets near the point at which Johnston and Beauregard rode upon the field, and Johnston's first act was to attempt to turn these beaten seekers of shelter into fighting infantry once more.

He called the flag bearer of the Fourth Alabama to his stirrup. They went, Johnston walking his horse to let the plucky soldier keep up. The rest of the regiment raised a cheer, shaky but earnest, and followed the colors, but they had no surviving officer above the rank of captain. Arbitrarily, Johnston called for one of

Bee's staff, young States' Rights Gist of South Carolina. The Alabamians knew and liked him; they accepted his leadership and went into line. Hampton, his companies badly shot up but still facing the front, took post on Jackson's right. At Jackson's left appeared the tardy Thirty-third Virginia. Beauregard, despite his dislike of speechmaking, harangued others of the broken and mingled units, reminding them most eloquently of their threatened homes, their duty as soldiers, the glory that awaited their success in battle. Some of them responded. Meanwhile, more fresh troops were coming up, to form on both sides of Jackson.

In front of Stonewall, Imboden fired those last shots and told his battery to pull out of the fight, but remained to help in whatever way he could. Alburtis' guns came up, in front of the gap between Jackson and Hampton. All three batteries began to fire at the Federals, three brigades of them in line, as they advanced once again.

To threaten Stonewall Jackson's left flank hurried two splendid Federal batteries, eleven rifled guns. They gained a position among trees beside the Sudley Springs-Manassas Road, unlimbered and began to fling shells that ripped gashes in the Confederate ranks. Other batteries fired from positions along the Federal line, past both sides of the Henry house.

Judith Henry, eighty-four years old and bedridden, was carried out of her back door by her two sons; but she begged so frantically to be taken back that they yielded, returned, and laid her down in her room again. Just then a shell burst through the wall, and Judith Henry died, as long she had thought she would die, in her own bed.

The volleys and explosions seemed to crowd the whole universe, as though some archangel of pandemonium had brought upon Henry Hill all the thunderstorms and hurricanes that ordinarily would suffice for a century. Here and there, horror-crazed Southern soldiers fled from the ranks. In vain did Beauregard, Johnston, and others plead, command and threaten. Imboden tried to bar the way of a headlong private of Hampton's Legion. A blind thrust of the fellow's bayonet pitchforked Imboden to one side, his red flannel sleeve torn away and his arm gashed.

But there were also steady spirits who kept their places, faced the shells and fought back. Bartow rallied a remnant of the butchered Seventh Georgia and led it to Jackson's left. Still the Federal batteries yelled murderously.

Bee was down, dying. So, almost at the same time, was Bartow. So were other officers, so were many of the men. Then, just as the clamor of those enemy guns at the left seemed unbearable, it ceased.

The Thirty-third Virginia, slow no more, had seen a regiment in gay Zouave uniforms move to support the batteries, and had charged. Jackson's other regiments supported the Thirty-third with the concentrated fire of all their muskets. The gunners fell around their pieces like reaped barley, the Zouaves reeled backward and away. A galloping rush of Jeb Stuart's cavalry completed the rout of the supporting infantry, and for a moment the Thirty-third held the guns as a prize. Fired on in turn, the Virginians were forced back to their original position; but the guns remained deserted and silent.

Shouting above all the cannonade, Beauregard begged Johnston to go to the rear and leave him to command on the field. At last Johnston did so, hurrying along more reinforcements from wherever he could lay hands on them.

The Sixth North Carolina had jumped off the train it had put into running order, dashed up and taken position at the left, beyond Virginia regiments that extended the line as the Federals extended theirs. It was two o'clock as the North Carolinians arrived, just in time to hear Beauregard's bugles blow the charge. The whole line surged forward, cheering.

That was a strange, high, quivering yodel of a cheer, perhaps remembered from the whoops of Indian warriors or the cries of fox hunters. Back and forth it rang, echoing above the loud guns, the blood-freezing first rebel yell.

Colonel Fisher led his regiment in among those rifled guns deserted by the Federals, and he died across one of them, pierced by a musket ball. His and other regiments drove the Union infantry back, back, almost away from the plateau; then, finding themselves reinforced, the Yankees fought bravely forward again, recapturing the ground they had lost. The battle still hung in the balance.

The blue line stretched away southward, curving in to sickle the gray left. Up came Cocke's troops, some strengthening the right, and one regiment flinging itself in at the left. After it came the Second and Eighth South Carolina, of Bonham's brigade.

Those two Palmetto regiments had fought in the delaying action of the 17th at Fairfax Court House, and across the fords on the 18th. By so much light skirmishing, they were more seasoned than any of the troops on Henry Hill. The ear-bursting bombardment, the cries of the wounded, shook but did not stampede them. They fired through smoky air, reloaded and fired again. Bluecoats fell before them. Still the line opposite stretched and writhed, seeking to flank them.

One of the Second South Carolina had not reached the battle.

Edmund Ruffin had hobbled all the way from Manassas Junction to Mitchell's Ford, four miles on blistered feet, and it had taken him all of four hours. He found the Second South Carolina gone to the fight on Henry Hill, and his beloved Palmetto Guards with it. Feebly he tried to follow. At last, utterly exhausted, he came to a halt.

And all around him, going the other way, scurried deserters from the fight.

Frantically the old man cried out for them to stop and make a stand. They dashed past him without pausing or listening. Unable to rally them, certain that the whole army had been routed, Ruffin himself stood all alone on the grass in his homespun gray. Probably he could not have taken another step, forward or backward, but that did not occur to him. With his white hair tumbled around his crinkled old face, he peered toward the awful noise of conflict. He clutched his musket with skinny hands that shook from age but not from fear. If the South was indeed beaten, he, Ruffin, refused to survive it. Let the pursuing Yankees come this way. He would defy them, he would fire and fall, would leave his ancient bones upon the lost field. . . .

Stronger of limb and wind if weaker of courage, the fugitives had flowed almost as far as Manassas Junction where, at about one o'clock, Kirby Smith's rear-guard brigade left its train.

Smith ordered his men to fling aside their heavy knapsacks and formed them for marching, regiment behind regiment. He rode along beside them, holding the back of his open hand in front of his cap.

"This is the signal, men," he roared out. "The watchword is 'Sumter.' "

They set off at the double, with the racket yonder to guide them. Elzey, the senior colonel, led the way with his Marylanders. They encountered throngs of walking wounded, and other throngs neither wounded nor walking, but hasty-footed in terror. These quavered out warnings of disaster:

". . . getting cut to pieces this time . . ."

". . . catching hell . . ."

". . . sure to be whipped . . ."

Elzey loudly cursed the pallid skulkers out of the way, and on the brigade pushed, and on. Riding ahead, Kirby Smith had found Johnston and had been pointed by him toward that threatened left flank.

They moved south of the Manassas Road, approaching at an angle to the front held by the Second and Eighth South Carolina. Even as they came into position, Smith fell from his horse, shot through the neck. At first he seemed dead. Elzey spurred forward to take command in Smith's place.

Opposite them, within easy range, stood infantry drawn closely into line among veils of dust and smoke. Friend or foe? Elzey snatched a field glass from an aide, thrust it to his eyes and stared at those troops across from him. As he did so, a puff of hot wind caught the flag at the center of the formation and spread it out. Elzey knew that flag; he had followed it into battle against Indians in Florida, Mexicans at Vera Cruz and Churubusco.

"Stars and Stripes!" he bellowed at the top of his lungs. "Stars and Stripes! Give it to them, boys."

His waiting brigade gave it to the regiment that flew the old flag, gave it a terrible point-blank volley that hurled it backward. The battle stubbornly extended itself by the length of Elzey's command. Just then, the extreme left of the Confederates and the extreme right of the Federals stood almost exactly opposite each other, and each side flailed the other with iron and lead. A few troops, only a few, brought into the right place by either army—that might well give the victory.

Even as that realization dawned upon Beauregard, troops were seen afar, hurrying from the south. What troops?

Beauregard, almost at mid-point of the line that had stood like a stone wall, had his own glass to his eye. Alexander's signalmen said that must be the advance guard of Patterson's army, coming at last from the Shenandoah Valley to join McDowell and make the Federal triumph sure.

Beauregard tried to fight down his dismay. It was past four o'clock, but hours of summer daylight remained, enough to witness the destruction of the Confederate army. A strong reinforcement of McDowell's right would crumple Elzey and the regiments next to him, get the rest of the stubborn line on the run from Henry Hill into the lower ground to eastward. The only sane policy was to draw in that left flank, disengage the whole row of regiments and retreat, saving what could be saved.

Like Elzey a short time before, Beauregard peered through his glass. The new column marched purposefully toward the Confederate left flank. And, as Elzey had seen a flag, so Beauregard saw a flag, carried at the head of the marching men but hanging limply and unrecognizably about its staff.

Beauregard spoke to an officer beside him; let Johnston be found and told to form what reserves he could to support a retirement from Henry Hill. Then, as the officer reined around to make off, Beauregard called out for him to stay.

"Let us wait a few minutes, to confirm our suspicions," said Beauregard, glass to eye again, "before finally resolving to yield the field."

The column had drawn nearer. Beauregard's glass made it seem very near indeed. Then a breeze flung the flag out, clear to the view.

Not the gridiron Stars and Stripes this time, but Stars and

Bars, the broad bars of the Confederate flag borne by Jubal Early's brigade.

Early had come from far to the Confederate right, had marched seven or eight blazing miles, brushing aside squalling deserters as Elzey had done. With Early had advanced Kemper's battery, and, as on the retreat from Fairfax Court House, Kemper's men had found the half-fainting Edmund Ruffin and had hoisted him to a gun carriage. The guns had turned off to the right, and Early, facing left, had passed along the rear of Jackson, Cocke, and Elzey, and had come out beyond the Manassas Road.

A thrill of triumph shot like electricity all along the gray line. Again rose the shrill, vibrating rebel yell.

The moment of decision was upon both hosts there on Henry Hill. Stonewall Jackson divined it and seized it. He commanded the center of his brigade to charge. The men sprang up, with yells that topped the volleys. The rest of the line swept forward with them.

The stone wall became a sudden bounding, crushing avalanche. It struck everywhere at once, piercing the Yankee positions, shredding them, flogging them clear of men.

Those abandoned guns were captured at last, and the captors slewed them around and fired them into their late owners. The blue infantry broke its formations, churned aimlessly, sagged backward, was captured in great chunks, from privates to brigadiers. Thrust down from Henry Hill, the invaders tried to stand again, on the far side of the Warrenton Turnpike and Young's Branch. But the Confederate infantry was at them, yelling, firing, thrusting. The Confederate batteries struck at them from both flanks and all along the front.

Jefferson Davis had arrived at Manassas Junction. He found a horse and rode through a cloud of skulkers who wailed that the battle was lost. He arrived on Henry Hill in time to see, but not in time to command as he had dreamed, the final moment of victory. And when Kemper's battery unlimbered, Edmund Ruffin was allowed, as at Sumter, to fire a gun. With bloodthirsty relish he saw the shell explode among Yankees; but those were Yankees in flight, they had run without his doing anything to show them the way north from Manassas. Like Davis, Ruffin had had no real part in winning that final grapple.

All the invaders were running. They abandoned their wounded on the field. They left their cannon, every cannon that had crossed Bull Run. They flung away muskets, bright bayonets, knapsacks, canteens. They jammed Stone Bridge, they clogged the fords, they floundered miserably in the waters of Bull Run, trying only to get away if they could.

Staggering with weariness, throttled with dust, thirsty, hungry, streaming sweat, the Confederates pursued until they, too, had lost all organization and lagged to a halt at last. They gazed after the vanishing backs of the driven foe. Nearly four hundred of their comrades had been killed, including some of their bravest. Perhaps fifteen hundred more were wounded. But, croaked each to his neighbor as the sun went down, they had won.

This was the victory for which they had caught up their weapons and formed their volunteer companies. The battle was over—the war was over. They had won the battle and the war. They had established the independence of the Confederate States of America. Now they could go home again and live happily ever after.

Afterword

THEY were wrong, of course. Far from ending the war at Manassas Junction, they had only begun it.

The Northern army they had driven back rallied and held its lines along the Potomac for months. Other Northern armies came south again. When Kentucky's hope of neutrality died, the entire Confederacy lay open to invasion. Guns howled in furious hunger, blood leaped bright under thirsty steel, at places with good-humored rustic names—Pea Ridge, Brandy Station, Cedar Creek. Eleven thousand fell at Seven Pines, and, during the Seven Days, thirty-six thousand. Murderous immortality came to the names of towns like Sharpsburg, Gettysburg, Vicksburg, to the names of streams like Antietam, Gravelly Run, Chickamauga. Atlanta burned, and a score of cities besides, to light the way of the destroyer. State capitals fell one by one before the trampling of ungainsayable hosts, and with them fell the states themselves, and the armies of the states.

Stonewall Jackson was killed in May of 1863, even as he gave the Confederacy its greatest victory at Chancellorsville. He was one of more than seventy general officers who died for the Dixie they could not save. With them perished hundreds of thousands, each mourned somewhere by someone, while the hammer of the North at last wore out the anvil of the South. Surrendering, Robert E. Lee and Joseph Eggleston Johnston wished they too had died fighting. So also must have wished Jefferson Davis, hunted like a fox and run to earth and captured and chained.

At the end of things as at the beginning, Edmund Ruffin chose to die rather than survive the Confederacy. The last words he set down in his journal, before he put a gun muzzle in his mouth and pulled the trigger, cursed "the perfidious, malignant and vile Yankee race. . . ."

Mary Chesnut, living on in beaten, starved and prostrate Dixie, finished her diary, too: "Enough! I will write no more."

Notes

I. MARCHING ON

The last day of John Brown's life has been described in several good studies and a number of bad ones. In the present account, much reliance is placed on Oswald Garrison Villard's *John Brown 1800–1859: A Biography Fifty Years After*, pp. 553-7; Marcus J. Wright's *Trial and Execution of John Brown* in *American Historical Association Papers* (hereinafter cited as *AHAP*), Vol. IV, pp. 437-52; and eyewitness accounts by J. T. L. Preston in Elizabeth Preston Allan's *Life and Letters of Elizabeth Junkin Preston*, pp. 111-17, and Thomas Jonathan Jackson in Mary Anna Jackson's *Memoirs of "Stonewall" Jackson* (hereinafter cited as *Mrs. Jackson*), pp. 129-32. The fine weather is described by Preston.

Jefferson Davis' publicly expressed opinion of Brown's guilt and deserts, in *Congressional Globe*, Vol. XXX, pp. 553-4, is calm and rational for a Southern leader of the time. Robert Toombs' more savage viewpoint, as summed up after the execution in his famous "door-sill" speech, is quoted in Pleasant A. Stovall's *Robert Toombs* (hereinafter cited as *Stovall*), pp. 171-4.

Mary Boykin Chesnut is a fascinating and articulate voice of her class and era. She wrote a diary of many hundred pages. As *A Diary from Dixie*, it was first published in 1905 as edited by Mrs. Chesnut's friends Isabella D. Martin and Myrta Lockett Avery (this edition hereinafter cited as *Mrs. Chesnut 1905*), and again in 1949 as edited by Ben Ames Williams (this edition hereinafter cited as *Mrs. Chesnut 1949*), each edition including matter omitted in the other and otherwise differing. The verb "to Brown" appears on p. 1 of both. Uneasiness of Southerners at the danger of abolitionist raids and slave uprisings is described in many contemporary accounts. A good one is that of Mrs. Burton Harrison in *Battles and Leaders of the Civil War* (hereinafter cited as *B&L*), Vol. I, pp. 160 ff.

Approval of Northern abolitionists, with some of the John Brown memorial ceremonies, is told in *Villard*, pp. 558-60. Lincoln's calm opinion appears in the same book, p. 564, quoting the Topeka, Kan., *Capital*, October 25, 1908.

The letters of Preston and Jackson, previously cited, tell the story of the execution from the viewpoint of the Virginia Military Institute cadets. Other details are in William Couper's *100 Years at V. M. I.* (hereinafter cited as *Couper*), Vol. II, employing papers of the Institute. A question that has vexed many—whether Jackson wore a beard in 1859—seems decided by John Power Smith, later on Jackson's staff, who on the first page of *With Stonewall Jackson in the Army of Northern Virginia* (hereinafter cited as *Smith's Jackson*) in *Southern Historical Society Papers* (hereinafter cited as *SHSP*), Vol. XLIII, tells of being introduced to the "well bearded" Jackson at a wedding during midsummer of that year. Industrious debunkers strive to characterize Jackson as uncouth in appearance and behavior, but the statements of many who knew him long before he became famous tend to show that, on the contrary, he was of fine presence though restrained, and there are many evidences that women admired him.

Very few contemporary accounts mention Edmund Ruffin as a volunteer with the Virginia Military Institute cadets. The present account of his experiences at Charlestown depends on Avery Craven's *Edmund Ruffin, Southerner* (hereinafter cited as *Craven*), pp. 176-8, with quotations from Ruffin's diary for December 2, 1859. Ruffin's long essay advocating secession appeared in *De Bow's Review* as a four-installment serial, in the June, September, October and November, 1857, issues. Yancey's crediting the formation of the League of United Southerners to Ruffin is quoted in *Craven*, p. 162. Apparently Ruffin wanted Yancey to have full credit and leadership.

Several commentators say that John Wilkes Booth was in Company F. Painstaking study of Booth family records leads Stanley Kimmell to say, in *The Mad Booths of Maryland*, pp. 156 f., that Booth was with Jennings Wise in the Richmond Grays. Like Ruffin, Booth was an impromptu volunteer. See accounts in the Richmond *Enquirer*, November 29, 1859, and the New York *Tribune*, November 28, 1859.

Brown's last conversations with the officers who guarded and attended him are approximately the same in various authoritative accounts. Several apocryphal reports of what he said are denied in a notarized deposition of Jailer John Avis, which is included as an Appendix in *Villard*, pp. 670-1. Preston's letter, p. 113, mentions the illusion of Brown's knees trembling. Both Jackson and Preston heard the final order of Colonel Smith to Sheriff Campbell. Ruffin's secret thoughts he summarized in his diary, quoted in *Craven*, pp. 177-8. Booth's request for whiskey is mentioned by Kimmell, p. 156.

Brown's last written statement has been quoted many times. A facsimile, showing Brown's peculiar underlinings and punctuation, appears in *Villard*, opposite p. 554.

II. WHERE THEY WERE BORN IN

Of the many books describing Southern ways and attitudes in slavery times, one of the best known and most useful is Ulrich B. Phillips' *Life and Labor in the Old South*. Statistics of free and slave populations, and of slave ownership, are from the *Eighth Census of the United States* (1860), *passim*.

Relatively few historians comment upon Jefferson Davis' comparative moderation before the John Brown raid. Dunbar Rowland, ed., *Jefferson Davis, Constitutionalist* (hereinafter cited as *Rowland*), Vol. III, pp. 271-305, includes some of the speeches he made on a New England tour in 1858. In his address to the Mississippi Legislature on November 16 of that year, in *ibid.*, III, pp. 339-60, he told of his friendly reception in the North and said earnestly: "I hold the separation from the Union . . . to be the last remedy and the final alternative" in solving the vexed situation between North and South.

Davis' Congressional allies mostly have good biographies. Among these are Pleasant A. Stovall's *Robert Toombs, Statesman, Speaker, Soldier, Sage* (hereinafter cited as *Stovall*); John Witherspoon DuBose's *The Life and Times of William Lowndes Yancey;* and Robert Douthat Meade's *Judah P. Benjamin: Confederate Statesman*. Also helpful is Rembert W. Patrick's *Jefferson Davis and His Cabinet* (hereinafter cited as *Patrick*).

The lag of secession enthusiasm in South Carolina during the 1850's is sketched in Chauncey Samuel Boucher's *South Carolina and the South on the Eve of Secession, 1852 to 1860*, in *Washington University Historical Studies*, Vol. VI, pp. 84-129. A calm and practical speech that helped cool South Carolina passions is *Speech of Hon. Wade Hampton on the Constitutionality of the Slave Trade, Delivered in the Senate of South Carolina, Dec. 10, 1859*, published as a 20-page pamphlet in Columbia, S.C., in January, 1860. Memminger's mission to Virginia is described in David Duncan Wallace's *History of South Carolina* (hereinafter cited as *Wallace*), Vol. III, p. 148. The Virginia song jeering at John Brown's fate is quoted in John S. Wise's *The End of an Era*, p. 136.

Craven, pp. 96-180, sums up Ruffin's rise to busy importance in the secession movement, without really explaining how and why Ruffin became so famous an apostle. I am indebted to Dr. Hugh Holman, chairman of the Department of English Literature at the University of North Carolina, for scholarly demonstration that Southerners devotedly read farm journals, to which Ruffin was a frequent and admired contributor. *Craven* also assesses, p. 183, Ruffin's happiness over the Democratic split at the Richmond convention, and describes him at Columbia in rough gray homespun, p. 184.

The belles of the South have left a considerable literature of their own. Mrs. Clement Clay's memoirs, as prepared for publication by Ada Sterling under the title *A Belle of the Fifties,* include charming likenesses of Mrs. Clay herself, Aurelia Fitzpatrick, Mary Chesnut, Varina Davis, and Eugenia Phillips. Mrs. Burton Harrison, formerly Constance Cary, wrote of her adventures and her contemporaries in *Recollections Grave and Gay.* Varina Davis often is self-revealing in *Jefferson Davis, Ex-President of the Confederate States of America, A Memoir By His Wife* (hereinafter cited as *Mrs. Davis*). The delights of Mary Chesnut's diary have already been noticed. Considerable about these and other ladies appears in T. C. DeLeon's *Belles, Beaux and Brains of the Sixties* (hereinafter cited as *DeLeon's Belles*), and *Four Years in Rebel Capitals* (hereinafter cited as *DeLeon's Four Years*).

Jackson's intelligent survey and recommendation of the rifled Parrott guns are described in Jennings C. Wise's *The Long Arm of Lee,* I, pp. 63-4. *Mrs. Jackson,* pp. 33-5, tells of the Jacksons' trip North in the summer of 1860. *Craven* tells, pp. 133-5, of Ruffin's visit to White Sulphur Springs, without mentioning his brief dream of a May-December romance. That abortive idyll is described in Percival Renier's *The Springs of Virginia,* pp. 200-4, and Dr. J. G. de Roulhac Hamilton, director emeritus of the Southern Historical Collection at the University of North Carolina and a kinsman of the Ruffins, has supplied some details.

James Chesnut's election eve speech at Columbia was considered significant at the time. Part of it is quoted from the Charleston *Courier,* in Horace Greeley's *The American Conflict* (hereinafter cited as *Greeley*), Vol. I, p. 332. Chesnut's offer to "drink every drop of blood shed" is quoted in Charles Edward Cauthen's *South Carolina Goes to War,* in *James Sprunt Studies in History and Political Science,* Vol. XXXII, pp. 53-4. William Boyce's remarks are in *Greeley,* I, p. 332.

Craven, p. 192, says that Ruffin voted for Breckenridge. Jackson's vote is noticed in *Mrs. Jackson,* p. 139. National figures on election results are in *Greeley,* I, p. 328, and several other works.

Mrs. Chesnut 1905, pp. 1-3, describes events of late November and early December, 1860, as the diarist saw them, and are published under specific dates. *Mrs. Chesnut 1949,* pp. 1-3, adds details omitted from the earlier edition but without the dates. Ruffin's visit to Columbia and later to Charleston is in *Craven,* pp. 192-9, and in *Greeley,* I, p. 335. A typescript of a memoir by Charles Woodward Hutson in the Southern Historical Collection tells, p. 68, of meeting Ruffin in Columbia. Ruffin's speech from the hotel balcony in Charleston is partially quoted in *Craven,* p. 198, and indirectly and somewhat differently in *Greeley,* I, p. 335, which depends on newspapers.

The character of Robert Anderson puzzles many historians. His old friend and comrade of the Corps of Engineers, George W. Cullum, in *Biographical Register of the Officers and Graduates of the United States Military Academy* (hereinafter cited as *Cullum*), Vol. I, is kindly but critical in saying, p. 352: "Anderson, though possessing professional judgment and fair intelligence, had more of the elements of moral than intellectual greatness." The situation of the Charleston Harbor defenses is well described in a number of works, notably Samuel W. Crawford's *The History of the Fall of Fort Sumter* (hereinafter cited as *Crawford*), pp. 1-7, and *B&L*, I, pp. 50-7.

The approach to secession of South Carolina, and the secession courses of other states, are well told in Dwight Lowell Dumond's *The Secession Movement, 1860–1861,* as well as Congressional efforts to solve or delay the secession crisis by committees of compromise. Howell Cobb's resignation is quoted in many works. Toombs' merriment at Cobb's thrifty drawing of travel allowance is noticed in Richard Malcolm Johnston's and William Hand Browne's *Life of Alexander Stephens,* p. 386.

Petigru's Unionism has frequently been mentioned in histories of South Carolina's secession. His outspoken opinions in December of 1860, with friendly forbearance toward them, are quoted in William L. Grayson's *A Memorial of James Louis Petigru,* pp. 146-151. Almost no modern historian reminds that Petigru later became an earnest secessionist and Confederate.

The airy pronouncements of James Hammond and William H. Gist are quoted in *Wallace,* III, p. 157.

Francis W. Pickens' insistence on being born insensible to fear was seriously admired by many contemporaries. See *Greeley,* I, p. 347 n. *Mrs. Chesnut 1905* cracks the joke about it, p. 3. Incidents of the journey of the convention from Columbia to Charleston are told in a letter from Chesley Evans, one of the delegates, to his wife, written on December 18, 1860, and now with the Evans Papers in the Southern Historical Collection. Details of arrival of the delegates and early transactions are in the Charleston *Mercury,* Dec. 21, 1860.

Jackson's attitude toward dissolution of the Union is summed up in Robert L. Dabney's *Life and Campaigns of Lieut. Gen. Thomas J. Jackson* (hereinafter cited as *Dabney*), pp. 153-4. To his minister Jackson said: "Do you not think that all the Christian people of the land could be induced to unite in a concert of prayer, to avert so great an evil?" But that coercion was a greater evil than secession was a certainty to Jackson.

III. THE CRY ROSE NEAR AND FAR

Events of the secession of South Carolina are circumstantially and joyfully related in the Charleston *Mercury,* December 21, 1860, complete with a roll of the delegates. Ruffin's part in the dramatic proceedings is sketched in *Craven*, p. 201. Some details of the signing are in Anthony Toomer Porter's *Led On! Step by Step; Scenes From the Clerical, Military, Educational and Plantation Life in the South, 1828–1898* (hereinafter cited as *Porter*), p. 117. Porter is mistaken in placing his brother-in-law, Samuel T. Atkinson, at the head of the alphabetical list of delegates. Petigru's sour epigram about a "torch to constitutional liberty," often quoted, is in James Petigru Carson's *Life, Letters and Speeches of James Louis Petigru, the Union Man of South Carolina*, p. 364. His young companion on the street was J. D. Pope, later a South Carolina judge. *Mrs. Chesnut 1905* tells, p. 4, of the news coming to the Kirklands' plantation on the Combahee. William Kirkland, Mary Chesnut's host, was killed in action in the last year of the war.

The organization of South Carolina as an independent commonwealth is ably summarized in *South Carolina Goes to War*, pp. 79-91. Early musters of troops are described in *ibid.*, pp. 103, 111-2, and in many memoirs and local histories. The military atmosphere at Christmas is viewed somberly in the diary of J. B. Grimball, III, Dec. 25, 1860, and gaily in the memoirs of Charles Woodford Hutson and John Cheves Haskell. All three of these are in the Southern Historical Collection. The Christmas incident at Vauclose is told by Mrs. Burton Harrison in *B&L*, I, pp. 160-1.

Anderson's move from Moultrie to Sumter is described in *Crawford*, pp. 102-9, and in *B&L* by Abner Doubleday, I, pp. 44-7, and James Chester, I, pp. 51-2. All three of these were officers active in the surprise transfer. *Crawford* recounts, pp. 109-12, Pettigrew's demand for surrender. *Mrs. Chesnut 1905* quotes table conversations at the Kirklands', pp. 160-1. The man who spoke to James Chesnut on the Charleston Battery was the Reverend Mr. A. Toomer Porter. See *Porter*, p. 122. Early activity of raw but determined militia at posts along the harbor is described in the manuscript *Order Book of Wilmot Gibbes deSaussure, December 27, 1860–April 30, 1861* (hereinafter cited as *deSaussure's Order Book*), in the Southern Manuscript Collection, under dates of December 27 to 31, 1860. Under the latter date is a copy of Pickens' anxious message concerning a rumored relief expedition from the North.

Slemmer's stern defiance at Fort Pickens is described in *B&L*, I, pp. 26-32. Stronger in Northern sympathies than Anderson, and readier to fight at the post where he served, Slemmer was to win a deserved success where Anderson was to fail. The firing on the *Star of the West*, with attitudes of North and South, is described in *B&L*, I, pp. 46-7, *Crawford*, pp. 183-5, and in *Rebellion Record* (each volume of this work is in three divisions: Diary of Events, hereinafter cited as *D.*; Documents, hereinafter cited as *Doc.*; and Poetry, Rumors and Incidents, hereinafter cited as *P.*), Vol. I, *D.*, p. 13.

The incident of the flag displayed at Mississippi's moment of secession, with the immediate writing and singing of "The Bonnie Blue Flag," is recounted in Peleg D. Harrison's *The Stars and Stripes and Other American Flags*, pp. 397-9. Something about Harry McCarthy's career is told in *Confederate Veteran*, IX, pp. 213, 273, and *DeLeon's Belles*, p. 355.

Frances Kirby Smith's letters to her soldier-son, suggesting that the South expected supreme leadership from Jefferson Davis, are with the Edmund Kirby Smith papers in the Southern Historical Collection.

Clarence Phillips Denman's *The Secession Movement in Alabama*, pays special attention to the fierce but vain battle of Alabama Unionists to stave off secession. The decision to invite delegates from all seceded states to Montgomery for the formation of a new government, as inspired by A. P. Calhoun of South Carolina, is described in *American Historical Association Report*, 1910, pp. 178-87. The Alabama Unionist who deplored the fall of the Stars and Stripes in Montgomery was L. R. Davis. His letter is quoted in *The Secession Movement in Alabama*, p. 151.

The demand for surrender of Sumter by Jamison and Magrath is told in *Crawford*, pp. 192-4, as by an eyewitness. Jamison's rather uncharacteristic threat that the fort would be torn down by hand is quoted indirectly. Correspondence between Governor Pickens and Anderson is included in this account.

Mrs. Davis describes her husband's farewell to the United States Senate and her own reactions, I, pp. 686-96. Quotation of Davis' speech here is from *Rowland*, V, pp. 40-5. Many other quotations are available, not always agreeing with each other. *Rebellion Record*, I, *Doc.*, p. 22, tells of friendly farewells offered by Hale and Cameron, "the only Republican Senators that did so."

Jackson's actions and feelings at this period are fairly easy to trace. See *Mrs. Jackson*, pp. 139-42, for a statement of Jackson's political views early in 1861. His letter of December 29, 1860, to his sister Laura is in Thomas Jackson Arnold's *Early Life and Letters of General Thomas J. Jackson* (hereinafter cited as *Arnold*), pp. 291-2. The letter to his aunt, Mrs. Alfred Neale, is in Roy Bird Cook's *The Family and Life of Stonewall Jackson*, p. 91. The letter of January 26, 1861, to Jackson's nephew, is in *Arnold*, pp. 293-4.

IV. A BAND OF BROTHERS

Overcrowded, overexcited Montgomery in early 1861 is described in *DeLeon's Four Years*, pp. 23-6; William H. Russell's *My Diary North and South*, pp. 164-7; and, perhaps most cheerfully of all, the New York *Herald*, February 11, 1861. *Mrs. Chesnut 1905*, pp. 6-8, describes the arrival of South Carolina's delegates. Yancey's speech was printed as an extra by the Montgomery *Advertiser*, January 28, 1861.

The first stopgap legislation adopted by the delegates as a provisional Congress is in *B&L*, I, p. 102, n. The main and significant articles of the Confederate Constitution are in *Rebellion Record*, I, *Doc.*, pp. 29-30, with a note on resemblance to the United States Constitution. The strong and sometimes fierce differences of opinion as to who should be President are well remembered by Barnwell Rhett, Jr., in *B&L*, I, pp. 101-3. The New England remarks of Jefferson Davis misquoted by the elder Rhett are in *Rowland*, III, p. 273. In context they do not amount to a plea for Unionism. *Mrs. Chesnut 1905* sums up, p. 6, the feelings of the South Carolina delegation: "Everybody wants Mr. Davis to be General-in-Chief or President. Keitt and Boyce and a party preferred Howell Cobb for President. And the fire-eaters *per se* wanted Barnwell Rhett." That the citizens of the New Confederacy generally approved Davis' election is demonstrated in *Patrick*, pp. 29-31.

The flattering picture of the Confederate Provisional Congress by the New York *Herald* correspondent is in the issue of February 11, 1861, and is reprinted in the Montgomery *Weekly Mail*, February 22, 1861.

The reaction of Davis to his election is vividly told in *Mrs. Davis*, I, pp. 19-20. Davis' letter to Varina is in *Rowland*, I, p. 53, and *ibid.* quotes, I, pp. 47-9, an account in the Charleston *Mercury* for February 19, 1861, of Davis' arrival at Montgomery and his speech from the window of his hotel. His inaugural address is in *ibid.*, I, pp. 49-53. The unceremonious poking of Davis by Aurelia Fitzpatrick is somewhat toned down in *Mrs. Chesnut 1905*, p. 8, but *Mrs. Chesnut 1949* says, p. 6, that Mrs. Fitzpatrick "made herself conspicuous by being the only lady who sat with the Congress. After the inaugural, she poked Jeff Davis in the back with her parasol that he might turn and speak to her. What a woman!"

Occupation of posts in Texas is described by Mrs. Caroline Baldwin Darrow in *B&L*, I, pp. 33-9, with strong Union bias. Mrs. Darrow describes, p. 36, the gravity of Robert E. Lee, saying that his eyes filled with tears and that he seemed to murmur prayers.

Davis' Cabinet appointments were variously viewed at the time. Judgment in *B&L*, I, pp. 104-9, is not sympathetic. *Patrick* argues, pp. 48-52, that the appointments were expedient and as sensible as the emergency would allow.

Legislation to form an army is quoted in *Rebellion Record*, I, *Doc.*, p. 40. The first general officers, Beauregard, Bragg and Cooper, with dates of appointment in the provisional and Confederate States armies, are listed in *Memorandum Relative to the General Officers Appointed by the President in the Armies of the Confederate States, 1861–1865* (hereinafter cited as *Confederate Generals*), p. 13. This compilation by the Military Secretary's Office of the War Department from official records is not as comprehensive as some other works, but probably is the most accurate as to dates.

Mrs. Chesnut 1949 includes, pp. 7-10, some Montgomery society gossip edited out of *Mrs. Chesnut 1905*. The flag-trampling of Maggie Mitchell at the Montgomery Theater is remembered in *DeLeon's Belles*, pp. 112-3. Before the war was over, Miss Mitchell was trampling Confederate colors underfoot on Northern stages.

I am indebted to Mrs. Panthea M. Twitty of Warrenton, North Carolina, for information about Orren Randolph Smith as designer of the Stars and Bars. The claims of several to this distinction were examined by the Stars and Bars Committee of the Confederated Southern Memorial Association meeting at Richmond, June 1–3, 1915, and later by a committee reporting to the annual convention of the United Confederate Veterans at Tulsa, Oklahoma, on September 25, 1918. Both committee reports accepted Smith as designer. The flag raising is described in *Mrs. Chesnut 1905*, p. 14. Leroy Pope Walker's promise to raise the Stars and Bars in Boston is quoted in the Richmond *Enquirer*, April 15, 1861, and in the Charleston *Examiner*, April 17, 1861, with some differences in the reported language and dates.

Mrs. Davis vividly describes, II, p. 40, the industry and fatigue of Jefferson Davis at this time. See also *Mrs. Chesnut 1949*, p. 20, for Varina's wish that her husband had been made general in chief instead of President. For some reason this was deleted from *Mrs. Chesnut 1905*, as were Mary's meditations on the evils of slavery and her doubts about continuing her diary. These latter are in *Mrs. Chesnut 1949*, pp. 21-2.

V. INTO THE BLACK CLOUD

Beauregard has several biographies, mostly apologistic. Alfred Roman's *The Military Operations of General Beauregard in the War Between the States* (hereinafter cited as *Roman*), is considered to be in some measure the work of Beauregard himself. For his arrival in Charleston and reactions thereto, see *Crawford*, pp. 278. *Ibid.*, 123-5, and *B&L*, I, pp. 74-5, describe the work under Pickens' orders of occupying and strengthening positions around Sumter. Most commentators agree that this work was carried out with energy and sense. Distances from various points to Sumter are from Beauregard's own computations, included with the Charles Woodward Hutson papers. Beauregard's orders for stricter discipline are in *deSaussure's Order Book* under dates of March 5–13, 1861.

The complaint about life on Morris Island is in a letter from Lieutenant Robert Flaeger Graham to his wife, March 11, 1861, with Harllee Papers in the Southern Historical Collection. *Mrs. Chesnut 1949* tells, pp. 27-32, of gay times meanwhile in Charleston. Charles Hutson's typescript memoir, p. 68, and a letter from Chesley Evans to his wife, March 31, 1861, describe the tour of the harbor by members of the convention and other notables.

Details of the court-martial of Sergeant Leiber and Corporal Callais, resolutely refusing to recognize the humor of their clash, are in *deSaussure's Order Book* under date of April 3, 1861.

Mrs. Chesnut 1949 describes, p. 32, the flirtation of Lucy Pickens, whom she did not like, with Porcher Miles, whom she did. "She is silly and affected, looking love into the eyes of the men at every glance," says this account. In *Mrs. Chesnut 1905*, p. 30, the passage reads: "She is a consummate actress and he well up in the part of male flirt."

The critical situation in Charleston Harbor, with news of the coming relief expedition, is outlined in *B&L*, I, p. 75, *Crawford*, pp. 408-17, and *Rebellion Record*, I, pp. 21-2. Roger Pryor's "Shrewsbury Clock" speech at the Charleston Hotel has been variously reported. Quotation here is from Mrs. Roger Pryor, *Recollections of Peace and War*, pp. 120-1. *Mrs. Chesnut 1905* mentions the speech, p. 37, but does not quote Pryor.

Ruffin's adventures as a volunteer on Morris Island are in *Craven*, pp. 215-8, with, opposite p. 216, perhaps the best-known portrait of Ruffin, showing him in semi-uniform for the occasion.

Beauregard's April 11 demand for the surrender of Fort Sumter and Anderson's reply are in *War of the Rebellion: Official Records of the Union and Confederate Armies*, First Series (hereinafter cited as *OR;* other series than first will be indicated in parentheses after *OR*), Vol. I, p. 13. Some of the conversation with Anderson is directly quoted by Stephen D. Lee in *B&L*, I, p. 75, and in *Crawford*, p. 423. *Mrs. Chesnut 1905* tells, p. 34, of her husband's hasty borrowing of a sword and sash for the occasion.

Walker's telegram to Beauregard is in *OR*, I, p. 301. This last effort at peaceful solution of the difficulty is taken seriously by historians; it is often quoted: by *B&L*, I, p. 75; *Crawford*, p. 424; and *Roman*, p. 40, among others. Toombs' protest against bombardment of Sumter is in *Stovall*, p. 226.

Presentation of Beauregard's ultimatum is vividly described by Stephen D. Lee in *B&L*, I, pp. 75-6, and *Crawford*, pp. 425-6. The exact correspondence is in *OR*, I, p. 14. Lee's narrative in *B&L*, I, pp. 76-7, describes the departure of the Confederate emissaries from Sumter to Fort Johnson and circumstances of firing the first shot by Captain James. A. R. Chisholm, who was with Lee and Chesnut, adds some details, *ibid.*, I, p. 82.

VI. THROW AWAY THE SCABBARD

Mrs. Chesnut 1905 offers, pp. 35-6, by far the most vivid and moving firsthand account to be found of the effect of the first shots on residents of Charleston.

Persistent legend credits Ruffin with firing the first shot at Fort Sumter. *Craven*, p. 217, gives Ruffin the honor, after "the signal flashed." *Crawford* says, p. 426, that Ruffin fired the shot that immediately followed that of James. Ben Ames Williams says in *Mrs. Chesnut 1949*, 60-1, n.: "Edmund Ruffin . . . is usually accorded the 'first shot' distinction." Mary Chesnut's own entry of June 19, in *ibid.*, p. 61, reveals that there was argument, perhaps jealous: "That [first shot] is claimed by Captain James. Others say it was one of the Gibbeses." *South Carolina Historical Magazine*, July, 1911, sums up exhaustive research to accord the first shot to Captain James' gun, the second to Wade Hampton Gibbes, and the third to Ruffin. Ruffin is described as an observer for the gunners on Morris Island in *Craven*, pp. 217-18.

Anderson's brief and modest report of the bombardment is in *OR*, I, p. 12, and that of Beauregard in *ibid.*, pp. 29-34. Good narratives by participants on both sides are in *B&L*, I, pp. 66-73, 76-9 and 82-3, and *Crawford*, pp. 426-43. Various newspaper accounts are quoted in *Rebellion Record*, I, *D.*, pp. 23-4, and *Doc.*, pp. 51-9. Jokes of boys at bombarded Fort Moultrie are related in *Mrs. Chesnut 1905*, pp. 42-3. John Cheves Haskell's memoir describes the arrival of the College Cadets and the tales of Colonel Evans.

The near-riot at Lexington, Virginia, and Jackson's "scabbard speech" to the cadets of Virginia Military Institute are variously related in several works. Dependence here is upon the account of William A. Obenchain in *SHSP*, XVI, pp. 36-47. Obenchain, later president of Ogden College at Bowling Green, Kentucky, was present at the squabble in town, and later in the auditorium where Jackson and other professors addressed the cadets.

Fall of the flag above Fort Sumter and details of the surrender are told in *B&L*, I, pp. 72-3, 78-9 and 82-3, and *Crawford*, pp. 439-43, with virtual agreement on direct quotation. Written correspondence achieving the surrender is in *OR*, I, pp. 14-5. Jefferson Davis' friendly message to Anderson is quoted in *Roman*, p. 52.

Crawford describes, pp. 446-8, the evacuation of Fort Sumter, quoting Beauregard's report concerning Southern admiration for the valor of the garrison and scorn for the timid fleet offshore. *Craven* tells, p. 218, the entry of the Palmetto Guards with Ruffin as standard-bearer. The odd request of Franklin B. Moses, Jr., is noticed in *Wallace*, III, p. 167.

Moses, a young man of superficial grace and good looks, became a singularly spiteful and dishonest official of South Carolina's Reconstruction government. *Mrs. Chesnut 1949*, in telling of Moses' flirtation with Governor Pickens' beautiful wife, says: "It suggested the Devil whispering in Eve's ear," and quotes James Chesnut, as early as 1862, as calling Moses "a liar, a sneak. . . ."

My Diary North and South tells, pp. 101, 110, of celebration in Charleston. Other details are in *Mrs. Chesnut 1905*, pp. 37-42.

Lincoln's call for troops, as sent to the governor of each unseceded state, is in *Rebellion Record*, I, *Doc.*, pp. 63-4.

VII. SO SHALL THY STRENGTH BE

Full texts of the defiant telegrams of Southern governors to Washington are in *OR* (Third Series), I, as follows: Magoffin of Kentucky, p. 70; Ellis of North Carolina, p. 72; Letcher of Virginia, p. 76; Harris of Tennessee, p. 81; Jackson of Missouri, pp. 82-3; Rector of Arkansas, p. 99. The less savage query of Hicks of Maryland is in *ibid.*, pp. 79-80, and the disclaimer of official power by Burton of Delaware on p. 114.

John Beauchamp Jones' *A Rebel War Clerk's Diary* (hereinafter cited as *J. B. Jones*), tells, I, pp. 21-4, of secessionist enthusiasm in Richmond. Jubal Early's Unionist sympathy is in *Lee's Lieutenants*, I, p. 85, and Bedford Forrest's vote to stay in the Union in Robert Selph Henry's *"First With the Most," Forrest*, p. 29. The well-known story of Robert E. Lee's agonizing decision is best told in Douglas Southall Freeman, *R. E. Lee*, I, pp. 419-471.

Mrs. Chesnut 1905 describes, p. 45, the conversation with the family slave and the prediction of emancipation.

The occupation of Harpers Ferry by Virginia militia, with some details of Virginia secession, is told by Captain (later Brigadier General) John D. Imboden, who played an important part, in *B&L*, I, pp. 111-15. Jackson's departure for Richmond is tenderly remembered in *Mrs. Jackson*, pp. 144-5. *J. B. Jones*, I, p. 27, expressed immediate admiration for Jackson upon his arrival. Early's offer of his services is in Douglas Southall Freeman's *Lee's Lieutenants*, I, p. 85. Stuart has been a favorite subject for biographies, and the most recent and perhaps the best of all is Burke Davis' *Jeb Stuart: The Last Cavalier*. Magruder's offer of services is in *Lee's Lieutenants*, I, p. 16. That of Meade is mentioned in *B&L*, I, p. 49, with the comment that "his death occurred soon after." *Cullum* says, II, p. 675, that Meade died in July, 1862, and he was in active service as late as March of that year. See *OR*, LI, pt. 2, p. 486.

Randall's composition of "My Maryland" is related in *DeLeon's Belles*, pp. 362-4, with notice of postwar honors. Randall wrote various other

Confederate poems and songs, some of them movingly eloquent, but did not join the army. "My Maryland" was instantly popular in the South, and was early published in the Charleston *Mercury*, signed only with the initial R. See *Rebellion Record*, I, pp. 93-4.

Jackson's assumption of command at Harpers Ferry and his bleak reduction of consequential militia officers are well told in *B&L*, I, pp. 120-2. *Mrs. Jackson* quotes home letters, pp. 151-7.

Mrs. Chesnut 1905 describes, pp. 47-50, political and social activity in Montgomery during April and early May. Davis' April 29 message to Congress, with its oft-quoted plea that the Confederacy "be let alone," is in *Rowland*, V, pp. 67-84. The Montgomery *Weekly Mail's* editorial is in the issue of May 3, 1861, as is the note on North Alabama's farewell to Unionism, quoting a dispatch of April 26 from Florence. *Mrs. Chesnut 1905* describes, p. 54, the visit of R. M. T. Hunter, calling him "the sanest, if not the wisest, man in our new-born Confederacy." The Montgomery *Advertiser's* opinion of the move to Richmond is in the issue of May 11, 1861, as is Judge Campbell's letter to "Gen. Davis."

Toombs' angry witticism about the State Department being in his hat is in *DeLeon's Four Years*, p. 33. Advertisements of steamers for New York and reports on cotton sales are in the Montgomery *Advertiser*, May 9, 1861. *My Diary North and South* tells, p. 169, of falling prices for slaves.

E. Porter Alexander's *Military Memoirs of a Confederate* (hereinafter cited as *Alexander*), quotes, p. 6, McPherson's friendly and farseeing letter.

The beginning of war in Missouri is summarized by Thomas Snead, later chief of staff of the Confederate Army of the West and member of the Confederate Congress, in *B&L*, I, pp. 262-6. Civilian opinion is quoted in the Montgomery *Daily Advertiser*, May 9, 1861, together with the Spartan remark of the Missouri foster mother. Application for membership in the Crescent Rifles is from the manuscript archives of the Howard-Tilton Library, Tulane University. Arrival of the First South Carolina in Richmond, with welcome by the citizens, is described in a letter of April 25, 1861, from Lieutenant Robert Flaeger Graham to his wife, with Harllee Papers in the Southern Historical Collection. The Third Alabama's adventures on their trip to Lynchburg are told in Henry Hotze's *Three Months in the Confederate Army*, pp. 18-9. Letters of Kirby Smith to his mother for May 10, 16 and 29, 1861, describes Lynchburg and Smith's duties and reactions.

Ruffin's reputation as he left Charleston for Richmond is described in *Craven*, pp. 218-20. The Montgomery *Weekly Mail's* last editorial protesting the move of the Confederate seat of government is in the issue of May 17, 1861. Ruffin's message to Davis is in *OR*, LI, part 2, p. 92. For other matters concerning the move, see *Mrs. Chesnut 1905*, pp. 53-9.

VIII. GIVE US A FAIR FIELD

Mrs. Jackson quotes, pp. 154-7, Jackson's experience of command at Harpers Ferry. For the Confederacy's limited resources of trained military officers, see *Lee's Lieutenants*, I, Appendix II, pp. 701-15, which places emphasis on the situation in Virginia as the war there began. Jackson's sane and vigorous strengthening of his position is sketched in *B&L*, I, pp. 122-4, and *Lee's Lieutenants*, I, pp. 9-12.

Few commentators have stressed the importance of Kentucky's early neutrality claims in focusing the first major military action in Virginia. Some discussion of the situation is in *B&L*, I, pp. 373-6. For military approaches to Virginia, see *Lee's Lieutenants*, I, Appendix I, pp. 677-700.

Jackson's adroit seizure of Federal trains and supplies at Harpers Ferry is told in *B&L*, I, p. 123, and *Mrs. Jackson* adds, pp. 171-3, a good description of Jackson's historic war mount, Old Sorrel. Johnston's assumption of command is summarized in *Lee's Lieutenants*, I, pp. 12-3, and Hunter Mcguire's and George L. Christian's *Confederate Cause and Conduct of the War Between the States* quotes, p. 207, Johnston's disparagement of Virginia volunteers.

The Federal occupation of Alexandria, with contrasting opinions of Union and Confederate papers on the character of the slain Colonel Ellsworth, is told in *Rebellion Record*, I, Doc., pp. 277-8.

Davis' journey to Richmond is described in the Richmond *Enquirer*, May 30, 1861. Several reports are summed up in Clifford Dowdey's *Experiment in Rebellion*, pp. 30-32, 37-8. Davis' speech to the soldiers is in *Rowland*, V, p. 104.

The journey of Beauregard to Richmond is sketched in *Lee's Lieutenants*, I, pp. 1-4, with references to all available sources. The first song rhyming Beauregard with petard is quoted in Alfred Hoyt Bill's *The Beleaguered City*, p. 297. Another, perhaps a slightly different version of the first, is in *Experiment in Rebellion*, p. 25. None of these labored paeans are sung today. Beauregard's parting address to his South Carolina admirers is in W. P. Snow's *Southern Generals*, p. 214.

The conference of Davis, Lee, and Beauregard is most fully described, though without direct quotation, in *Roman*, I, pp. 66-7. References to Lee's visit to Manassas are in *OR*, II, pp. 890-2, and are the first reports of the significance of Manassas to come to hand. Lee's advice that the main defense be attempted there plainly was based on his visit and the report of Colonel Thomas Jordan as to troops and fortifications.

IX. TRUST IN GOD AND DAVIS

The story of the naming of Manassas Junction is told in *Dabney*, p. 207, with a rather lofty reference to the "insignificant Israelite." A comprehensive study of the terrain and points of interest throughout is Joseph Mills Hanson's *Bull Run Remembers*, on which the present account gratefully depends for many details. The country surrounding Manassas is in many aspects the same as in 1861, and is helpfully marked by the National Park Service.

The troops found by Beauregard at Manassas and nearby are listed in *OR*, II, pp. 841, 846 and 879. Beauregard's estimate of the terrain's defensibility is in *ibid.*, II, p. 441. As early as June 3, 1861, Beauregard was nervous in his position: see *ibid.*, II, p. 77. The small action at Fairfax was treated as a major victory by Federal officers and newspapers. See *Rebellion Record*, I, *D.*, p. 89, and *Doc.*, pp. 321-2. Captain Marr had been a member of the Virginia secession convention, and the Nashville *Union*, quoted in *ibid.*, called him "a gentleman of the highest position, social and political, of his native State."

Beauregard names his staff officers in *OR*, II, p. 446. His proclamation to the citizens of the region is in *ibid.*, II, p. 907. James Chesnut's departure from South Carolina to join Beauregard is dated June 10 in *Mrs. Chesnut 1949*, p. 57, June 12 in *Mrs. Chesnut 1905*, p. 62.

Joseph E. Johnston's appeal for reinforcements is in *OR*, II, p. 896, and Magruder's is in *ibid.*, II, p. 887. Magruder's earlier offer to take Washington with 5,000 men is told in *Lee's Lieutenants*, I, pp. 14-5.

Information on Confederate money here is from Claude E. Fuller, *Confederate Currency and Stamps, passim*. Stamps and bills are on display at the Confederate museum in Richmond. Notes on stationery with appropriate emblems and rhymes are in Bell Irvin Wiley's *The Life of Johnny Reb*, pp. 194-6. The general order concerning official Confederate uniforms is in *OR* (Third Series), IV, pp. 369-73, under date of June 6, 1861. The New Orleans *Picayune* of May 25 mentioned the plans for uniforms of various ranks and branches. See *Rebellion Record*, I, *P.*, pp. 98-9.

DeLeon's Belles describes, pp. 59-65, the arrival of Deep Southern leaders of politics and society in Richmond, and the social adjustment. This is among accounts summarized in *Experiment in Rebellion*, p. 75.

The battle of Big Bethel is reported by Magruder and Hill in *OR*, II, pp. 91-7. More details are in Walter Clark, ed., *Histories of the Several Regiments and Battalions from North Carolina in the Great War 1861–65* (hereinafter cited as *N. C. Regiments*), Vol. I, pp. 83-102.

James Chesnut's letters about arrival in Richmond, and later at

Manassas Junction, are in *Mrs. Chesnut 1949*, pp. 62, 67-8. The same work describes, pp. 53-64, early wartime activities in South Carolina. Mustering of Wade Hampton's Legion is told in Mary Conner Moffett, ed., *Letters of General James Conner, C.S.A.* (hereinafter cited as *Conner*), pp. 26-30, and in various home letters of Charles Hutson for May and June, 1861. Adventures of the Washington Artillery in its journey from New Orleans to Richmond are in William Miller Owen's *In Camp and Battle With the Washington Artillery*, pp. 8-14.

Jefferson Davis' proclamation of a day of fasting and prayer is in *Rebellion Record*, I, *Doc.*, p. 274. The angry witticism of Robert D. Bone is in a home letter to Minerva Bone, undated but plainly of June, 1861, kindly supplied by his granddaughter, Mrs. Mildred Bone Barkley of New Orleans. Adjutant General Cooper's orders of June 13 are in *OR*, II, pp. 923-5. Jackson's home letter describing events of the 13th is in *Mrs. Jackson*, pp. 161-2. Mrs. Bradford's letter is in *Mrs. Chesnut 1949*, pp. 61-2. The June 13 prayer of Overseer I. A. Randall is in the Magnolia Plantation Record Book in the Southern Historical Collection, and has been quoted in several works, though not always with identification of Randall.

X. NOW THAT WE HAVE STUNG THEIR PRIDE

Richmond full of soldiers is described in *The Beleaguered City*, pp. 66-8, summarizing many accounts. Travel adventures of the Sixth Alabama are in John B. Gordon's *Reminiscences of the Civil War* (hereinafter cited as *Gordon*), pp. 26-8, 32. The coming of Hampton's Legion to Richmond is described in *Conner*, pp. 21-4, with experiences in the new camp told in Charles Hutson's letters of June 30 and July 6, 1861. Flattering accounts of the Legion's arrival are in the Petersburg *Express*, June 29, 1861, and the Richmond *Dispatch*, July 1, 1861. The young North Carolinian enchanted with Richmond was James A. Whitehead, whose home letters are in the Manuscript Department of Duke University.

Beauregard's preparations for attack are summarized in *Roman*, I, pp. 72-83. His letter to Wigfall is in Mrs. D. Giraud Wright's *A Southern Girl in '61* (hereinafter cited as *Mrs. Wright*), pp. 71-2. His plan of campaign is in *Roman*, I, pp. 77-8, with Davis' reply.

Jackson's account of the move from Harpers Ferry to Winchester is in *Mrs. Jackson*, pp. 161-3. The skirmish with the trainload of Federals is in *OR*, II, pp. 124-8, and an eyewitness account is in a letter from Robert Flaeger Graham to his wife. *J. B. Jones* says, I, pp. 52-3, of the retirement from Harpers Ferry: ". . . for the first time, I heard rumors against the government." Jones himself admired and trusted Davis.

Promotions of Samuel Cooper and Robert E. Lee are listed in *Confederate Generals*, p. 3, and promotions to brigadier in *ibid.*, pp. 14-5. The military situation in mid-June is sketched in *Lee's Lieutenants*, I, pp. 39-41.

Jackson's actions and attitudes are summed up in *Mrs. Jackson*, pp. 163-8. An account of the destruction of the Baltimore and Ohio trains, as carried in a contemporary newspaper, is in Festus P. Summers' *The Baltimore and Ohio Railroad in the Civil War*, p. 94. The fight of Romney, with the death of Richard Ashby and Turner Ashby's grim reaction, is told in Virgil Carrington Jones' *Gray Ghosts and Rebel Raiders*, pp. 27-8.

Mrs. Chesnut 1905 describes, pp. 68-70, the journey to Richmond. The two Northern schoolteachers on the train may have been Maria Florilla Flint and Miss Mary Bannister. Miss Flint's manuscript memoir, lent by W. Lunsford Long of Warrenton, North Carolina, tells a similar incident happening at the same time. *Mrs. Chesnut 1905* continues, p. 75, with an account of the visit to the troops, and Miss Flint's memoir grudgingly admires the Black Horse Cavalry and the Texas Rangers.

Ruffin's venture to the front is told in *Craven*, pp. 226-7.

The comet is mentioned in several accounts. The Richmond *Whig and Advertiser* carries a poem about it, in the issue of July 5, 1861, and *Mrs. Chesnut 1905* refers to it, p. 79.

XI. BATTLE SUMMER

Jackson's delaying action against Patterson's overwhelming force is modestly reported in *OR*, II, pp. 185-6, and he describes the fight in a letter to his wife, in *Mrs. Jackson*, pp. 164-6. Details of the handling of guns are told by Pendleton in *The Long Arm of Lee*, I, pp. 125-6. Mrs. Johnston's hysterically dramatic cry and Varina Davis' calming rebuke are in *Mrs. Chesnut 1949*, p. 75, and are omitted from *Mrs. Chesnut 1905*. Lee's letter to Jackson, informing the latter of his promotion to brigadier general, is in *Mrs. Jackson*, p. 166, with, p. 167, Jackson's own happy comments.

The observation balloon above Manassas Junction is mentioned in Robert Flaeger Graham's letter of June 25, 1861. *Alexander* tells, pp. 15-6, of setting up his signal stations and the work of perfecting his system of communications.

Events of Mary Chesnut's trip to Fauquier White Sulphur Springs are in *Mrs. Chesnut 1949*, pp. 76-80, including several incidents and repartees edited from *Mrs. Chesnut 1905*.

Lee's Lieutenants sketches, I, pp. 23-37, the fighting in northwestern Virginia in early July of 1861, summarizing various reports and narratives.

Rose Greenhow, Beauregard's Washington informant, is anonymized as Mrs. G—— in *B&L*, I, p. 200. Beauregard's letter of unasked advice to Johnston is in *Roman*, I, p. 87, and James Chesnut's memory of his written suggestions for grand strategy as submitted to Davis and Lee is in *OR*, II, pp. 506-7. *Mrs. Chesnut 1949* tells touchingly, pp. 82-3, of the glimpse of her husband at Davis' door, the meeting with him afterward, and immediately subsequent matters.

XII. SEND FORWARD ANY REINFORCEMENTS

Organization of McDowell's army is listed in *B&L*, I, pp. 94-5, and in *Bull Run Remembers*, pp. 9-10, the latter work including notes on graduation from West Point of some of the officers and, pp. 14-25, discussion of armament, training and rations. Fighting at Fairfax Court House is described in *OR*, II, pp. 61-3. Ruffin's experience in this skirmish is in *Craven*, pp. 227-8.

Beauregard's early disposition of troops along Bull Run is in *OR*, II, p. 440. His dispatch to Richmond is in *Roman*, I, p. 90, and his appeal to Johnston in *OR*, II, p. 480. The departure of Hampton's Legion for Manassas is described in *Conner*, pp. 36-7, 40. Toombs' resignation from Davis' Cabinet is quoted in *Stovall*, p. 235, dating his brigadier's commission as of July 21, 1861. *Confederate Generals* dates it, p. 15, as of July 19. According to *J. B. Jones*, I, p. 60, this transfer of Toombs from the Cabinet to the army had been predicted for some days.

Plainly Richmond was successfully guarded from the disquieting news of the threat toward Manassas. See *The Beleaguered City*, pp. 68-9.

Beauregard's frantic wire of July 17, 1861, to Cooper is in *OR*, II, p. 980. Ruffin's plight in the rain is described in Craven, pp. 228-9.

Joseph E. Johnston, *Narrative of Military Operations* (hereinafter cited as *Johnston's Narrative*), describes, pp. 33-4, receipt of the orders to march to Manassas. See also *OR*, II, p. 478. Johnston's dispositions of sick troops, with muster of scanty defenses for Winchester, are described in *Johnston's Narrative*, pp. 34-5. See also Judith Brockenbrough McGuire's *Diary of a Southern Refugee*, p. 37.

Johnston's Narrative mentions, pp. 38-9, the query about seniority over Beauregard, but this dispatch is not in *OR*.

Beauregard's move of headquarters is in *B&L*, I, p. 201. The skirmish across the fords, considered a major battle at first, is described in *OR*, II, pp. 440-3, 461-3. Davis' telegram of congratulation to Beauregard is in *ibid.*, p. 981. See *B&L*, I, pp. 163-4, for arrival of wounded at Bristoe Station.

XIII. STEP OUT LIKE MEN

Jackson's march from Winchester to the relief of Beauregard is related in a home letter, apparently of July 20, 1861, in *Mrs. Jackson*, p. 175. The order of brigades on the march is in *Johnston's Narrative*, pp. 37-8. A tradition persists, and is accepted by several historians, that Jackson stayed awake all the first night to guard his sleeping camp. See *Dabney*, p. 212. This may stem from Jackson's own words in the letter cited above: ". . . my men were so exhausted that I let them sleep while I kept watch myself."

Johnston's move on July 18 and through the ensuing night is described in *Johnston's Narrative*, pp. 38-9. Kirby Smith's march at the rear is remembered in McHenry Howard's *Recollections of a Maryland Confederate Soldier* (hereinafter cited as *McHenry Howard*), pp. 30-3.

John O. Casler, *Four Years in the Stonewall Brigade* (hereinafter cited as *Casler*), tells, pp. 21-2, of arrival at Piedmont Station. Jackson's account is in *Mrs. Jackson*, p. 177. For the lagging of the Thirty-third Virginia, see *Casler*, p. 22.

Beauregard's meditations at Manassas while he waited for Johnston are hinted in *Roman*, I, pp. 94-5. Cooper's telegram is in *OR*, II, p. 983. Arrival of the first reinforcements from Winchester is reported in *OR*, II, p. 473. For the weather at Manassas that evening, see *Craven*, p. 228, and *McHenry Howard*, p. 33. Ruffin's doleful dropping out of the line of battle next morning is described in *Craven*, p. 229.

Johnston's account of receiving Beauregard's suggestions for a surprise of McDowell, with his departure for Manassas with Bee's troops, is in *Johnston's Narrative*, pp. 39-41. Davis' assurance concerning Johnston's seniority is in *OR*, II, p. 985. Johnston tells of his own exhausted acceptance of Beauregard's plan to assail McDowell's left flank in *B&L*, I, pp. 245-6.

A number of commentators notice the failure of the Manassas Gap Railroad. Its repair by mechanics in the ranks of the Sixth North Carolina is described in *N. C. Regiments*, I, p. 341. The full text of Beauregard's order of battle is in *OR*, II, pp. 479-80. Sober comment on its vagueness of terms and impracticality of organization has been offered by several, best of which is *Lee's Lieutenants*, I, pp. 50-1.

XIV. SOLDIER, I STAY TO PRAY FOR THEE

Charleston's sketchy impression of what had happened at Blackburn's Ford is reported in J. B. Grimball's diary, July 19, 1861. *J. B. Jones*, I, p. 63, gives the War Department clerk's enthusiastic reactions as the news reached Richmond. *Mrs. Chesnut 1949*, pp. 84-5, tells of rather nervous conversations at the Spotswood. The departure of Hampton's Legion for Manassas is in *Conner*, p. 40. Some details are in Charles Hutson's letter to "Dear Father and Mother," July 22, 1861.

Diary of a Southern Refugee, p. 41, and the diary of Betty Maury in Katherine M. Jones' *Heroines of Dixie*, p. 53, show reactions of these ladies on news of the preliminary fighting along Bull Run. Events and feelings of Bristoe Station are described in *B&L*, I, p. 164.

Kate E. Staton's *Old Southern Songs of the Confederacy* includes, pp. 85-6, the song "Soldier I Stay to Pray For Thee," with a note on the legend of its inspiration and composition early in the war. It has been almost forgotten. Secretary Walker's petulant remarks to his clerk are in *J. B. Jones*, p. 64, with description of the office in an atmosphere of conflicting rumors and nervous anticipation. Arrival of Federal prisoners in Richmond, with Mrs. Wigfall's gentle sympathy for them, is described in *Mrs. Wright*, p. 73.

Mrs. Chesnut 1949, pp. 85-6, sets forth the diarist's thoughts on the eve of First Manassas. Jefferson Davis' message to Congress as of July 20, 1861, is in *Rowland*, V, pp. 114-8, and his appeal to Governor Brown of Georgia in *ibid.*, p. 118.

Davis' sudden departure for the front did not greatly excite Mary Chesnut, who may have been exhausted with worry. See *Mrs. Chesnut 1949*, pp. 85-6. Reactions of someone officially closer to the President are in *J. B. Jones*, I, p. 64. Jones' expectation that Davis could and would exercise supreme military command seems to have been shared in high places of the Confederacy.

Mrs. McLean, in *Harper's Magazine*, February, 1914, tells of Mrs. Davis' inquiry on the street and the news that fighting had begun at Manassas. Many historians take this account as proof that Mrs. Davis herself did not know of the battle, and Mrs. Davis' own memoirs say nothing to show that she had information. *J. B. Jones*, I, p. 64, sets the arrival of the news as "early in the evening."

XV. LIKE A STONE WALL

Beauregard's orders to Ewell are in *Roman*, I, pp. 447-8. *Gordon* tells, pp. 27-8, of the conversation with Ewell in the dawn. Longstreet's report of his own movement is in *OR*, II, pp. 543-4. Information by Bonham's scouting force of Federal movements to the Confederate left is in *ibid.*, II, p. 518. The reconnoitering officer was Colonel W. W. Kirkland of North Carolina.

Evans' force and armament are given in *OR*, II, pp. 474, 488. The movement of troops to the left of Beauregard's line is sketched in *Lee's Lieutenants*, I, pp. 56-8, summing up various reports. Imboden tells in *B&L*, I, pp. 230-2, of Bee's first movements and his own part in them. The wakening of Ruffin to the noise of battle is described in *Craven*, p. 229.

The historically important signal message that warned of McDowell's flanking movement is related in *Alexander*, pp. 30-1.

Evans' prompt and valiant response to the critical situation has perhaps lacked proper appreciation. His report is in *OR*, II, pp. 558-60. *B&L*, I, pp. 184-5, contains praise of Evans by McDowell's assistant adjutant general, Captain (later Major General) James B. Fry. Beauregard's comment is found in the same volume, p. 206. Betrayal of the farm ford by Wheat's loudly defiant scouts is also recounted by Beauregard, p. 207.

Imboden tells, *B&L*, I, p. 232, of Bee's first intention to face the flanking Federals on Henry Hill, and the account of Bee's advance to support the hard-pressed Evans, in *ibid.*, pp. 206-7, describes him as "generously yielding his own better judgment to Evans's persistence. . . ."

The Federal column that crossed the ford revealed by Wheat's scouts was led by William Tecumseh Sherman. See *Memoirs of Gen W. T. Sherman*, I, p. 211.

The disorganized retreat of Bee and Evans is told in *B&L*, I, p. 210, where Beauregard says they were "fleeing in disorder." Beauregard's report in *OR*, II, 490-1, attempts to say that the retreat was orderly and at command of Bee. Hampton's stand is vividly described in *Conner*, pp. 41-2, and in Charles Hutson's home letter of July 22, 1861. For praise and appreciation of this gallant effort to check the Federal advance, see Beauregard's account in *B&L*, I, p. 210, and Johnston in *ibid.*, I, p. 247. Hampton's report is in *OR*, II, pp. 566-7. Imboden tells of his own retreat in *B&L*, I, p. 234.

Jackson's report of the battle, characteristically modest, is in *OR*, II, pp. 481-2. Lagging of the Thirty-third Virginia is told in *Casler*, p. 25. Jackson wrote more proudly of his adventures to his wife, and the letter is in *Mrs. Jackson*, pp. 177-8. G. F. R. Henderson's *Stonewall Jackson and the American Civil War* includes, I, pp. 177-9, much material gathered on this aspect of the battle. Imboden describes his meeting with Jackson, *B&L*, I, p. 234.

Bee's exchange with Jackson and his "stone wall" speech to his troops are told in the Charleston *Mercury*, July 25, 1861, and have been repeated many times. One or two commentators have sought to argue that Bee compared Jackson to a stone wall in angry protest because Jackson had not advanced to join the stand on Matthews Hill. This attitude seems to stem from a statement in J. C. Haskell's manuscript memoir, quoting friends of Bee; but Bee's own first plan to hold his line on Henry Hill, which he gave up only when his close friend Evans frantically begged for his help, would suggest that Bee should have fully understood and approved Jackson's tactics. A study of the terrain will convince any observer that Jackson took and held the best position. Within only a few days Jackson was "Stonewall" throughout the Confederacy. See the entry of July 24 in *Mrs. Chesnut 1949*, p. 88, and summation of the name's origin in *Lee's Lieutenants*, I, Appendix V, pp. 733-4.

XVI. LIVE AND DIE FOR DIXIE

Johnston's account of his morning at Manassas is in *Johnston's Narrative*, pp. 48-53. *Alexander* gives, pp. 34-5, a firsthand report of actions and conversations of Beauregard up to the moment of departure for Henry Hill. Rallying of the shaken troops is described in *OR*, II, pp. 475, 491-2; *Johnston's Narrative*, p. 48; *B&L*, I, pp. 210, 248. Imboden's retirement of his guns and later conversation with Jackson are in *ibid.*, I, pp. 235-6.

The tragic death of Judith Henry is told in *Bull Run Remembers*, pp. 88-90, summarizing the apparent truth in several slightly conflicting accounts.

The line of battle as formed on Henry Hill has perplexed many historians. *Lee's Lieutenants*, I, Appendix IV, pp. 728-32, is here most gratefully followed. A map on p. 729 is particularly helpful.

Coming of the Thirty-third Virginia into line and its subsequent bloody experience are remembered in *Casler*, pp. 25-8. The action of the Sixth North Carolina, with the death of brave Colonel Fisher, is included in *N. C. Regiments*, I, pp. 343-6. Arrival of Bonham's regiments is reported in *OR*, II, p. 522. Andrew T. Harllee's letter to his brother, July 23, 1861, describes his adventures of the day as a private of the Eighth South Carolina. Ruffin's pitiful tottering to join the fight is recounted in *Craven*, pp. 229-30.

Arrival of Kirby Smith's brigade and its hurrying into the fight are described in *McHenry Howard*, pp. 34-9.

The incident of Early's coming into action, with Beauregard's anxious peering to identify the flag, was dramatically described by Beauregard himself during a visit to New Orleans the following October, and an account in the New Orleans *Delta* is reprinted in the Richmond *Whig*, November 20, 1861. James Chesnut, who may have been close to Beauregard at the time, later told a similar story to his wife, saying the flag was Kirby Smith's. See *Mrs. Chesnut 1949*, p. 90.

The final sweeping of the Federal troops from the field is gleefully reported in *OR*, II, 556-7. See also Beauregard's narrative in *B&L*, I, p. 215, and the doleful account of Fry of McDowell's staff in *ibid.*, I, pp. 191-3. Davis tells gravely of his arrival in *Rise and Fall of the Confederate Government*, I, pp. 348-55; and *McHenry Howard*, p. 42, and *N. C. Regiments*, I, p. 346, give firsthand glimpses of him as he rode upon the field at the moment of victory.

Ruffin's firing of a gun into the fleeing enemy is told in *Craven*, pp. 230-1. Kemper's report in *OR*, II, mentions, p. 536, "the venerable Edmund Ruffin" as firing the first shot of Kemper's battery in the action, and adds that "a prisoner subsequently stated that the effect was frightful."

More than a score of memoirs mention the belief that the end of the battle of First Manassas meant the end of the war. Several newspapers predicted this on the following day. But *Mrs. Chesnut 1949,* in the entry of July 27, 1861, p. 91, says with bleak and clear foresight: ". . . this victory will be our ruin. It lulls us into a fool's paradise of conceit at our superior valor, and the shameful farce of the Federal's flight will wake every inch of their manhood."

Bibliography

Here are listed the books, periodicals, and papers most frequently consulted, or containing matter of special importance in the study, among hundreds which have been of use.

BOOKS

ALEXANDER, E. P.: *Military Memoirs of a Confederate*. New York, 1907. Particularly valuable in its consideration of First Manassas.

ARNOLD, Thomas Jackson: *Early Life and Letters of General Thomas J. Jackson*. New York, 1916. A memoir by a near kinsman, including several revealing letters.

Battles and Leaders of the Civil War. 4 vols. New York, 1884-1887. A compilation of articles by veterans and other observers on both sides, one of the necessities in studying the conflict.

BILL, Alfred Hoyt: *The Beleaguered City: Richmond, 1861-1865*. The intriguing tale of the Confederate seat of government, summarizing many firsthand accounts.

BOUCHER, Chauncey Samuel: *South Carolina and the South on the Eve of Secession*, in *Washington University Studies*, VI. St. Louis, 1919. A scholarly and dispassionate study of how South Carolina became the first state to secede.

BROWN, Maud Morrow: *The University Grays, Company A, Eleventh Mississippi Regiment, Army of Northern Virginia, 1861-1865*. Valuable here for an account of Deep Southern soldiers at the beginning of hostilities. Includes good home letters.

CASLER, John O.: *Four Years in the Stonewall Brigade*. Girard, Kan., 1906. A recognized classic from Confederate ranks, by one who got in dangerously close to his work at First Manassas.

CAUTHEN, Charles Edward: *South Carolina Goes to War*. Chapel Hill, N. C. 1950. A comprehensive and splendidly researched and annotated essay.

CHESNUT, Mary Boykin: *A Diary From Dixie*, edited by Isabella D. Martin and Myrta Lockett Avery. New York, 1905. The fascinating private emotions and opinions of a gallant, wise and witty Southern lady, here invaluable. The lady editresses omitted many entries they considered scandalous.

————: *A Diary From Dixie,* edited by Ben Ames Williams. Boston, 1949. Editor Williams put back much of the material left out of the earlier edition, and offers numerous footnote comments, not all of them accurate.

CLARK, Walter, ed.: *Histories of the Several Regiments and Battalions From North Carolina in the Great War, 1861-'65.* 5 vols. Raleigh, N. C., 1901. Surely the best war history of a Confederate state.

COOK, Roy Bird: *The Family and Early Life of Stonewall Jackson.* Richmond, 1925. Has revealing letters written by Jackson at the first secession.

COUPER, William: *One Hundred Years at V.M.I.* 4 vols. Richmond, 1939. A history of the school that gave the Confederacy many of its bravest and most useful soldiers.

CRAVEN, Avery: *Edmund Ruffin, Secessionist.* New York, 1932. Depends on a careful and intelligent study of Ruffin's voluminous journal and notices his ante-bellum importance in bringing about secession.

CRAWFORD, Samuel W.: *The History of the Fall of Fort Sumter.* New York, 1898. In some editions the title is *Genesis of the Civil War.* This work of Fort Sumter's surgeon is articulate and amazingly unbiased, with considerable detail of the first secessions and the political affairs in Washington and Montgomery.

CULLUM, George W.: *Biographical Register of the Officers and Graduates of the United States Military Academy.* 6 vols. Boston, 1891-1920. Includes records of the pre-war service of many Confederate officers, but almost nothing of their careers in the Confederacy.

DABNEY, Robert Lewis: *Life and Campaigns of Lieutenant-General Thomas J. Jackson.* New York, 1866. Dabney knew Jackson in both peace and war, and served on his staff.

DAVIS, Burke: *Jeb Stuart: The Last Cavalier.* New York, 1957. The latest and probably the best biography of the glittering cavalry general.

————: *They Called Him Stonewall: A Life of Lt. General T. J. Jackson, C.S.A.* New York, 1954. Wide research went into this study, but it seems to miss certain gentle and graceful traits of Jackson's character.

DAVIS, Jefferson: *The Rise and Fall of the Confederate Government.* 2 vols. New York, 1881. The Confederacy's President writes gravely, carefully, and with assurance that he has vindicated his decisions and actions.

DAVIS, Varina: *Jefferson Davis, Ex-President of the Confederacy: A Memoir by his Wife.* 2 vols. New York, 1890. Admiring and affectionate, often self-revealing.

DELEON, T. C.: *Belles, Beaux and Brains of the Sixties.* New York, 1909.

A Confederate *bon vivant* remembers, usually with admiration and always with affection, his companions of the war.

————: *Four Years in Rebel Capitals.* Mobile, Alabama, 1892. An earlier work, similar to the later.

DuBose, John Witherspoon: *The Life and Times of William Lowndes Yancey.* 2 vols. New York, 1942. A careful and admiring biography, without full understanding of why Yancey did not deserve and get the highest Confederate office.

Dumond, Dwight Lowell: *The Secession Movement, 1860-1861.* New York, 1931. A good book with which to begin a study of the subject.

Freeman, Douglas Southall: *Lee's Lieutenants: A Study in Command.* 3 vols. New York, 1942-1944. The highly instructive and dramatic story of the officers of the Army of Northern Virginia. Magnificently documented, its notes open many avenues of further study. Surely the best of Confederate military histories.

————: *Robert E. Lee: A Biography.* 4 vols. New York, 1934-1935. And surely the best of Confederate biographies.

Gordon, John B.: *Reminiscences of the Civil War.* New York, 1904. One of Lee's lieutenants tells his story, with justifiable pride but with scant bitterness.

Hanson, Joseph Mills: *Bull Run Remembers . . . The History, Traditions and Landmarks of the Manassas (Bull Run) Campaigns Before Washington, 1861-1862.* Manassas, Va., 1953. An able summary by the former superintendent of Manassas National Battlefield Park. An excellent companion for a trip to the battlefield itself.

Henderson, G. F. R.: *Stonewall Jackson and the American Civil War.* 2 vols. New York, 1898. An Englishman's admiring but intelligent appraisal of a Confederate hero.

Hotze, Henry: *Three Months in the Confederate Army.* University, Ala., 1952. Facsimile reproduction of Hotze's letters from camp as published in the London *Index* in 1862. The facts and the fancies as they existed at the beginning of the war.

Howard, McHenry: *Recollections of a Maryland Confederate Soldier.* Baltimore, 1914. They are vivid recollections, of one who helped to win at First Manassas.

Jackson, Mary Anna: *Memoirs of "Stonewall" Jackson.* Louisville, Ky., 1895. By the one who knew Stonewall best; as close an insight as can be had into the rich and loving heart beneath the austere public manner.

Johnston, Joseph E. *Narrative of Military Operations.* New York, 1874. Full of information about the war's beginnings, with a mighty effort at self-justification in various squabbles.

Johnston, R. M.: *Bull Run: Its Strategy and Tactics.* Boston, 1913. The best history of this campaign so far, but not a perfect one.

JONES, John Beauchamp: *A Rebel War Clerk's Diary*. 2 vols. Philadelphia, 1866. This successful author took a job with the Confederate War Department in order to produce a publishable journal, and succeeded.

JONES, Katherine M., ed.: *Heroines of Dixie: Confederate Women Tell Their Story*. Indianapolis, 1955. Firsthand accounts of the Confederacy and the war, by women and girls who knew how to write.

McGUIRE, Judith Brockenbrough: *Diary of a Southern Refugee*. New York, 1867. She was present in northwestern Virginia as hostilities broke out, and felt and wrote poignantly.

Memorandum Relative to the General Officers Appointed by the President in the Armies of the Confederate States, 1861-1865. Washington, 1905. A concise compilation from the Official Records by the Military Secretary's Office. It seems to be more accurate than other such listings as to dates of appointment, rank, and Congressional confirmation.

OWEN, William Miller: *In Camp and Battle with the Washington Artillery*. Boston, 1885. A loyal gunner's memory of how his crack outfit did its part in the war.

PATRICK, Rembert W.: *Jefferson Davis and His Cabinet*. A well-documented study of Confederate politics and politicos.

PHILLIPS, Ulrich B.: *Life and Labor in the Old South*. Boston, 1929. Indispensable to a study of ante-bellum Southerners and their ways.

Population of the United States in 1860: Compiled from the Original Returns of the Eighth Census. Washington, 1864. Statistics, bald and ungainsayable, as to the slavery situation that brought on the war, and as to the fantastic inequality of the odds in that war.

PORTER, A. Toomer: *Led On! Step by Step: Scenes From Clerical, Military, Educational and Plantation Life in the South, 1828-1898*. New York, 1898. The Reverend Mr. Porter was close to the men who procured South Carolina's secession and began the war by firing on Fort Sumter. Later he was a military chaplain.

ROMAN, Alfred: *Military Operations of General Beauregard in the War Between the States*. 2 vols. New York, 1884. Beauregard himself assisted greatly in preparing this work for publication. It is full of information, but never once suggests that Beauregard was wanting in ability, judgment or modesty.

ROWLAND, Dunbar, ed.: *Jefferson Davis, Constitutionalist: His Letters, Papers and Speeches*. 10 vols. Jackson, Miss., 1923. Indispensable in any serious study of Davis.

RUSSELL, William Henry: *My Diary North and South*. New York, 1863. This English journalist was at Charleston and Montgomery at the beginning of things, and wrote revealingly, though not always kindly, of what he saw.

SNOW, W. P.: *Southern Generals*. New York, 1866. Especially good for early careers of various Confederate heroes.

STERLING, Ada, ed.: *A Belle of the 'Fifties: Memoirs of Mrs. Clay of Alabama.* New York, 1904. Mrs. Clay knew the great men and women of the Confederacy as well as her friend Mary Chesnut, and wrote about them nearly as well.

STOVALL, Pleasant A: *Robert Toombs: Statesman, Speaker, Soldier, Sage.* New York, 1892. In varying degrees, Toombs was all the things his biographer says he was.

VANDIVER, Frank E. *Mighty Stonewall.* New York, 1957. The most recent biography of Stonewall Jackson, readable as well as respectable.

VILLARD, Oswald Garrison: *John Brown 1800-1859: A Biography Fifty Years After.* Boston, 1910. With splendid documentation on Brown's final adventure.

WALLACE, David Duncan: *History of South Carolina.* 3 vols. New York, 1934. Comprehensive on secession and Sumter.

War of the Rebellion: A Compilation of the Official Records of the Union and Confederate Armies. 128 vols. Washington, 1880-1901. The backbone of Civil War research.

WILEY, Bell Irvin: *The Life of Johnny Reb.* Indianapolis, 1943. Much about the common Confederate soldier, from primary sources.

WISE, Jennings C. *The Long Arm of Lee.* 2 vols. Lynchburg, Va., 1915. The history of the artillery of the Army of Northern Virginia.

WISE, John S.: *The End of an Era.* New York, 1899. The young son of Virginia's governor loved the era he saw end, and fought to prolong it.

PERIODICALS

Charleston *Examiner.*
Charleston *Mercury.*
Confederate Veteran.
Harper's Magazine.
Harpers' Weekly.
Leslie's Weekly.
Montgomery *Advertiser.*
Montgomery *Weekly Mail.*
New Orleans *Delta.*
New York *Herald.*
Petersburg *Express.*
Richmond *Dispatch.*
Richmond *Enquirer.*
Richmond *Whig and Advertiser.*
South Carolina Historical and Genealogical Magazine.
Southern Historical Society Papers.

UNPUBLISHED MATERIAL

(A great number of single manuscript items were consulted, but the seven large collections listed here, all in the Southern Historical Collection of the Louis Round Wilson Library at the University of North Carolina, were particularly helpful.)

DeSaussure, Wilmot Gibbes. Order Book, Dec. 27, 1860-April 30, 1861. A record of deSaussure's command of South Carolina State troops during the siege and capture of Fort Sumter in Charleston Harbor.

Evans, Chesley D. Evans wrote a series of letters to his wife, dealing with the South Carolina Secession Convention of which he was a member and the tense situation regarding Fort Sumter.

Grimball Family Papers. These include the diaries for 1860 and 1861 of John B. and Meta Morris Grimball, also the letters of their son Lewis who fought at Manassas.

Harllee Family Papers. This tremendous collection includes several series of letters from soldiers at the start of the war, notably Robert Flaeger Graham of the First South Carolina Regiment and Robert Armstrong Harllee and Andrew Turpin Harllee of the Eighth South Carolina.

Haskell, John Cheves. A typescript of Haskell's unpublished memoirs, which should go unpublished no longer, was given the Southern Historical Collection by Mrs. Preston Hampton Haskell, Jr., of Birmingham, Alabama. It includes sharp-eyed observations of the start of things in South Carolina.

Hutson, Charles Woodward. He lived a long and useful life as educator and writer. His papers include home letters from Manassas and elsewhere, and later reminiscences of war years and other adventures.

Smith, Edmund Kirby. General Kirby's letters and those of his mother, written early in 1861, tell much of secession, the Confederacy's beginnings, and the outbreak of hostilities.

Index

Adams, James H., at South Carolina secession convention, 42, 43

Adventures of Simon Suggs, by Johnston Jones Hooper, 62

Alabama: Slave power in, 21; antebellum senators, 22; proposes reopening of slave trade, 23; secedes, 37, 49, 51-2; seizes forts, 49; besieges Fort Pickens, 52; Unionism in, 52, 109; State House of, 60-1; Montgomery delegates, 62

Alabama troops: Seize forts, 49; go to Virginia, 113-4, 167; Montgomery Blues, 70; Ruffin Dragoons, 114; Fourth Regiment, 174, 178, 205, 207-8; Sixth Regiment, 141-2, 193-4

Alexander, Brig.-Gen. E. Porter, CSA: Resigns from U. S. Army, 111-2; signal officer at Manassas, 156; warns of Federal flanking movement, 196-7; mentioned, 111, 212

Alexandria, Va.: Federals enter, 123, 127, 131; mentioned, 143, 144, 145, 164

Alexandria, Loudon and Hampshire Railroad, 130

Alexandria and Orange Railroad, 145

Allison, R. T., at South Carolina secession convention, 43

Anderson, Maj.-Gen. Robert, USA, at Charleston: Description, record and Southern sympathies, 36; his officers and troops, 37; leaves Fort Moultrie for Fort Sumter, 47; refuses to surrender, 47, 48, 53, 82; salutes Washington's Birthday, 69; not allowed to buy provisions, 79; thought signaling U. S. fleet, 80; receives ultimatum, 86; returns fire of shore batteries, 89; surrenders Fort Sumter, 95-7; departs, 99; mentioned, 48, 74, 76-7, 78, 98, 147

Apostate, The, John Wilkes Booth stars in, 70

Appleby, D. S., at South Carolina secession convention, 43

Arkansas: Slaves in, 26; Lincoln asks for troops, 101; rejects call, 102; secedes, 103, 190

Arlington Heights, Va., 144, 145

Ashby, Richard, 17, 107, 148-9

Ashby, Brig.-Gen. Turner, CSA: At John Brown's execution, 16, 17, 19; as cavalry leader, 107, 120, 148-9

Ashby's Gap, Va., 169, 175

Avis, John, John Brown's jailer, 14, 17

Bahr, Madame ———, Washington Artillery's vivandière, 137

Baltimore, Md., 27, 105

Baltimore and Ohio Railroad, 122, 148

Ball's Ford, near Manassas, 131, 166, 170, 182

Barnwell, Robert W.: At South Carolina secession convention, 42; delegate to Montgomery, 60, 63, 64

Barry, William S., announces Mississippi's secession, 50

Bartow, Col. Francis S., CSA: Georgia secessionist, 38; seizes Fort Pulaski, 49; delegate to Montgomery, 62; marches to Manassas, 174, 177; supports Longstreet, 178; supports Bonham, 182; in battle, 199, 206, 207; mortally wounded, 209

Beauregard, Gen. Pierre Gustave Toutant: Ordered to Charleston, 69; description and career, 74; surveys and improves Charleston harbor defenses, 74-6; halts Fort Sumter's food purchases, 79; his staff appointments, 81, 131-2, 150; demands Fort Sumter's surrender, 47-8, 82, 84, 96-7; reports Anderson's refusal to Montgomery, 83; is told he may attack, 84; aides under fire, 90; Fort Sumter surrendered to, 97-8; praises subordinates, 98-9; at victory reception, 100; praised, 114; called to Richmond, 125-6; celebrated in song, 126; confers with Davis and Lee, 126-8; commands at Manassas, 128, 131; his address to citizens, 132; wears old U. S. uniform, 134; his plans for battle at Manassas, 136, 144-5, 157, 159; receives reinforcements, 141, 145; his brigade commanders, 147; sends Chesnut to Rich-